Contributions to Finance and Accounting

The book series 'Contributions to Finance and Accounting' features the latest research from research areas like financial management, investment, capital markets, financial institutions, FinTech and financial innovation, accounting methods and standards, reporting, and corporate governance, among others. Books published in this series are primarily monographs and edited volumes that present new research results, both theoretical and empirical, on a clearly defined topic. All books are published in print and digital formats and disseminated globally.

More information about this series at http://www.springer.com/series/16616

Umberto Sagliaschi • Roberto Savona

Dynamical Corporate Finance

An Equilibrium Approach

Springer

Umberto Sagliaschi
Quaestio Capital SGR SpA
Milan, Italy

Roberto Savona
Department of Economics and Management
University of Brescia
Brescia, Italy

ISSN 2730-6038 ISSN 2730-6046 (electronic)
Contributions to Finance and Accounting
ISBN 978-3-030-77852-1 ISBN 978-3-030-77853-8 (eBook)
https://doi.org/10.1007/978-3-030-77853-8

This Springer imprint is published by the registered company Springer Nature Switzerland AG.
The registered company address is: Gewerbestrasse 11, 6330 Cham, Switzerland

Contents

Chapter 1
Introduction

1.1 Introduction

The way in which leverage and its expected dynamics impact on firm valuation is very different from the assumptions of the traditional static capital structure framework. The purpose of this book is to re-characterize the firm's valuation process within a dynamical capital structure environment, by drawing on a vast body of recent and more traditional theoretical insights and empirical findings on firm evaluation, also including asset pricing literature. We offer a new setting in which practitioners and researchers are provided with new tools to anticipate changes in capital structure and setting prices for firm's debt and equity accordingly.

We introduce the reader to selected theoretical models in corporate finance that can be used to understand investment and financial decisions on the firms' side, their interdependence and related impacts on the value of corporate securities, such as stocks and bonds. The book is then intended mostly for graduate/phd students, researchers and financial professionals who are interested in modeling asset prices and corporate strategy decisions. Our approach is sometimes referred as "supply-side" or "investment-based" asset pricing, and it complements with the more traditional approach deriving from the application of optimal portfolio theory. The success of this approach (see Zhang 2017), is the possibility to leverage the large availability of corporate data and partly overcome aggregation problems, as opposed to demand side models, such as the Consumption Capital Asset Pricing Model (e.g., Rubinstein 1976; Lucas 1978; Breeden 1979), which instead requires to know investors' preferences. To some extent, dynamic corporate finance is the crossroads where equilibrium asset pricing meets the scope of firms' production, investment and financing decisions. In this regard, the book is also intended to provide a guidance for an advanced practice of equity valuation. To make an example, consider the practical problem of valuing the *debt tax shield*. At which rate should we discount future tax benefits of debt, and how future financial leverage

U. Sagliaschi, R. Savona, *Dynamical Corporate Finance*, Contributions to Finance and Accounting, https://doi.org/10.1007/978-3-030-77853-8_1

decisions should be factored in the same valuation process? This book is conceived to give theoretical and pragmatical answers to questions such as these.

We have decided to keep the book intentionally synthetic, exploring in more depth only those parts we believe to be relevant for both academics and practitioners. While we do not cover the complete literature on dynamical capital structure, we provide a large number of references for the readers wishing to understand in more depth the technical details of the topics we deal with. However, some topics of corporate finance theory have been intentionally excluded for reasons of scope and space. The major exclusion is the field of security design, for which a huge literature was developed in the last 20 years of the past century (see Hart 1995). In other words, in all our models we take as given the contractual features of corporate securities (e.g. common stocks have certain characteristics, such as shareholders' limited liability). In this regard, we shall be clear from the beginning that the models presented in the book can be applied only to non-financial corporations. This is an intended consequence, motivated by three different reasons related to the nature of financial corporations. Firstly, banks, insurance companies and asset managers are delegated investors/financial intermediaries using their leverage in a very different way relative to non-financial firms. Secondly, financial intermediaries are regulated. Their capital structure decisions are constrained by tight *capital adequacy* rules, that are primary intended to reduce their contribution to systemic risk. Thirdly, the structure of their balance sheet is significantly different from that of non-financial corporations, and therefore different accounting conventions must be taken into account. For the interested reader, a synthetic introduction to the dynamic corporate finance for banks and insurance companies can be found respectively in Chapters 4 and 5 of Moreno-Bromberg and Rochet (2018).

1.2 The Realm of Corporate Finance

At an abstract level, firms can be described in terms of production, investment and financing decisions, which are interrelated one each other. To get an idea of the underlying complexity of the corporate finance decision process, we may start by observing that production depends on firm's assets, which in turns are the outcome of investment decisions. The optimal use of the production capacity is then depending on the market competition, which affects the marginality of the firm, and, consequently, financial resources available for new investments. For instance, if inventories of intermediate inputs must be purchased before production eventually becomes available for sales, the firm must be able to finance the working capital required to achieve its production target. Likewise, investment decisions may be affected by the level of indebtedness of the firm, with shareholders being little motivated to invest in new projects when default is impending.

The example is enough to clarify why we need a theory of corporate finance, which must be *dynamic* given the intertemporal nature of investment decisions.

Otherwise, a similar complexity could be never resolved by simply looking at data in a unstructured fashion.

How do we build corporate finance models? First of all, it is necessary to establish which questions are relevant, and in which order. Shareholders typically control the firm and they try to maximize the value of their claims. The first task is therefore that of putting in relation the cash flows that can be distributed to shareholders with the equity value of the firm, which is a mere exercise of combining basic accounting with the way in which stocks are priced as a function of their future stream of dividends. After doing this, we must extend the analysis to the pricing of any generic type of security that the firm may want to issue consistent with its budget constraint. This process, in a sense, is equivalent to descriptive statistics in data science. Given a set of available data, we learn how to present them in a consistent fashion, which corresponds, in this case, to show how the budget constraint of the firm affects the total value of the securities. In a nutshell, we will show that given any (feasible) path for investment and financing decisions, the sum of the market values of all the securities issued by the firm can be always traced back to the sum of few components. Next, we can go back to the original problem of determining which decisions are consistent with the shareholders optimizing behavior, exploring which managerial conditions are needed to do this. We deal with such an extremely complicated problem in Sect. 2.3.3, without entering into technical details, for which the interested reader may refer to Tirole (2005). When presenting and discussing the model in Chap. 3 through Chap. 7 we always assume that firms are effectively managed in order to maximize shareholders value.

In sum, we are interested in shareholders optimal financing and investment decisions, possibly conditional on the industrial organization setting of the firm. As said, our interest is on the impact on firm value and its securities outstanding, as well as the associated expected returns. Having clarified the corporate finance perspective we assume, now we focus on the theoretical tools we need to build consistent models.

We adopt an equilibrium approach and in the next section we provide the basic elements for a correct understanding of all the models presented in the following chapters, without entering too much into technical details in order to keep the discussion self-contained.

1.3 Equilibrium Approach, Market Structure and Corporate Governance

The concept of equilibrium is of central importance in our book and needs to be contextualized within our framework. To do this we rely on Kreps (1990), Fudenberg and Tirole (1991), Osborne and Rubinstein (1994) and Gatcher (2013).

A theoretical model is an artificial economy where different agents, such as investors and firms, interact with each other. As such, the role of an artificial economy is the same as the laboratories for natural scientists, namely performing controlled experiments assuming ideal conditions. An artificial, or "model", economy is always characterized by an institutional framework, which defines the aggregate resource constraints and the way in which agents can interact with each other. A *situation* is an outcome of the artificial economy. An *equilibrium* is a situation in which each agent is doing as best as it can, given the institutional framework and the behaviors of all other agents.[1] The concept of equilibrium is intended to be a composite principle to determine a plausible outcome for the model economy, that is, a *solution concept*. The axiomatic explanation for this approach is that an equilibrium defines a situation in which no agent has incentive to behave in a different way given the behavior of other agents. In this regard, it is important to observe that an equilibrium is always a property of the model, and not of the real world. Hence, being the general definition of equilibrium a theoretical abstraction, we may wonder why we should adopt an equilibrium approach in the first place. For this reason, we adopt a set of more primitive principles, which jointly motivates the use of equilibrium as *solution concept* for economic models.

There are two principles which are always assumed valid in economics, *aggregate consistency* (e.g. Barro 2001) and *optimization* (e.g. Varian 2011). Aggregate consistency requires that individual actions must conform with the institutional constraints. For instance, the quantity purchased of an object cannot be different from its quantity sold. Likewise, the total amount of securities within a market must correspond to the total securities held by all investors. In this perspective, we state that the actions of agents must be compatible with each other and with the institutional framework. Optimization relates to the absence of unexploited opportunities. This principle states that every agent select the best choice available to her, depending on her informational set. This principle captures the basic idea that we generally act in what we believe to be in our best interests. There is a key caveat underlying the optimization principle to clarify. Indeed, in many circumstances, the consequences of a certain decision may be affected by the behavior of other individuals. As such, individual decisions may be driven by what each agent believes about the simultaneous and subsequent behavior of others, depending on whether individual act simultaneously or according to a a priori ordering. As a consequence, without a principle describing how agents develop their conjectures about the behaviors of other, we cannot characterize the outcome of the model as a whole. The most common solution is to introduce the hypothesis of *correct beliefs* as a third principle, which states that each agent takes as given the behaviors of others.

Since the assumption of *correct beliefs* is an important integrand part our models, it is worth giving a little bit more of context. Essentially, the principle of *correct*

[1]The "optimality" concept embedded in the definition of equilibrium is intended from an ex-ante perspective, i.e. before the uncertain and random events materialize. To put the point into perspective, consider, for e.g., an investor optimizing her portfolio, who then experiences a considerable financial loss due to an adverse exogenous shock. Ex-ante, she formulates expectation on key variables and takes her optimal asset allocation decision, while ex-post, due to a random event which was not included in her decision process, she suffers a substantial loss.

beliefs translates into practice depending on what it is intended with the expressions "doing" and "behaviors of others" in the definition of an *equilibrium*. Broadly speaking, we can identify three situations. In simultaneous interactions with perfect information, the principle of *correct beliefs* requires that each agent takes as given the actions *simultaneously* played by others, which is the usual Nash requirement. A trivial example is the one-shot *prisoner's dilemma*, where the common knowledge of rationality is enough for each prisoner to deduce that the other will confess the crime. With imperfect information, this requirement is modified by imposing that each agent takes as given the state-contingent actions of other agents, which are commonly referred as *strategies*. To make an example, consider a *sealed-bid* auction, in which the various participants submit their bids for a certain object without knowing the reservation values of others, which are drawn from a common probability distribution. In this case, the principle of correct beliefs requires that each participant takes as given the functions (*strategies*) mapping the reservation prices of other players' into their corresponding bids. While a bit abstract at first, the *epistemic* motivation for the assumption of correct beliefs in simultaneous interactions is that the *common knowledge* of the optimization principle and the institutional framework should guide each individual to deduce the simultaneous behaviors of others (Aumann and Brandenburger 1995; Polak 1999). Likewise, in sequential interactions, either with perfect or imperfect information, the principle of correct beliefs requires the player moving first to correctly anticipate how her decisions will affect those of the second movers.[2] The reason for this assumption is again that the common knowledge of optimizing behavior should allow the first mover to correctly map its actions into those of second movers, which may be still permeated by an element of uncertainty depending on the information structure of the economy.[3] In this regard, it is important to note that "sequentiality" needs not be necessary intended in terms of passing time, but extends to decisions taking place at a same instant albeit according to a predetermined "virtual" ordering. One example is the basic model of monopolistic competition, in which the monopolist maximizes its profits correctly anticipating the aggregate demand schedule deriving from consumers' optimizing behavior. This assumption is of extreme importance for corporate finance models, in which at a certain point in time[4] more events can occur according to a virtual sequentiality (e.g. at time $t \in \mathbb{N}$ the firm produces a certain amount of goods, collect revenues and then decide whether to default on its debt obligations or not).

Taking together the principles of *aggregate consistency*, *optimization* and *correct beliefs* we get an equilibrium approach in which every agent is doing as best as it can, given the institutional framework and the behaviors of other agents. In the

---

[2]In other words, when an agent is moving before others, she takes as given the function mapping her decisions into the actions that second movers will play in response to her decision. In game theory, this is the usual requirement of *subgame perfection* for Nash equilibria.

[3]Or, more appropriately, the characteristics of the *sequential game*.

[4]A point in time is a point on a subset of the real line ($\mathbb{R}$).

same way, the solution of any economic model based on *aggregate consistency, optimization* ad *correct beliefs* principles is an equilibrium. While the definition of equilibrium is potentially more general,[5] this is how the equilibrium approach is generally intended in applied economic theory. In this book, the principles of *aggregate consistency, optimization* ad *correct beliefs* are always assumed valid to build economic models, and, consequently, we are always considering *equilibrium behaviors*. From a technical perspective, notice that, having assumed correct beliefs for sequential interactions, we always consider *subgame perfect* equilibria. This point is particularly relevant for Chap. 6, in which we analyze a *dynamic game* between shareholders and bond holders of a given company.

It it important to observe that the *equilibrium approach* is intended to obtain economic relations that, being valid in the model, should be tested empirically before using by practitioners. For this reason, it is often convenient to focus on a subset of agents, taking for granted the aggregate consistency of their equilibrium behavior with the rest of the model economy. In this case, we refer to *partial equilibrium* models. This is very common in corporate finance, and it is a characteristic of all the models that are discussed in the next chapters. This simplification is motivated by our primary interest to understand the equilibrium dynamics of firm's decisions for a given asset pricing kernel, the latter being a concept of utmost importance we will discuss in Sect. 1.3.2.

1.3.1 Building on the Neoclassical Synthesis

The equilibrium approach is just a very general recipe to build economic models. Consequently, it is important how economists translate it in practice, depending on the context and the research questions that should be analyzed with the aid of a specific model. Despite the vast array of different modeling choices, most of corporate finance models are built on the *neoclassical synthesis*, which is based on the following assumptions:

(1) *perfectly rational* individuals;
(2) rational expectations (RE).

By perfectly rational individuals, we intend that each agent is always able to decide whether an action is preferred or not to another, according to a binary preference relation satisfying the transitive property and the axiom of independence of irrelevant alternatives. This ensures that the optimization principle can be cast into a mathematical optimization problem, consisting in the maximization of an expected utility function subject to the constraints faced by each decision maker in

[5] An example is the assumption of self-confirming beliefs (Fudenberg and Levine 1993) instead of correct beliefs, which is typical of the Nash tradition. Both assumptions lead to a situation where the general definition of equilibrium is valid.

the model. The reader may refer to Mas-Colell et al. (2011) or Varian (1992) for the more details. Expectations, in turn, depend on the probabilities that each agent attributes to random events not yet realized at the time of its decision. In general, the agents in the model may ignore the probabilistic structure of the *exogenous* random variables, and have different *priors* in a Bayesian sense. In this regard, the *rational expectations* (RE) hypothesis requires that individuals have *common priors* for exogenous random variables, and that such a prior coincides with their objective distribution. Additional references on this topic may be found in Ljungqvist and Sargent (2018). Rational expectations are useful to introduce model discipline. Indeed, without RE it would be very hard to obtain testable predictions, as we can almost always find a set of heterogeneous priors to obtain a target outcome as the equilibrium outcome of a given model. In fact, structural estimation and testing of equilibrium models is possible only for rational expectations models (Hansen and Singleton 1982).[6]

The neoclassical synthesis offers a plenty of potential modeling choices. Due to the scope of our models, in our book we introduce few additional hypothesis regarding the structure of financial markets and the informational set (i.e. the *institutional framework*):

(1) perfect information;[7]
(2) Walrasian secondary financial markets;
(3) zero profits for intermediaries, which do not take risky positions on their own as they do not trade directly in the firm's securities (i.e. *brokers* rather than *dealers*).

Perfect information is not a strict requirement, and a large body of literature in corporate finance does not share this hypothesis. However, in our context it takes the meaning of simplifying the set of equilibria that may be observed, particularly in terms of how the price of corporate securities are determined on secondary financial markets. By secondary financial markets we mean the trading venues in which corporate securities are negotiated right after their issuance. The issuance of new securities is generally intermediated by specific agents, such as coordinating brokers, which could demand a fee in exchange of their services. Sometimes these fees may be not negligible, although in recent years pure intermediation costs have fallen significantly. The issuance process takes place on what we call primary, or capital, markets. In all our models, this process takes place immediately and translate into a corresponding listing of the newly issued securities on secondary markets. We will come back at the end of this section on the role and potential frictions of capital markets.

[6]DeJong and Dave (2011) provides an excellent reference to structural estimation methods, although pretty much focuses to macroeconomics applications. Strebulaev and Whited (2014) is a concise and hands-on discussion of structural estimation in dynamic corporate finance models.

[7]More formally, we say that all information is common knowledge, that is, at each date, the information set of each agent is the same of any other.

We assume that secondary markets are organized as Walrasian auctions. In a Walrasian market, there is a single market price at which the participants can buy and sell any amount of a certain object, for instance the stocks of a company. In other words, investors face as only restriction their own budget constraints and do not need to take into account the behavior of other traders. Aggregate consistency is ensured by an anonymous auctioneer that sets beforehand a price at which the resulting trades are mutually compatible (see Kreps 1990). Such a price is called *market-clearing* price, and the resulting price and trades constitute a *competitive equilibrium*.[8] Real financial markets are not exactly consistent with the ideal setting of the market-clearing model. However, for thick trading posts, a competitive equilibrium is effectively a convenient approximation. The underlying idea is that, when the number of investors is large, trading protocols[9] should not be the driving force behind corporate finance decisions.

Once we will add the hypothesis of market completeness (see Sect. 1.3.3), corporate securities are always "correctly" evaluated, in the sense that we can rule out the presence of *bubbles*, whether rational or not. This certainly precludes any possibility to statistically profit from information frictions. Warusawitharana and Whited (2015) is probably the only dynamic corporate finance model with equity "misevaluation" due to imperfect information (e.g. Merton 1987; Grossman and Stiglitz 1980) or heterogeneous beliefs (see Back 2017).

We now discuss in more details the role of primary, or capital, markets in our models. As said, the issuance of new securities take place instantaneously on these markets. However, financial intermediaries just coordinate the issuance of new securities, without holding any of newly issued securities on their books. Effectively, this setting is equivalent to the one in which newly issued securities are listed immediately on the secondary financial market, and the issuer pay the associated flotation costs, if any, to financial intermediaries as additional expenses that are not included in the financial conditions of the securities issued. In all our models, we shall rely implicitly on this equivalence.

[8]The major drawback of the market-clearing model is that it doesn't explain how the auctioneer *clears* the market. At a theoretical level, the most convincing argument is that the auctioneer knows the aggregate excess demand schedule and, right before the trades take place, sets a price vector that ensures aggregate consistency of subsequent trades (Qin and Yang 2019). In this case, sequential moves are taking place at a certain market instant, with the price being announced before trades are executed. In a simultaneous moves setting, Arrow and Debreu (1954) shows that a competitive equilibrium can be obtained if the auctioneer minimizes the net worth of aggregate excess demand function (see also Villar 2000 and Tian 1992). However, a controversial assumption is implicit in the Arrow and Debreu model. The auctioneer has "deep pockets", and aggregate consistency does not matter, in the sense that, out of equilibrium, the auctioneer can always satisfy the aggregate excess demand using her own resources (Shapley and Shubik 1977). Despite the difficulties in developing a convincing *mechanism* that implements a competitive equilibrium, the market-clearing model remains a good proxy for real market in several circumstances.

[9]Market microstructure is a very interesting field, and we invite the reader to explore this field. Excellent references are Harris (2003) and De Jong and Rindi (2010).

The next question is therefore when transaction costs can be assumed equal to zero. The answer is embedded in the assumption of zero profits for capital markets intermediaries. When intermediation is costless, competition drive flotation costs (intermediaries' revenues) to zero. Whenever we believe reasonable to assume the flotation of new securities as a costless process, we can set flotation costs equal to zero. Clearly, this argument implicitly assumes absence of information asymmetries, which is indeed one of our working hypothesis. There are however securities that requires intermediaries (or sometimes the firm) to bear specific issuance costs. A notable example is that of secured debt contracts, such as leveraged loans, in which the firm pledges one or more assets as collateral. There are several legal and monitoring activities involved in the lien process, which is usually delegated to one or more intermediaries. As a result, capital markets intermediaries will charge a fee to the firm in order to cover the related costs, unless the firm pay directly for this expense. In both cases, we shall assume that the resulting flotation costs are not paid within the terms of securities, but as direct costs charged to the firm. As a result, the issuance price of a security will be always equal to its secondary market equilibrium price. In other words, there will be no difference in our models between primary and secondary listing prices.

1.3.2 Market Completeness, Pricing Kernel and the Objective of the Firm

In our book, we assume markets to be *complete*, in the same spirit of Radner (1972) model of sequential trading. Roughly speaking, completeness means that investors can trade any form of state contingent contract. In other terms, the market includes assets for every possible state of the world. Under the complete markets assumption, also imposing perfect information and rational expectations, the competitive equilibrium of secondary financial markets ensures the existence of a unique strictly positive stochastic process $\{M_t\}_{t\geq 0}$ $(M(t)$ in continuous time), commonly known as *stochastic discount factor* (SDF) or *asset pricing kernel*, such that the price (p_t) of a generic security must satisfy,

$$\begin{cases} \begin{cases} p_t = \mathbb{E}_t \sum_{s=0}^{\infty} \frac{M_{t+s}}{M_t} y_{t+s} \\ \lim_{T\to\infty} \mathbb{E}_t \left[\frac{M_T}{M_t} p_T n_{T+1} \right] = 0 \end{cases} & \text{Discrete time models,} \\ \begin{cases} p_t = \mathbb{E}_t \int_0^{\infty} \frac{M(s)}{M(t)} y(s)\, ds \\ \lim_{T\to\infty} \mathbb{E}_t \left[\frac{M(T)}{M(t)} p(T)\, n(T) \right] = 0 \end{cases} & \text{Continuos time models,} \end{cases} \tag{1.3.1}$$

where $\{y_t\}_{t\geq 0}$ ($y(t)$ in continuous time) is the stochastic process characterizing the cash flows paid by one unity of the security to its holder, while n_{t+1} ($n(t)$ in continuous time) is the amount in circulation at time t. In Sect. 2.1 we clarify the reason why we set n_{t+1} instead of n_t, although it is a matter of convenience in discrete time dynamic corporate finance applications.[10] A competitive equilibrium is always arbitrage free, in the sense that a) it prevents risk-free trading opportunities with unbounded profits, and, b) all risk-free assets have the same rate of return.

We recall that firms do not participate in secondary financial markets directly. However, firms take as given the SDF. As each firm is the monopolist of its own securities, it is natural to expect that its capital structure decisions will take into account the related price impact (if any), just as the monopolist producer of a certain good takes into account the pricing constraint induced by the demand schedule for its products (see Sect. 4.2). The point is discussed in Chap. 6, in which we study the dynamic game between shareholders and debt holders relative to the optimal issuance of unsecured debt. In general, firms take the process M_t ($M(t)$ in continuous time) as given, while they might affect the distribution of the cash flows of their securities through production, investment and financing decisions. In other words, the firm, or who is in charge for its management, take as given the way in which market-clearing prices are determined as a function of its strategy.

We assume that shareholders do not invest in other liabilities issued by their firm and agree unanimously with the maximization of the market value of the firm's equity. This is known as the *shareholders value* approach (Tirole 2001, 2005). As we discuss in the next chapters, equity value maximization does not necessary correspond to maximization of the total value of the firm, which is by definition the sum of the market values of the securities issued by the firm, net of cash and other risk-free investments held as liquidity reserves. Nevertheless, there might be situations in which shareholders may fail in their objective of maximizing the value of equity. As firms are generally run by a group of managers, equity value maximization requires a preemptive alignment of managerial incentives with shareholders objectives. This is a type of principal-agent conflict, which may be anything but easy to solve in practice. However, except for a few illustrative examples, all the models we discuss from Chaps. 3–7 assume the existence of a corporate governance mechanism that perfectly aligns the interests of shareholders with that of managers. For the same reason, we move under the same hypothesis for which the firm is directly managed by shareholders.

As introduced in this section, there is a fundamental difference between partial and general equilibrium models. General equilibrium models consider closed-ended environments, in which *primitives* such as individuals preferences and production technologies are mapped into equilibrium prices and asset allocations.

[10] In macroeconomics models this convention is instead more uncomfortable, and it is generally used n_t to denote the amount of securities outstanding at date t, instead of n_{t+1} as we do here.

Instead, partial equilibrium models are concerned with the behavior of one or more individuals, holding everything else constant. Most of corporate finance models are indeed partial equilibrium models, in which the main interest in deriving the firm's equilibrium relative to asset pricing kernel, which is assumed as given for each firm. The models discussed in the book pertain to this group, as our objective is to fully understand the effects of shareholders' optimizing behavior in terms of production, investment and financing decisions on market value of the firm as well as the value of its securities, given a certain SDF. Hence, the implications and results proposed with the models discussed throughout the book assume that each firm is small enough relative to the market as a whole. This is a common assumption among practitioners which is easy to verify empirically.

The extension within a general equilibrium models setting is not trivial, as aggregating investors' preferences could be problematic.[11] To do this, the compromise between partial and general equilibrium approaches is commonly proposed, which consists in assuming a parametric form for the SDF, then computing find the values for those parameters ensuring the aggregate consistency of the firms' decisions. This approach is nonetheless likely to have more success in empirical applications, instead of deriving the SDF from a direct specification of investors preferences, which is the crux of the equity premium and risk-free rate puzzles (Mehra and Prescott 1985; Weil 1989). The reason is that aggregation problems across firms tend to be less severe, making investment-based asset pricing a prominent direction to obtain empirically robust pricing models (Lin and Zhang 2013). We discuss this point in Chaps. 3 and 4, when introducing the Investment CAPM (Zhang 2017) as a corollary of investment and financing decisions with risk-free debt.

A word of caution. Without complete markets, or in presence of externalities or imperfect product market competition, the maximization of the equity value may not be the best choice for all the shareholders (Grossman and Hart 1979; Milne 1995; Carceles-Poveda and Coen-Pirani 2009; Hart and Zingales 2017). The objective of the firm becomes the outcome of a voting problem, since depending on the preferences of the majority of shareholders. Under some specific conditions, shareholders may still agree on maximizing the equity market value (Sabarwal 2004). Despite that, asset prices may be sometimes disjoint from their fundamentals, as there might be rational bubbles as in the case of *sunspots equilibria* (Maskin and Tirole 1987).

Furthermore, with incomplete markets, there might be situations in which criteria other than shareholders value maximization may be adopted, especially if the firm generates externalities that cannot be hedged. In this regard, many are debating on whether social and environmental impacts should be included in the objectives of

[11] This is a consequence of the Sonnenschein-Mantel-Debreu ("anything goes") theorem (Sonnenschein 1972; Sonnenschein 1973; Debreu 1974; Mantel 1974; Andreu 1982; Chiappori and Ekeland 1999).

the firm (Hart and Zingales 2017). This may complicate the analysis for sure. Also, growing discussion is focusing on the hypothesis that firms may increase their value by paying more attention on environmental and social issues, which is a sort of "doing good by doing better" concept. As is obvious, such assumption derives from the idea that managers are not maximizing the value of the firm, and, therefore, shareholders could improve their value by taking corrective measures, although this implicitly requires that environmental and social performances can be correctly measured by outsiders.[12] If true, the ESG paradigm would resolve in the last letter of its acronym: governance. To date, there is no clear consensus on this issue, and then we have stick on the canonical assumption of equity value maximization, which is a more robust theoretical framework when having conflicting objectives. After all, maximizing the firm's value is equivalent to agree to run the firm at an "average" optimized risk-return profile.

1.4 Roadmap

1.4.1 Plan of the Book

The remainder of the book is organized as follows.

Chapter 2 introduces the reader to the main concepts in corporate finance, and to all other topics we deal with in the next chapters. We focus, in more depth, on the value of the firm and its determinants, which is consistent with the book's philosophy. The natural starting point are the Modigliani and Miller theorems (MM), which marked the birth of modern corporate finance in the 50's. The ideal conditions of the MM theorems are progressively abandoned in favor of richer and more sophisticated environments. We briefly overview agency problems such as debt overhang, the importance of efficient corporate governance mechanisms, and illustrate how to describe in general terms bankruptcy procedures. A general expression for the value of the firm is provided, which proves to be particularly helpful in the following chapters.

Chapter 3 introduces debt dynamics and investment decisions. We assume the presence of a collateral constraint that ensures that firms will never default. These models are useful in several circumstances, especially once endogenous investment decisions are introduced. In this regard, we analyze shareholders' optimal investment and financing program in the case of perfect product market competition, also introducing the presence of convex investment adjustment costs.

[12]The quality of environmental (E) and social (S) performances may be subject to a strong information gap between managers and shareholders. As externalities represent a tangible operational and financial risk to shareholders, managers may be motivated to report E&S performances in the most convenient way possible. Camodeca et al. (2018) formalizes this idea using different game theoretical models of strategic information transmissions, with particular emphasis to the case of partitioning equilibria as in the cheap talk model of Crawford and Sobel (1982).

The model is used to obtain a large number of useful insights on the firm's leverage dynamics and the relation between investment and stock markets returns.

The limits of the model are discussed in Chap. 3 and focus on the industrial organization setting, since, except for some commodity producers, the majority of firms have some degree of market power. Hence, in Chap. 4 we introduce the effects of imperfect competition in the firm's product market. The model also includes the role of the working capital, in terms of inventories of intermediate inputs used in the production process.The model offers a more realistic and insightful relation between investment and stock returns. For this reason, we present a specific version of the model in terms of stochastic processes for the exogenous variables, which can be proficiently used in several applications, from empirical research in asset pricing to equity valuation.

Until Chap. 4 all models are presented in discrete time. Continuous time methods are introduced in Chap. 5, which is based on the Leland (1994) model. Differently from the previous two chapters, the focus is on unsecured, unprotected and *pari passu* (equal seniority) debt securities. Despite being a static representation of the capital structure, this model turns out to be a very useful tool for more advanced dynamic models. Besides, it helps to frame the economic intuition behind agency problems such as strategic default, debt overhang and risk-shifting.

In Chap. 6 we extend the Leland model to the study of optimal dynamic capital structure decisions, following the recent model developed by DeMarzo and He (2020). The striking result of this framework is that, in a continuous time Markov Perfect Equilibrium (MPE), the equity market value is the same as in the case that shareholders commit to not issue additional debt in future. We analyze the impact of this result to leverage dynamics and the firm's cost of capital. We also provides a discrete time version of the model, which helps to understanding the economic mechanisms at work, and can be also used as a building block for quantitative models.

Chapter 7 is the last chapter in which we are eventually able to introduce several extensions that might be of particular relevance in practice. Firstly, we formulate a model, both in discrete and continuous time, where the firm can issue either secured risk-free debt or unsecured, unprotected, *pari passu* debt. The model is an efficient combination of what is developed in the previous chapters, and can be used for quantitative analysis. Indeed, it allows to model very heterogenous capital structures, as a combination of risk-less secured debt and unsecured debt can be used most of the time to represent also the case of risky secured debt. In any case, the model has two limitations. First, it is based on Markov perfect strategies. Second, it needs to be solved numerically. We discuss each of these points, and also provide a brief introduction to structural econometric methods in finance.

1.4.2 Prerequisites

In Sect. 1.3 we summarize some very important, synthetic, while incomplete, prerequisites for the reader. We suggest the readers who are unfamiliar with those concepts to refer on equilibrium asset pricing literature, such as Cochrane (2009), Duffie (2010), Ma (2011), Dumas and Luciano (2017) or Back (2017). There are in any case some other prerequisites that will help the reader to comfortably navigate through the technical details of the book. First, a good understanding of static optimization methods (linear and concave programming) in several variables is more than essential, as well as an intermediate knowledge of stochastic processes, both in discrete and continuous time. Hamilton (1994), Oksendal (2003) and Bjork (2009) are very useful references for the theory of stochastic processes, while De la Fuente (2009) and Simon and Blume (1994) provide a very good overview of static optimization methods. As is natural, a complete understanding of the theory of stochastic processes require a sound knowledge of probability theory and mathematical statistics. Second, a basic knowledge of stochastic dynamic programming (SDP) is absolutely necessary for a thorough comprehension of dynamic corporate finance models. Miao (2020) and Stokey and Lucas (2004) are excellent references for discrete time SDP. Dixit (1993), Dixit and Pindyck (1994), Bjork (2009) and Stokey (2009) are useful references for continuous time dynamic programming methods in finance. The basics of corporate finance are, of course, the starting point to explore more advanced concepts. Berk and DeMarzo (2019) is an excellent reference to this purpose. Although not essential, a prior knowledge of more theoretical aspects of corporate finance are helpful. Amaro de Matos (2001) and Tirole (2005) are strongly suggested readings. Tirole (1988) provides, instead, a comprehensive overview of the theory of industrial organization, which may be useful to have in mind the effects of product market competition. After all, profitability drives investment and financing decisions, so it is quite relevant to understand where it comes from. Finally, a basic knowledge of accounting is essential.

Acknowledgments We are intellectually and personally indebted with many friends and colleagues who have provided us with invaluable comments and discussions regarding the topics exposed in this book. We wish to thank Quaestio Capital Management, in particular Christian Prinoth, Alessandro Potestà, Mario Baronci, Federico Valesi, Giacomo Saibene and Francesco Ceci, as well as all the members and participants of the Investment Committee. We thank Luca Bertazzi (University of Brescia), Renato Camodeca (University of Brescia) and all the PhD program faculty in Analytics for Economics and Management, University of Brescia, Department of Economics and Management. And finally, a special thank goes to our families, Elena with Leonardo, and Marika with Luca and Nicolò.

References

Amaro de Matos, J. (2001). *Theoretical foundations of corporate finance*. Princeton University Press.

Andreu, J. (1982). Rationalization of market demand on finite domains. *Journal of Economic Theory, 28*(1), 201–204.

Arrow, K. J., & Debreu, G. (1954). Existence of an equilibrium for a competitive economy. *Econometrica, 22*(3), 265.

Aumann, R., & Brandenburger, A. (1995). Epistemic conditions for Nash equilibrium. *Econometrica, 63*(5), 1161.

Back, K. E. (2017). *Asset pricing and portfolio choice theory* (2nd ed.). Oxford University Press.

Barro, R. J. (2001). *Macroeconomics*. MIT Press.

Berk, J., & DeMarzo, P. M. (2019). *Corporate Fiance*. Pearson.

Bjork, T. (2009). *Arbitrage theory in continuous time*. Oxford University Press.

Breeden, D. T. (1979). An intertemporal asset pricing model with stochastic consumption and investment opportunities. *Journal of Financial Economics, 7*(3), 265–296.

Camodeca, R., Almici, A., & Sagliaschi, U. (2018). Sustainability disclosure in integrated reporting: Does it matter to investors? A cheap talk approach. *Sustainability, 10*(12), 4393.

Carceles-Poveda, E., & Coen-Pirani, D. (2009). Shareholders' unanimity with incomplete markets. *International Economic Review, 50*(2), 577–606.

Chiappori, P. A., & Ekeland, I. (1999). Aggregation and market demand: An exterior differential calculus viewpoint. *Econometrica, 67*(6), 1435–1457.

Cochrane, J. H. (2009). *Asset pricing*. Princeton University Press.

Crawford, V. P., & Sobel, J. (1982). Strategic information transmission. *Econometrica, 50*(6), 1431.

De Jong, F., & Rindi, B. (2010). *The microstructure of financial markets*. Cambridge Univ. Press.

De la Fuente, A. (2009). *Mathematical methods and models for economists*. Cambridge University Press.

Debreu, G. (1974). Excess demand functions. *Journal of Mathematical Economics, 1*(1), 15–21.

DeJong, D. N., & Dave, C. (2011). *Structural macroeconometrics*. Princeton Univ. Press.

DeMarzo, P. M., & He, Z. (2020). Leverage dynamics without commitment. *The Journal of Finance, 76*(3), 1195–1250.

Dixit, A. K. (1993). *The art of smooth pasting*. Harwood Academic Publishers.

Dixit, A. K., & Pindyck, R. S. (1994). *Investment under uncertainty*. Princeton University Press.

Duffie, D. (2010). *Dynamic Asset Pricing Theory*. Princeton University Press.

Dumas, B. and Luciano, E. (2017). *The economics of continuous-time finance*. The MIT Press.

Fudenberg, D., & Levine, D. K. (1993). Self-confirming equilibrium. *Econometrica, 61*(3), 523.

Fudenberg, D., & Tirole, J. (1991). *Game theory*. MIT Press.

Gatcher, S. (2013). *Rationality, social preferences, and strategic decision-making from a behavioral economics perspective* (pp. 33–71). Stanford University Press.

Grossman, S. J., & Hart, O. D. (1979). A theory of competitive equilibrium in stock market economies. *Econometrica, 47*(2), 293.

Grossman, S. J., & Stiglitz, J. E. (1980). On the impossibility of informationally efficient markets. *The American Economic Review, 70*(3), 393–408.

Hamilton, J. D. (1994). *Time series analysis*. Princeton University Press, Princeton

Hansen, L. P., & Singleton, K. J. (1982). Generalized instrumental variables estimation of nonlinear rational expectations models. *Econometrica, 50*(5), 1269.

Harris, L. (2003). *Trading and exchanges*. Oxford University Press.

Hart, O., & Zingales, L. (2017). Companies should maximize shareholder welfare not market value. *Journal of Law, Finance, and Accounting, 2*(2), 247–275.

Hart, O. D. (1995). *Firms, contracts, and financial structure*. Clarendon Press.

Kreps, D. M. (1990). *A Course in Microeconomic Theory*. Princeton University Press.

Leland, H. E. (1994). Corporate debt value, bond covenants, and optimal capital structure. *The Journal of Finance, 49*(4), 1213–1252.

Lin, X., & Zhang, L. (2013). The investment manifesto. *Journal of Monetary Economics, 60*(3), 351–366.
Ljungqvist, L., & Sargent, T. J. (2018). *Recursive macroeconomic theory*, (4th ed.). MIT Press.
Lucas, R. E. (1978). Asset prices in an exchange economy. *Econometrica, 46*(6), 1429.
Ma, C. (2011). *Advanced asset pricing theory*. Imperial College Press.
Mantel, R. R. (1974). On the characterization of aggregate excess demand. *Journal of Economic Theory, 7*(3), 348–353.
Mas-Colell, A., Whinston, M. D., & Green, J. R. (2011). *Microeconomic theory*. Oxford Univ. Press.
Maskin, E., & Tirole, J. (1987). Correlated equilibria and sunspots. *Journal of Economic Theory, 43*(2), 364–373.
Mehra, R., & Prescott, E. C. (1985). The equity premium: A puzzle. *Journal of Monetary Economics, 15*(2), 145–161.
Merton, R. C. (1987). A simple model of capital market equilibrium with incomplete information. *The Journal of Finance, 42*(3), 483–510.
Miao, J. (2020). *Economic dynamics in discrete time*. MIT Press.
Milne, F. (1995). *Finance theory and asset pricing*. Oxford University Press.
Moreno-Bromberg, S., & Rochet, J. C. (2018). *Continuous-time models in corporate finance*. Princeton University Press.
Oksendal, B. K. (2003). *Stochastic differential equations*. Springer.
Osborne, M. J., & Rubinstein, A. (1994). *A course in game theory*. MIT Press.
Polak, B. (1999). Epistemic conditions for nash equilibrium, and common knowledge of rationality. *Econometrica, 67*(3), 673–676.
Qin, C.-Z., & Yang, X. (2019). On the equivalence of rational expectations equilibrium with perfect Bayesian equilibrium. *Economic Theory, 69*(4), 1127–1146.
Radner, R. (1972). Existence of equilibrium of plans, prices, and price expectations in a sequence of markets. *Econometrica, 40*(2), 289.
Rubinstein, M. (1976). The valuation of uncertain income streams and the pricing of options. *The Bell Journal of Economics, 7*(2), 407.
Sabarwal, T. (2004). A consistent firm objective when markets are incomplete: Profit maximization. *SSRN Electronic Journal*.
Shapley, L., & Shubik, M. (1977). Trade using one commodity as a means of payment. *Journal of Political Economy, 85*(5), 937–968.
Simon, C. P., & Blume, L. (1994). *Mathematics for economists*. W. W. Norton and Company.
Sonnenschein, H. (1972). Market excess demand functions. *Econometrica, 40*(3), 549.
Sonnenschein, H. (1973). Do Walras' identity and continuity characterize the class of community excess demand functions? *Journal of Economic Theory, 6*(4), 345–354.
Stokey, N. L. (2009). *Economics of inaction: Stochastic control models with fixed costs*. Princeton University Press.
Stokey, N. L., & Lucas, R. E. (2004). *Recursive methods in economic dynamics*. Harvard Univ. Press.
Strebulaev, I. A.,& Whited, T. M. (2014). *Dynamic models and structural estimation in corporate finance*. Now Publishers.
Tian, G. (1992). Existence of equilibrium in abstract economies with discontinuous payoffs and non-compact choice spaces. *Journal of Mathematical Economics, 21*(4), 379–388.
Tirole, J. (1988). *The theory of industrial organization*. MIT Press.
Tirole, J. (2001). Corporate governance. *Econometrica, 69*(1), 1–35.
Tirole, J. (2005). *The theory of corporate finance*. Princeton University Press.
Varian, H. R. (1992). *Microeconomic analysis*. Norton.
Varian, H. R. (2011). *Intermediate microeconomics*. Norton
Villar, A. (2000). *Equilibrium and efficiency in production economies*. Springer.

Warusawitharana, M., & Whited, T. M. (2015). Equity market misvaluation, financing, and investment. *Review of Financial Studies, 29*(3), 603–654.

Weil, P. (1989). The equity premium puzzle and the risk-free rate puzzle. *Journal of Monetary Economics, 24*(3), 401–421.

Zhang, L. (2017). The investment CAPM. *European Financial Management, 23*(4), 545–603.

Chapter 2
The Value of the Firm and Its Securities

This chapter has the fundamental role to introduce the reader to the basics of corporate finance. Broadly speaking, corporate finance is the branch of economic science which deals with the financing and investment decisions of firms, and how these decisions affect the value of corporate securities and their financial returns. A security is a contingent claim liability issued by a company, which attributes certain control rights to its holders. Control rights include, but are no restricted to, receiving certain cash flow streams. For instance, common stocks attribute the right to shareholders to receive dividends, as well as equal voting rights. Firms are not directly tradable, while their liabilities are. The set of the outstanding securities characterizes the ensemble of the control rights, and therefore the set of individuals that are entitled to split the (free) cash flows generated by the firm. Accordingly, the value of a firm is defined as the market value of its securities, net of cash and other equivalent risk-free assets. Netting for liquidity allows to identify the going concern value of the business, which is generally higher than the accounting book value of invested capital (fixed assets plus trade working capital). Many motivations explain such a underlying difference, which becomes more evident in the next chapters, in particular in Chap. 3 and 4. In short, firms may extract valuable rents from their operations, depending on the competitive landscape and the efficiency level of their assets. Besides, firms may have valuable growth options, whose value cannot be preemptively recognized in the balance sheet statement. In the end, what really matters for the total value of the firm is the total cash flows that all security holders can split between themselves. The purpose of this chapter is to clarify this point, namely, how the value of a firm and its securities are related to the free cash flows generating process.

The chapter is organized as follows. In Sect. 2.1 we introduce the main notations, the concept of unlevered free cash flows and a very basic model of the firm's budget constraint. Section 2.2 presents the Miller and Modigliani (MM) theorems, which state that, under certain conditions, financing decisions are irrelevant. As a consequence, the only effect of financial leverage is to increase expected equity

U. Sagliaschi, R. Savona, *Dynamical Corporate Finance*, Contributions to Finance and Accounting, https://doi.org/10.1007/978-3-030-77853-8_2

returns, consistent with the higher risk for shareholders, who are the residual claim holders (i.e. the most *junior*) in the firm's capital structure. The main assumptions of the MM theorems are: (a) exogenous investment decisions, (b) absence of transaction costs, (c) no tax benefits from the use of debt financing and (d) absence of bankruptcy costs. In Sect. 2.2 we introduce tax effects of debt financing and bankruptcy costs, and provide a general expression for the value of the firm.

Section 2.3 introduces a first analysis on the optimal investment decisions and agency costs. A notable example is debt overhang, which is presented in Sect. 2.3.1. We also provide specific examples of agency problems related to corporate governance frictions, by limiting the discussion of these problems only in this chapter. In Sect. 2.4 we provide a general formula for the value of the firm. We introduce the concept of abstract security, and show that regardless the number and the design of the securities actually issued, the value of the firm can be always obtained as the sum of few distinct components. Sect. 2.4 concludes with practical examples, which is a first attempt to estimate the expected stock returns based on equilibrium corporate finance principles.

To summarize, with this chapter the reader should have a clear picture of which elements affect the valuation of the firm and its securities, and how financing and investment decisions can interact with each other. The topics covered in this chapter are important prerequisites to fully understand more advanced discussions and models we present throughout the book.

2.1 Notation and Basic Setting

Our analysis of corporate finance begins with a discrete time setting, in which all agents interact with each other only at a countable set of decision instants, or dates, $t \in \mathbb{T} \subseteq \mathbb{N}$. As anticipated in Sect. 1.3, this does not mean that at a generic time t everything take place simultaneously. Rather, different events or actions may take place sequentially, according to a predetermined ordering. However, as t is a point on the real line, everything takes place instantaneously and the ordering has to be intended as a virtual one. For the same reason, instants are also referred as periods, although they are specific points in time. In the same way, when we consider a variable at the end of period t, we intend its value after all the decisions in t took place, which include all payments executed/received by the firm. Likewise, when we observe the value of the firm's securities at the beginning of time t, we must include any cash flow that might be paid in the same period. Hence, we use the definition *cum cash flows* or even, *cum dividend* market values. Instead, market values at the end of the period are observed after all payments are made, and therefore they are *ex cash flows* or *ex dividend*. This flexibility is very important to achieve consistency with accounting data thereby representing the right timing of different decisions within the model.

The natural starting point of our discussion is the firm's budget constraint, which relates the use of resources to the evolution of the firm's liquidity balance.

Table 2.1 Overview of recurrent notation

Symbol	Description
M_t	Stochastic discount factor (SDF)[a]
$M_{t,t+j} := \frac{M_{t+j}}{M_t}$	The j-periods ahead pricing kernel at time t
$r_{t+1} = \left[\mathbb{E}_t\left(\frac{M_{t+j}}{M_t}\right)\right]^{-1} - 1$	The risk-free rate at time t
IC_{t+1}	The book value of the firm's invested capital at end of period t
L_{t+1}	The liquidity of the firm at the end of period t
F_{t+1}	The nominal amount of debt outstanding at the end of period t
$ebit_t$	Earnings before Interests Expenses and Taxes (EbIT)
T_t^c	Taxation of EbIT
$nopat_t := ebit_t - T_t^c$	Net operating earnings after taxes (NoPAT)
$x_t = NOPaT_t - (IC_t - IC_{t-1})$	Unlevered free cash flows (UFCF)
π_t	Debt tax shield
$T_t = T_t^c + \pi_t$	Total taxes paid in t
$x_t + \pi_t$	Free cash flows to the firm

[a]See Sect. 1.3 for a quick reference

By liquidity, we mean callable deposits, term deposits or other equivalent *risk-free* securities in which the firm invests its savings. Put in other terms, we assume that the firm's savings (if any), are invested at the risk-free rate, although we can also include specific transaction costs (e.g. a tax on call deposits). Before presenting the first model of the firm's budget constraint, it is important to present a synthetic overview of the relevant notation; see Table 2.1.

The risk-free rate at time t (r_{t+1}) is equal to the coupon received in $t+1$ for a dollar invested at time t in a risk-free security. Except specific cases (e.g. taxes), the difference between capital and lowercase letter serves to make distinction between stock and flow variables, which is important from an accounting perspective. Invested capital is the sum of firm's fixed assets and trade working capital, which is in turn equal to the book value of trade receivables plus that of inventories and minus that of trade receivables. Unlevered free cash flows are the free cash flows to the firm before any direct impact of debt financing. This does not means that the financing policy will not affect them, as investment decisions may be *indirectly* affected by capital structure decisions. In other words, for a given *investment policy*, unlevered free cash flows corresponds to the dividends paid by an all-equity firm which does not accumulate cash.

As anticipated in the previous chapter, the value of the firm is defined as the sum of the market values of all its securities outstanding, net of liquidity (L_{t+1}). In this regard, it is important to observe that we can consider cum-dividend or ex-dividend valuations, although securities will be always traded at their ex-dividend price.

Needless to say, the two cases are essentially equivalent, in that the former differs from the latter only by the inclusion of the same period cash flows. Nevertheless, as investment and financing decisions must be taken before dividends are paid, it is the *cum dividend* value of equity that matters for their optimal decisions at each date t. For this reason, the cum-dividend value of equity is also commonly referred as *shareholders value*. These are important considerations that are valid in general. To simplify the discussion, from here on out when we speak of *value of the firm*, or that of a certain class of securities, we always intend ex-dividends values.

As for the probabilistic structure of discrete time models, we limit to say that the economy is characterized by a probabilistic space $\left(\Omega, \{\mathcal{F}_t\}_{t\geq 0}, \mathbb{P}\right)$ spanned by a set of exogenous source of randomness $\{\mathbf{z}_t\}_{t\geq 0}$. The bold notation is intended to denote a vector of real variables. The symbol Ω is the sample space of $\mathbf{z}_t$, while $\mathbb{P}$ is an *objective* probability measure define over Ω. The collection $\{\mathcal{F}_t\}_{t\geq 0}$ is the natural filtration generated by $\mathbf{z}_t$. All the other stochastic processes involved in our analysis are assumed to be adapted to $\mathcal{F}_t$, once the correct timing (and notation) conventions are properly taken into account.

2.1.1 Budget Constraints and Policies

Our analysis of corporate finance decisions starts from a simple setting in which the company can issue common stocks and a bond with one period maturity (i.e. bonds issued in t expire in $t+1$), and there are no transaction costs on capital markets. At each date, the bonds issued are all of equal seniority, and pay a predetermined coupon rate equal to c_{t+1}. The face value of each bond is equal to one unit of the relevant *numeraire*, we name as *dollar*. Consequently, the number of bonds issued in t is equal to F_{t+1}. Hence, provided that the firm is solvent[1] at date t, its budget constraint is given by

$$\underbrace{s_t\left(n_{t+1}-n_t\right)+p_t F_{t+1}+y_t}_{\text{Inflows from capital markets}}-\left[\underbrace{d_t n_t+F_t\left(1+c_t\right)}_{\text{Outflows related to existing liabilities}}\right]=L_{t+1}-L_t\left(1+r_t\right), \tag{2.1.1}$$

where n_{t+1} is the number of shares outstanding at the end of period t, and d_t is the dividend per share paid to *incumbent* shareholders. Basically, the change in end of period liquidity is the sum of the following components: (i) the free cash flows to firm (y_t), (ii) the interest income on existing liquidity ($r_t L_t$) and (iii) the net proceeds from financial markets $s_t\left(n_{t+1}-n_t\right)+p_t F_{t+1}-\left[d_t n_t+F_t\left(1+c_t\right)\right]$. This consideration holds in general, as we show in Sect. 1.4.1.

[1] We use the term solvent as a synonym of a active (non-defaulted) firm at a generic time t.

Notice that in the current example, bonds are *unsecured*.[2] A debt instrument is secured if, in case of the firm's default, its holders can seize a specific asset of the firm. Therefore, the recovery value of secured debt can never fall below the net proceeds from the sales of the pledged asset. On the other hand, the recovery value of unsecured debt instruments is tight to the going concern value of the firm at default. We analyze in detail the difference between the two cases in the next chapters, as the correlative borrowing mechanisms have different consequences. From a technical perspective, the issuance of unsecured debt is known as *borrowing against cash flows*, while we use the term *borrowing against assets* or *collateral* in case of secured debt.

The value of the firm (V_t), or *enterprise value*, is given by the following equation

$$V_t = V_t^E + p_t F_{t+1} - L_{t+1}, \tag{2.1.2}$$

where $p_t F_{t+1}$ is the market value of debt, while $V_t^E = p_t^E n_{t+1}$ is the market value of equity. On this regard, n_{t+1} is the number of shares outstanding at the end of t, i.e. after all payments for the same period are settled. Admittedly, the use of $t+1$ in spite of t may be misleading at first. However, as for the case of debt's face value and liquidity, this notation is convenient to set up the dynamic programs characterizing shareholders optimizing behavior in the following chapters. In short, the number of shares in circulation and the face value of debt at the end of each date are the *control variables* for shareholders. On the contrary, the amount of debt and shares inherited from the previous period are *state variables*. Rearranging Eq. (2.1.1), the budget constraint of the firm can then be expressed as,

$$\underbrace{V_t + x_t + \pi_t}_{\text{Cumdividend value of the firm}} = (p_t + d_t)\, n_t + F_t\,(1 + c_t) - L_t\,(1 + r_t)\,, \tag{2.1.3}$$

which simply states that the cum-dividend value of the firm is equal to the sum of cum-dividend value of incumbent security holders, net of the liquidity available at the beginning of the period $(1 + L_t r_t)$. This relation is of utmost importance, as it suggests that, after all, the only thing that matters is the total amount of free cash flows generated by the firm, which depends on production, investment and financing decisions.

A policy is a state contingent rule which maps the set of measurable events at each date in a specific decision. For ease of exposure, we often include production decisions in the firm's investment policy, although sometimes we need to be more explicit, as in Chap. 4 and Sect. 7.1 of Chap. 7. For the moment, we assume that both financing and investment decisions are exogenously given. In this case, we can model a given investment policy in terms of the associated unlevered free cash flows process $\{x_t\}_{t\geq 0}$. Likewise, a financing policy is intended to be a multivariate

[2] As a technical aside, notice that in this example there could be no role for debt covenants, as debt is due at the same date at which new information is released.

stochastic process $\{d_{t+1}, n_{t+1}F_{t+1}, c_{t+1}, L_{t+1}\}_{t\geq 0}$ for the firm's capital structure. We define the firm's synthetic dividend (D_t) as,

$$D_t := d_t n_t + p_t (n_{t+1} - n_t), \tag{2.1.4}$$

which is the sum of actual dividends paid plus cash flows related to share buybacks (minus, if shares are issued). As is clear, for a given investment policy, we can consider only feasible financing policies, in the sense that Eq. (2.1.1) must be valid at each date in which the firm is solvent.

While it should be immediate to conclude that the firm can adopt only feasible financing policies, it is less obvious whether we should consider any restriction on $\{x_t\}_{t\geq 0}$. If we were taking explicitly into account shareholders optimizing behavior, the answer would be certainly negative, as shareholders have always the option to shut down the firm if there is no way to make it profitable. However, when the investment policy is exogenously given, as if it was written in the corporate bylaws rather than being dynamically optimized in the best interests of shareholders, it is convenient to restrict our attention only to policies with a positive net present value (NPV), that is,

$$\mathbb{E}_t \sum_{j=0}^{\infty} \frac{M_{t+j}}{M_t} x_{t+j} \geq 0. \tag{2.1.5}$$

A policy that satisfies Eq. (2.1.5) is *individually rational*. To understand the meaning of this condition, consider the case of an all-equity firm without liquidity, i.e. $x_t = D_t$. It is easy to show that the left hand side (LHS) of Eq. (2.1.4) is the cum-dividend equity value of the firm $\left(\hat{V}_t^E = d_t n_t + V_t^E\right)$. The proof comes from rearranging Eq. (1.3.1) and Eq. (2.1.3) (see Sect. 2.2.1), from which we obtain

$$V_t^E = s_t n_{t+1} = \mathbb{E}_t \left[\frac{M_{t+1}}{M_t} \left(V_{t+1}^E + x_{t+1} \right) \right]. \tag{2.1.6}$$

Solving forward the previous expression, under the transversality condition $\lim_{T\to\infty} \mathbb{E}_t \left[\frac{M_T}{M_t} s_T n_{T+1} \right]$ deriving from Eq. (1.3.1), we eventually obtain,

$$\hat{V}_t^E = \mathbb{E}_t \sum_{j=0}^{\infty} M_{t,t+j} x_{t+j}. \tag{2.1.7}$$

A policy that is not individual rational will be never adopted by the shareholders of the firm, as it is equivalent to a collection of *projects* with strictly negative NPV. Therefore, it is quite natural to rule out this case while we are working under the hypothesis of an exogenously given investment policy.

Notice that, in order to obtain the previous result, we made use of the transversality condition from Eq. (1.3.1), $\lim_{T\to\infty} \mathbb{E}_t \left[\frac{M_T}{M_t} s_T n_{T+1}\right]$. Similarly, another important constraint must be always imposed when financing decisions are exogenously given, that is,

$$\lim_{T\to\infty} \mathbb{E}_t \left(\frac{M_T}{M_t} L_{T+1}\right) = 0. \tag{2.1.8}$$

As liquidity reserves are invested in risk-free assets, $\lim_{T\to\infty} \mathbb{E}_t \left(\frac{M_T}{M_t} L_{T+1}\right) > 0$ would be equivalent to allow for the existence of a Ponzi scheme in the supply-side of risk-free assets. In equilibrium, this eventuality is ruled out by the dynamics of the risk-free rate. Consequently, the value of the firm satisfies the transversality condition,

$$\lim_{T\to\infty} \mathbb{E}_t \left(\frac{M_T}{M_t} V_T\right) = 0. \tag{2.1.9}$$

Notably, the effect of Eq. (2.1.9) is that of restricting further the set of admissible financing policies, by requiring that the growth of cash balances is bounded above by the risk-free rate process $\{r_{t+1}\}_{t\geq 0}$.

2.1.2 Default and Bankruptcy Procedures

The remainder of the section is dedicated to discuss what happens if the firm renege on its debts. This is a very important part of every corporate finance model, as it shapes the conflict of interests between share and debt holders. First of all, recall that equity holders are protected by limited liability, which means that in the worst case they get nothing out of a bankruptcy procedure. Holding the investment policy fixed to the one exogenously given, shareholders always opt for default if there exists no feasible financing policy $\Gamma_t = \{F_{s+1}, L_{s+1}\}_{s\geq t}$ such that $\hat{V}_t^E(\Gamma_t) \geq 0$. However, the assumption of an exogenous investment policy is just a way to initially separate investment from financing decisions. When production and investment decisions are explicitly modeled, it is customary to impose that default always occurs after production takes place. This hypothesis serves to rule out indirect asset sales before trading becomes possible at a certain date. This is a very technical point which we clarify further in the next chapter.

The first type of bankruptcy procedure which we examine is inspired by the *Chapter 11* of the United States Bankruptcy code. Basically, we consider a *restructuring* of the firm's liabilities through a *debt-for-equity* swap. Let t_d be the default date; then, the process goes as follows:

(1) the firm, on behalf of its shareholders, declares the intention to renege on its debts;[3]
(2) investment, financing decisions are temporary suspended, and all the outstanding securities are converted in a new class of ordinary shares;
(3) the incumbent share and debt holders split between themselves, according to some *allocation mechanism*, the cum-dividend value of the new shares, obtaining respectively a non-negative payoff equal to to R_{td}^E and R_{td}^B ;
(4) the legal and administrative expenses related to the balance sheet restructuring $\left(bc_{t_d}\right)$ are paid;
(5) investment and financing decision for date t_d are taken.

Based on the timing of these events, we can formulate the following equation in t_d,

$$R_{t_d}^E + R_{t_d}^B = x_{t_d} - bc_{t_d} + \left(1 + r_{t_d-1,t_d}\right) L_{t_d} + V_{t_d} \tag{2.1.10}$$

which reflects the fact that sum of the recovery values, net of the available liquidity, is equal to the cum-dividend value of the firm. As there are no interest payments at t_d, compared to the case in which the firm is solvent, dividends are lowered by direct bankruptcy costs $\left(bc_{t_d}\right)$ and the loss of tax shield on current interests expenses $\left(\pi_{t_d} = 0\right)$. The debt-for-equity swap is essentially a procedure in which the firm continues to operate, but there is a change in its ownership. The fact that shareholders may retain a positive recovery value, therefore violating the absolute priority of debt holders, may depend on the strategic design (see Section 6.3.5), as in Mella-Barral and Perraudin (1997). Notice that a debt-for-equity swap is feasible if and only if $0 \leq bc_{t_d} \leq V_{t_d} + x_{t_d} + \left(1 + r_{t_d-1,t_d}\right) L_{t_d}$, as a result of shareholders' limited liability.

Instead, on the other side we have Chap. 7-like procedures, which entail the liquidation of the firm. The general schematic description of a liquidation is the following:

(1) an event of default takes place (e.g. coupon payments are skipped);
(2) the firm's assets are seized and grouped into different lots;
(3) a contract is written with an agent in charge of maximizing the proceeds from the assets sale;
(4) depending on their priority, the incumbent security holders obtain a non-negative recovery value;
(5) the firm ceases to exist and its securities are written off.

The total proceeds from assets sales are equal to the sum of the recovery values of debt and equity holders, where the latter will typically obtain nothing in this case. It is convenient to represent the sum of recovery values introducing a random variable

[3]In the legal jargon, the firm *fills for bankruptcy protection*.

bc_{t_d} defined as,

$$bc_{t_d} := \mathbb{E}_{t_d} \sum_{j=0}^{\infty} \frac{M_{t_d+j}}{M_{t_d}} x_{t+j} - R_{t_d}^E + R_{t_d}^B, \tag{2.1.11}$$

which can be interpreted as the difference between the NPV of the cash flows that could be extracted from the firm's assets and their liquidation value. Typically, we should expect to see this difference to be positive, which means that liquidation is costly. Shleifer and Vishny (1992) provides a general equilibrium explanation for the presence of liquidation costs, which could be useful to understand how macroeconomic conditions influence the outcome of bankruptcy procedures. With these notions, we are ready to present the Modigliani and Miller (MM) theorems, which marked the birth of modern corporate finance theory.

2.2 The Modigliani and Miller Theorems

The MM theorems are valid under specific conditions, which are often labelled as "ideal" to give a sense of how far they are from reality. And it is indeed for this reason that the propositions are of fundamental importance, as we can understand when and why capital structure and dividend policy decisions may affect the value of firms when relaxing the MM assumptions. We illustrate the theorems by considering the simple capital structure described above. Nevertheless, a more sophisticated capital structures is possible, and it is actually a specific result of the general case we discuss in Sect. 1.4.1. The MM theorems divide in a statement about the irrelevance of dividend policy, and one about the irrelevance of the financing policy as a whole. While we could present just the latter result, it is useful to proceed step by step, as the methodology developed in this section will prove to be a very useful tool in more general circumstances.

2.2.1 *Irrelevance of Dividend Policy*

Consider a firm which makes no use of debt and does not hold cash reserves. By Eq. (2.1.1), unlevered free cash flows are paid out as dividends plus share buybacks (shares offerings, if negative), and the value of the firm is equal to $V_t = \mathbb{E}_t \sum_{s=1}^{\infty} M_{t,t+s} x_{t+s}$, consistent with Eq. (2.1.7). Suppose that either taxation is null or interest income is tax-free ($\pi_t = 0$). We now allow the firm to hold cash reserves. Absent debt, the firm dividend policy $\{d_t \geq 0, n_{t+1} \geq 0, L_{t+1}\}_{t \geq 0}$ must be consistent with the budget constraint,

$$s_t (n_{t+1} - n_t) + x_t = d_t n_t + L_{t+1} - L_t (1 + r_t), \tag{2.2.1}$$

as well as with Eq. (2.1.8). As a result, the budget constraint can be written as $V_{t+1} + x_{t+1} = n_{t+1}(p_{t+1} + d_{t+1}) + L_{t+2} - L_{t+1}(1 + r_{t+1})$, where $V_t = p_t n_{t+1} - L_{t+1}$. Financial markets equilibrium requires that,

$$
\begin{aligned}
p_t n_{t+1} &= V_t + L_{t+1} = \mathbb{E}_t\left[M_{t,t+1}(p_{t+1} + d_{t+1})\, n_{t+1}\right] = \\
\mathbb{E}_t &\left\{\frac{M_{t+1}}{M_t}\left[V_{t+1} + x_{t+1} + L_{t+1}(1 + r_{t+1})\right]\right\} = \\
&= \mathbb{E}_t\left[\frac{M_{t+1}}{M_t}(V_{t+1} + x_{t+1})\right] + L_{t+1}\mathbb{E}_t\left[\frac{M_{t+1}}{M_t}(1 + r_{t+1})\right] \\
&= \mathbb{E}_t\left[\frac{M_{t+1}}{M_t}(V_{t+1} + x_{t+1})\right] + L_{t+1}. \qquad (2.2.2)
\end{aligned}
$$

Hence, we can write the value of the firm as,

$$
V_t = \mathbb{E}_t\left[\frac{M_{t+1}}{M_t}(V_{t+1} + x_{t+1})\right]. \qquad (2.2.3)
$$

To solve this equation we can then use Eq. (2.1.9), thereby obtaining the following expression for the value of the firm.

$$
V_t = \mathbb{E}_t \sum_{j=1}^{\infty} \frac{M_{t+j}}{M_t} x_{t+j}. \qquad (2.2.4)
$$

Thus, we have the following result.

Proposition 2.1 *Suppose the firm's capital structure includes only common stocks, and the investment policy $\{x_t\}_{t\geq 0}$ is exogenously given. If there are no transaction costs, and no taxes on liquidity reserves, then the value of the firm is independent from its dividend-liquidity policy and shareholders gain nothing regardless the policy assumed by the firm.*

Proof The first part of the proposition has been shown above. To prove that shareholders value is independent from the dividend-liquidity policy adopted, it is sufficient to observe that $\hat{V}_t^E = x_t + L_t(1 + r_t) + \mathbb{E}_t \sum_{j=1}^{\infty} \frac{M_{t+j}}{M_t} x_{t+j}$, which is independent from the continuation policy $\{d_j \geq 0, s_{j+1} \geq 0, L_{j+1}\}_{j\geq t}$. Since the same argument holds for all $t \geq 0$, we conclude that shareholders value is unaffected by dividend-liquidity decisions. □

As a corollary to the proposition, since L_t is taken as given at time t, the only driver for the value the shareholders can focus on is the investment policy of the firm.

2.2.2 The Irrelevance of Financing Policy

The result we obtained in the previous section can be generalized by including debt financing. If this result was actually true, the theory of capital structure would probably end up in this section. This is not the case, as several hypothesis, such as the absence of tax effects of debt financing, are counterfactual. However, the importance of the *irrelevance* result contained in Proposition 2.2 is twofold. On one hand, it shows under which ideal conditions we should not be caring about financing decisions, which may be a useful approximation in several cases. On the other, it suggests that investment decisions will be a primary driver of the value for shareholders, which is a generally accepted result, both in theory and practice.

We give a formal statement for the capital structure described in Sect. 2.1, and provide a formal proof in the case that an event of default is resolved with a debt-for-equity swap, in which bond holders have absolute priority. The alternatives of liquidation and multiple debt securities can be obtained as special cases of the general analysis presented in Sect. 1.4.1.

Proposition 2.2 *Suppose the investment policy* $\{x_t\}_{t\geq 0}$ *is exogenously given, independently from the financing policy, and that* $\{\pi_t = bc_t = 0\}_{t\geq 0}$. *If the absolute priority rule is satisfied in case of default,* $R^B_{t+1} = \min\{F_{t+1}(1+c_{t+1}), x_{t+1} + L_{t+1}(1+r_{t+1}) + V_{t+1} - bc_{t+1}\}$*, the value of the firm* $(V_t = s_t n_{t+1} + p_t F_{t+1} - L_{t+1})$ *is independent from its financial policy* $\{d_{t+1}, n_{t+1}F_{t+1}, c_{t+1}, L_{t+1}\}_{t\geq 0}$ *and it is equal to* $V_t = \mathbb{E}_t \sum_{j=i}^{\infty} M_{t,t+j}x_{t+j}$. *Moreover, shareholders value is independent from financing decisions.*

Proof Let δ_t be an indicator function that is equal to 1 if bankruptcy occurs at date t, or zero otherwise. At each point in time, the asset pricing equations for bonds and shares are,

$$p_t = \mathbb{E}_t \left\{ \frac{M_{t+1}}{M_t} \left[(1+c_{t+1}) \cdot (1-\delta_{t+1}) + \frac{R^B_{t+1}}{b_t}\delta_{t+1} \right] \right\} \tag{2.2.5}$$

$$s_t = \mathbb{E}_t \left\{ \frac{M_{t+1}}{M_t} \left[(s_{t+1}+d_{t+1}) \cdot (1-\delta_{t+1}) + \frac{R^E_{t+1}}{n_t}\delta_{t+1} \right] \right\} \tag{2.2.6}$$

Let $\mathscr{C}_{t+1} \subseteq \mathcal{F}_{t+1}$ the set of events for which default does not take place in $t+1$. If we let $\mathbb{P}_t$ the conditional probability measure at time t, the value of the firm can be written as,

$$\begin{aligned} V_t = s_t n_{t+1} + p_t F_{t+1} - L_{t+1} = \\ \int_{\omega\in\mathscr{C}_{t+1}} \frac{M_{t+1}}{M_t}\left[(s_{t+1}+d_{t+1})\,n_{t+1} + (1+c_{t+1})\,F_{t+1}\right] d\mathbb{P}_t(\omega) + \\ \int_{\omega\in\overline{\mathscr{C}}_{t+1}} M_{t,t+1}\left(R^E_{t+1} + R^B_{t+1}\right) d\mathbb{P}_t(\omega) - L_{t+1}. \end{aligned} \tag{2.2.7}$$

Furthermore, $\forall \omega \in \mathscr{C}_{t+1}$ the firm's one-period ahead budget constraint is equal to,

$$(p_{t+1}+d_{t+1})\,n_t + (1+c_{t+1})\,b_t = V_{t+1} + x_{t+1} + (1+r_{t+1})\,L_{t+1} \tag{2.2.8}$$

while for $\forall \omega \in \overline{\mathscr{C}}_{t+1}$, the following expression holds valid,

$$R^E_{t+1} + R^B_{t+1} = V_{t+1} + x_{t+1} + (1+r_{t+1})\,L_{t+1}. \tag{2.2.9}$$

Therefore,

$$\begin{aligned} V_t = \int_{\omega \in \mathcal{F}_{t+1}} \frac{M_{t+1}}{M_t} \left[V_{t+1} + x_{t+1} + L_t\left(1 + r_{t,t+1}\right)\right] d\mathbb{P}_t - L_{t+1} = \\ \mathbb{E}_t\left[\frac{M_{t+1}}{M_t}\left(x_{t+1} + V_{t+1}\right)\right]. \end{aligned} \tag{2.2.10}$$

Recall the transversality condition $\lim_{s\to\infty} \mathbb{E}_t\left(\frac{M_{t+s}}{M_t} V_{t+s}\right) = 0$. Solving Eq. (2.2.10) we obtain,

$$V_t = \mathbb{E}_t \sum_{j=1}^{\infty} M_{t,t+j} x_{t+j}, \tag{2.2.11}$$

To prove the second part of the proposition we can proceed as in the proof of Proposition 2.1. Since the absolute priority rule holds, shareholders will default only if their recovery value is null. In fact, in order to obtain a positive recovery value, we must have $SH_t := x_t + L_t\,(1+r_t) + \mathbb{E}_t \sum_{j=1}^{\infty} \frac{M_{t+j}}{M_t} x_{t+j} - F_t\,(1+c_t) > 0$, which is equivalent to having positive shareholders value and conditional upon the decision to repay debt and coupon. Hence, shareholders value is equal to $\max\{0, SH_t\}$, which is independent from the continuation policy $\left\{d_{j+1}, n_{j+1} F_{j+1}, c_{j+1}, L_{j+1}\right\}_{j\geq t}$. □

Proposition 2.2 asserts that, if (i) there are no bankruptcy costs, (ii) the are no transaction costs associated to issuing new securities, (iii) taxation is unaffected by financing choices, and (iv) the firm's investment policy is independent from financing choices, then both the value of the firm and shareholders value are not affected by financing choices. The intuition is trivial. We can imagine debt and equity as different slices of a pie, where the pie is the market value of the firm. By non-arbitrage, although the firm's unlevered cash flows are not directly traded, there exists always a portfolio of securities that replicates its dynamics. Such a portfolio is indeed composed by the firm's financial liabilities, that are freely tradable on the market. Hence, if the financial liabilities mix has no effects on the free cash flows stream of the firm, the size of the pie remains unchanged, and the total market value of the firm depends only on $\{x_t\}_{t\geq 0}$.

At this point, we may wonder what is the effect of financial leverage, as it is eventually irrelevant for shareholder value. Suppose that c_{t+1} is such that $p_{t+1} = 1$

always, that is, debt is issued at *par value*. Intuitively, higher debt makes future dividends riskier for shareholders. As such, after time t dividends are paid, we should expect the ex-dividend equity value to be lower the higher the leverage ratio $\frac{F_{t+1}}{V_t^E}$ is. Equivalently, the stocks of more levered firm, *ceteris paribus*, should be associated to higher expected returns. Similarly, higher liquidity levels should reduce expected returns, as they dilute the weight of cash flows risk. However, since the value of the firm is unchanged, we should not expect the weighted average of stocks and bonds to be affected by the financing mix. This result is actually a corollary of Proposition 2.2, which comes from Hamada (1972) for the case of risk-free debt (see Sect. 3.3). Two considerations appears useful from a practitioner's perspective, at least assuming that Proposition 2.2 can thought as a good approximation of what happen in the real market. First, financial leverage can be used to shift the risk-return profile of a stock. Hence, holding everything else constant, investing in stocks with higher leverage should generate higher expected returns on average, but, at the same time, it should also be associated to higher portfolio volatility. Second, if we wish to neutralize the effect of leverage, but still get exposure to the firm's free cash flows, we should invest both in stocks and bonds, in the same proportion of their relative market capitalizations.

Proposition 2.3 *Assume that c_{t+1} is such that $p_t = 1$ for all t. Let $\chi := \{x\}_{t\geq 0}$ the firm's investment policy, and $r_{t+1}^{\chi} := \frac{V_t^E}{V_t} r_{t+1}^E + \frac{F_{t+1}}{V_t} r_{t+1}^B - \frac{L_{t+1}}{V_t} r_{t+1}$, $r_{t+1}^E := \frac{(d_{t+1}+s_{t+1})(1-\delta_{t+1})+R_{t+1}^E \delta_{t+1}}{s_t}$ and $r_{t+1}^B = (1+c_{t+1})(1-\delta_{t+1}) + R_{t+1}^B \delta_{t+1}$ the total returns firm, stocks and bonds at time $t+1$, respectively. Then, r_{t+1}^{χ} is independent from the firm's financing policy. Furthermore, $\mathbb{E}_t\left(r_{t+1}^E\right)$ is increasing in $\frac{F_{t+1}}{V_t^E}$ and decreasing in $\frac{L_{t+1}}{V_t^E}$.*

Proof The first part is trivial. Simply, $\frac{V_t^E}{V_t} r_{t+1}^E + \frac{p_t F_{t+1}}{V_t} r_{t+1}^B - \frac{L_{t+1}}{V_t} r_{t+1} = \frac{x_{t+1}+V_{t+1}}{V_t}$ from the application of the firm's budget constraint. Hence, r_{t+1}^{χ} does not depend on the firm's financing policy. The second part, instead, is more complicated. To see why, consider that the effect of leverage is ambiguous in principle. On one hand, higher leverage increases the risk for shareholders to see their dividends slashed in the following period, if they decide to repay debt. On the other, higher leverage increases the option value of default, that is, the possibility for shareholders to rationally renege on the firm's debt.

Formally, our goal is to show that $\frac{\partial \mathbb{E}_t\left(r_{t+1}^E\right)}{\partial F_{t+1}} \geq 0$. In order to do so, the first step is to recognize the expression of time $t+1$ shareholders value $\left(\hat{V}_{t+1}^E\right)$ the numerator of r_{t+1}^E, so that we can write $r_{t+1}^E = \frac{\hat{V}_{t+1}^E}{V_t^E}$. From Proposition 2.2, we have $\hat{V}_t^E = \max\left\{0, x_t + L_t(1+r_t) + \mathbb{E}_t \sum_{j=1}^{\infty} \frac{M_{t+j}}{M_t} x_{t+j} - F_t(1+c_t)\right\}$, which can be used to obtain the following expression for equity returns,

$$1 + r_{t+1}^{E} = \frac{1}{V_t^E} \max\left\{0, x_{t+1} + V_{t+1} + L_{t+1}\left(1 + r_{t+1}\right) - F_{t+1}\left(1 + c_{t+1}\right)\right\}, \tag{2.2.12}$$

Consider the scenarios in which the firm is not defaulted, $\delta_{t+1} = 0$. Then, debt holders are paid back in full, $r_{t+1}^{\chi} = \frac{V_t^E}{V_t} r_{t+1}^{E} + \frac{p_t F_{t+1}}{V_t^E} c_{t+1} - \frac{L_{t+1}}{V_t} r_{t+1}$ and we can write Eq. (2.2.12) as,

$$r_{t+1}^{E} = \max\left\{r_{t+1} + \left(1 - \frac{L_{t+1}}{V_t^E}\right)\left(r_{t+1}^{\chi} - r_{t+1}\right) + \frac{F_{t+1}}{V_t^E}\left(r_{t+1}^{\chi} - c_{t+1}\right), -1\right\}. \tag{2.2.13}$$

Let $u_{t+1} := r_{t+1}^{\chi} - \frac{L_{t+1}}{V_t^E}\left(r_{t+1}^{\chi} - r_{t+1}\right) + \frac{F_{t+1}}{V_t^E}\left(r_{t+1}^{\chi} - c_{t+1}\right)$. Since the investment policy is individually rational, $r_{t+1}^{\chi} \geq -1$ and, consequently, $\Pr_t\left\{u_{t+1} > 1 + \alpha\right\} > \Pr_t\left\{u_{t+1} > 1 - \alpha\right\}$ for every $\alpha > 0$. The resulting positive skew implies that $\mathbb{E}_t\left(r_{t+1}^{E}\right) = \mathbb{E}_t\left\{\left[u_{t+1}, -1\right]^{+}\right\}$ is increasing in the variance of u_{t+1}. Since the latter is increasing in $\frac{F_{t+1}}{V_t^E}$ and decreasing in $\frac{L_{t+1}}{V_t^E}$, we conclude that $\mathbb{E}_t\left(r_{t+1}^{E}\right)$ is increasing in $\frac{F_{t+1}}{V_t^E}$ and decreasing in $\frac{L_{t+1}}{V_t^E}$ as we claim. □

2.2.3 *Debt Tax Shield and Bankruptcy Costs*

Most of countries adopted fiscal legislations that allows for tax effects of financial income and expenses. For instance, the interest income earned on liquidity reserves is often taxed at the same rate applied for operating earnings. Likewise, interests expenses are often tax deductible, although sometimes with limitations. At a very general level, we can say that a certain financing policy results in a net tax shield π_t which increases or reduces taxation in period t depending on the interests paid on debt and those earned on liquidity. To make a specific example, suppose that the corporate tax rate (τ) is constant[4] and it is applied to the firm's net income. In this case, we would have $T_t = \left(ebit_t - c_t F_t + r_t L_t\right)\tau$, and, consequently, $\pi_t = c_t F_t - r_t L_t$.

In the remainder of the section our interest is to understand the effects of introducing taxable financial income and bankruptcy costs in the MM framework. A debt-for-equity swap procedure remains the working hypothesis in case of default.

[4]A constant tax rate implies that the firm receives a net transfer from the government when its net income is negative. It is sometimes a good approximation in situations in which the loss carry-forwards can be quickly used.

As a result, in case of default the firm will loose its ability to deduce interests expenses from taxes in the same period that default takes place, as all bonds are converted in shares before coupons are paid. Although not essential, it may be convenient in this case to represent the debt tax shield as $\pi_t = dts_t\,(r_t L_t, (1-\delta_t)\,c_t F_t)$. We can then show that the following value of the firm is always valid,

$$V_t = \mathbb{E}_t \sum_{j=1}^{\infty} M_{t,t+j} x_{t+j} + DTS_t - BC_t \tag{2.2.14}$$

where $DTS_t \;:=\; \mathbb{E}_t \sum_{j=i}^{\infty} M_{t,t+j} dts_t\,(r_t L_t, (1-\delta_t)\,c_t F_t)$ is the net present value of the tax benefits from a given financing policy. The term $BC_t \;:= \mathbb{E}_t \sum_{j=i}^{\infty} M_{t,t+j} bc_{t+j}\delta_{t+j}$ is instead the NPV of all bankruptcy costs that the firm will experience in case of one or more default episodes.

The proof of Eq. (2.2.14) derives again from the firm's budget constraint. Starting from the asset pricing equation for the price of shares and debt, Eq. (2.2.5–2.2.6) respectively, we can write the value of the firm as,

$$\begin{aligned} V_t = s_t n_{t+1} + p_t F_{t+1} - L_{t+1} = \int_{\omega \in \mathscr{C}_{t+1}} \frac{M_{t+1}}{M_t} \left[(s_{t+1} + d_{t+1})\, n_{t+1} + (1 + c_{t+1})\, F_{t+1} \right] \\ \times (1 - \delta_{t+1})\, d\mathbb{P}_t\,(\omega) \\ + \int_{\omega \in \overline{\mathscr{C}}_{t+1}} \frac{M_{t+1}}{M_t} \left(R^E_{t+1} + R^B_{t+1} \right) \delta_{t+1} d\mathbb{P}_t\,(\omega) - L_{t+1}. \end{aligned} \tag{2.2.15}$$

Substituting Eq. (2.1.1) and Eq. (2.1.10) into the first and second integral of Eq. (2.2.15), respectively, the following difference equation is obtained,

$$V_t = \mathbb{E}_t \left\{ M_{t,t+1} \left[x_{t+1} + V_{t+1} + \pi_{t+1} - \delta_{t+1} bc_{t+1} \right] \right\}, \tag{2.2.16}$$

which admits the solution,

$$\begin{aligned} V_t = \mathbb{E}_t \sum_{j=1}^{\infty} \frac{M_{t+j}}{M_t} x_{t+j} + \mathbb{E}_t \sum_{j=1}^{\infty} \frac{M_{t+j}}{M_t} dts_t \left(r_{t+j} L_{t+j}, \left(1 - \delta_{t+j}\right) c_{t+j} F_{t+j} \right) \\ - \mathbb{E}_t \sum_{j=1}^{\infty} \frac{M_{t+j}}{M_t} bc_{t+j} \delta_{t+j}. \end{aligned} \tag{2.2.17}$$

Differently from the MM world, the value of the firm is now affected by the firm's financing policy. As a result, shareholders value may depend on capital structure decisions. The irrelevance of the firm's financing policy is now broken, and understanding the effects of dynamical capital structure decisions is of central importance.

2.3 Capital Structure and Corporate Governance

We have seen that introducing tax effects of debt financing and bankruptcy costs, the MM irrelevance results are no longer valid. However, one point we consider as unsatisfactory is about the investment and financing decisions which are assumed as exogenously given. In other words, while we could always formulate Eq. (2.2.17) for a given investment and financing pattern, a more robust theoretical framework is need to determine which patterns will be chosen. This will be actually the purpose of all the following chapters, but it is important to introduce from the beginning few very important concepts in relation to investment decisions and in which interests we should expect a firm to be managed.

2.3.1 *Investment Decisions and Agency Costs*

Let Υ be the set of all unlevered free cash flows processes $\chi = \{x_t\}_{t\geq 0}$, which depends on the firm's investment policy. To simplify our discussion, and without loss of generality, Υ can be assumed as the set of all available investment policies. Note that we are not imposing the *individual rationality* condition. Let assume that there exists an element $\chi^* \in \Upsilon$, $\chi^* = \left\{x_t^*\right\}_{t\geq 0}$, such that $\mathbb{E}_t \sum_{j=0}^{\infty} M_{t,t+j} x_{t+j}^* \geq \mathbb{E}_t \sum_{j=0}^{\infty} M_{t,t+j} x_{t+j}$ for every $\chi \in \Upsilon$. By definition, χ^* maximizes shareholders value for an all-equity firm that does not hold liquidity reserves. This lead us to following definition. A firm is said *unlevered* if these conditions hold: (i) the capital structure includes only common stocks, (ii) no cash reserves exist and (iii) the investment policy adopted is χ^*. In other words, the *unlevered firm* is an-all equity firm whose value, V_t^u, cannot be improved by any other investment strategy,

$$V_t^u = \mathbb{E}_t \sum_{j=0}^{\infty} M_{t,t+j} x_{t+j}^*. \tag{2.3.1}$$

The unlevered firm is an important benchmark, which can be used to gauge the real effects of dynamic capital structure decisions. To put the point into perspective, assume that, in order to the best interest of the *controlling stakeholder*, the firm is running under an investment policy $\chi \in \Upsilon : \chi \neq \chi^*$. The difference between $\mathbb{E}_t \sum_{j=1}^{\infty} M_{t,t+j} x_{t+j}^*$ and $\mathbb{E}_t \sum_{j=1}^{\infty} M_{t,t+j} x_{t+j}$ is called *agency costs* (AC_t),

$$AC_t := \mathbb{E}_t \sum_{j=1}^{\infty} M_{t,t+j} x_{t+j}^* - \mathbb{E}_t \sum_{j=1}^{\infty} M_{t,t+j} x_{t+j} \tag{2.3.2}$$

and it is a deadweight loss for the firm. It should be noticed that the notion of controlling stakeholder denotes the agent effectively in control of the firm's decision making process. While in general we conjecture that markets are complete and a representative shareholder is in control, there might situations in which this hypothesis is not appropriate. In Sect. 2.3.3 we briefly overview this important feature, which motivates the indispensable role of *corporate governance*. Still, even when a representative shareholder can be thought to be in control, there might be reasons for her to deviate from χ^*. Writing Eq. (2.2.17) equivalently as,

$$V_t = V_t^u + DTS_t - (AC_t + BC_t), \qquad (2.3.3)$$

we can guess that, in *equilibrium*, shareholders are trading-off the tax benefits of debt financing with the resulting agency and bankruptcy costs. Actually, this is the common trait of all the models we present in the following chapters, and well summarizes the kind of topics that are commonly considered part of dynamic corporate finance theory.

2.3.2 *Optimal Investments, Capital Budgeting and Debt Overhang*

Debt overhang is a notable example of agency costs, we briefly discuss in this section. Chapters 5, 6 and 7 explore in more depth the technical details and come up with more accurate quantitative predictions. Myers (1977) is the first to formalize the idea that shareholders may become reluctant to invest when indebtedness becomes very high relative to the firm's fundamentals. The model we present in this section is useful also to introduce the concept of *growth options* and *assets in place*.

Suppose there are neither taxes nor bankruptcy costs. The firm is endowed with capital stock K_0, which is assumed for simplicity not to depreciate over time. The optimal use of this capital stock allows shareholders to extract in each future time $t > 0$ an amount of *operating cash flows* equal to $A_t K_0$, where $\{A_t > 0\}_{t \geq 0}$ is a strictly positive exogenous stochastic process. Let assume also that the firm's capital stock cannot be increased, but in each period the firm has the *option to invest* a dollars amount equal to $I_t \in [0, I]$ in a new project. Each project becomes available at a specific time t, and the firm can invest in it only at the same date. In other words, there is no *option to delay* the investment in the growth option becoming available at a given point in time. Likewise, investment in each project is irreversible. A generic project[5] t generates a non-negative cash flows streams $\left\{y_{t+j}^{(t)} I_t > 0\right\}_{j>0}$, where I_t is the amount of dollar invested in the project. In addition, investment in each project is irreversible, meaning that the firm cannot divest from any of its earlier implemented projects.

[5] Projects are indexed by the date in which they are available, which corresponds to the time index of the economy.

If we let K_t be the firm's total invested capital,

$$K_t = K_0 + \sum_{j=1}^{t} I_t, \tag{2.3.4}$$

it easily turns out that unlevered free cash flows can be expressed as,

$$x_t = A_t K_0 + \sum_{j=1}^{t-1} I_t y_t^{(j)} - I_t. \tag{2.3.5}$$

The firm is endowed with a certain amount of debt, say $F_0 \geq 0$, which consists of a perpetual bond with coupon rate $c > 0$. The amount of the outstanding debt cannot be adjusted over time, and the firm does not hold or accumulate cash. A default event results in the firm liquidation and shareholders are assumed to lose everything. On this regard, the hypothesis is that the option to invest in future projects is lost in the bankruptcy process, as only the assets in place of the firm can be liquidated. Hence, the key question is whether shareholders will adopt the same investment policy $\{I_t\}_{t\geq 0}$ independently from F_0.

Consider first the case of an all-equity firm, that is, $F_0 = 0$. In all discrete time models we discuss, investment decisions at time t are always taken before dividends are paid. Hence, shareholders maximize their cum-dividend equity value, then obtaining the cum-dividend unlevered firm value $\hat{V}_t^u = V_t^u + x_t^*$. Thus, the unlevered firm's shareholders solve the following *dynamic problem*,

$$\hat{V}_t^u = \max_{I_t \in [0,I]} \left\{ A_t K_0 + \sum_{j=1}^{t-1} I_j y_t^{(j)} - I_t + \mathbb{E}_t \left(\frac{M_{t+1}}{M_t} \hat{V}_t^u \right) \right\}, \tag{2.3.6}$$

as $V_t^u = \mathbb{E}_t \left(\frac{M_{t+1}}{M_t} \hat{V}_t^u \right)$. The solution of the problem can be obtained by using a standard dynamic programming approach. However, in this specific case we can use a more direct approach, after having represented the LHS of Eq. (2.3.6) equivalently as,

$$\max_{I_t \in [0,I]} \left\{ A_t K_0 + \sum_{s=0}^{t} I_{t-s} y_t^{(t-s)} - I_t + \mathbb{E}_t \sum_{s=1}^{\infty} \frac{M_{t+s}}{M_t} \left[A_{t+s} K_0 + \sum_{j=1}^{t+s-1} I_j y_t^{(t+s)} - I_{t+s}^* \right] \right\}, \tag{2.3.7}$$

where I_{t+s}^* is the optimal investment decision in period $t \pm s$, $s \neq 0$. Notice that past and future investment decisions have no effect on the decision about investing in the currently available project. As a result, the optimal investment level in each period can be obtained as the solution of a *static problem*, namely,

$$I_t^* = \text{argmax}_{I_t \in [0,I]} \left\{ \left[-1 + \mathbb{E}_t \sum_{s=1}^{\infty} \frac{M_{t+s}}{M_t} y_{t+s}^{(t)} \right] I_t \right\}. \tag{2.3.8}$$

The expression $NPV_t^{(t)} := -1 + \mathbb{E}_t \sum_{s=1}^{\infty} M_{t,t+s} y_{t+s}^{(t)}$ is the NPV per dollar invested in the project t at the same date, which is constant and independent from the amount of dollars invested. As long as $NPV_t^{(t)} > 0$, it is optimal for shareholders to invest as much as possible in project t. Hence, the equilibrium investment policy for an all-equity firm is,

$$I_t^* = I\mathbb{I}\left(\mathbb{E}_t \sum_{s=1}^{\infty} \frac{M_{t+s}}{M_t} y_{t+s}^{(t)} \geq 1 \right) \tag{2.3.9}$$

This result is a restatement of the *positive NPV rule*,[6] which is a direct consequence of shareholders inability to postpone the investment decisions. Hence, the recursive application of Eq. (2.3.9) generates the maximum NPV for $\{x_t\}_{t \geq 0}$.

At this point, we need to understand whether introducing $F_0 > 0$ should motivate shareholders to deviate from the first-best *policy* $I_t^* = I\mathbb{I}\left(\mathbb{E}_t \sum_{s=1}^{\infty} M_{t,t+s} y_{t+s}^{(t)} \geq 1\right)$ for the NPV of unlevered free cash flows. To answer the question, we formulate the problem of the levered firms, which consists in maximizing shareholders value. However, differently from the unlevered case, we must take into account the effects of the option to default. Since the option to invest at time t project is lost in case of default, the levered firm's shareholders solve,

$$\hat{V}_t^E = \max \left\{ \max_{I_t \in [0,I]} \left\{ A_t K_0 + \sum_{j=1}^{t-1} I_j y_t^{(j)} - I_t - cF_0 + \mathbb{E}_t \left(\frac{M_{t+1}}{M_t} \hat{V}_t^E \right) \right\}, 0 \right\}. \tag{2.3.10}$$

First, we observe that for high levels of debt, relative to the current fundamentals, the continuation value $\max_{I_t \in [0,I]} \Big\{ A_t K_0 + \sum_{j=1}^{t-1} I_j y_t^{(j)} - I_t - cF_0$ $+\mathbb{E}_t \left(\frac{M_{t+1}}{M_t} \hat{V}_t^E \right) \Big\}$ could be negative. As such, shareholders prefer the default instead of paying coupons and continue to invest in positive NPV projects. Let δ_t be an indicator function of this occurrence. Then, it is straightforward to reformulate

[6] Usually assumed as benchmark rule in *optimal capital budgeting*.

shareholders problem as,

$$\hat{V}_t^E = \max \left\{ \max_{I_t \in [0,I]} \left\{ A_t K_0 + \sum_{j=1}^{t-1} I_j y_t^{(j)} - I_t - cF_0 + \right.\right.$$

$$\left.\left. \mathbb{E}_t \sum_{s=1}^{\infty} \frac{M_{t+s}}{M_t} \left[A_{t+s} K_0 + \sum_{j=1}^{t+s-1} I_j y_t^{(t+s)} - I_{t+s} - cF_0 \right] (1 - \delta_{t+s}) \right\}, 0 \right\}. \tag{2.3.11}$$

Suppose at time t $\max_{I_t \in [0,I]} \left\{ A_t K_0 + \sum_{j=1}^{t-1} I_j y_t^{(j)} - I_t - cF_0 + \mathbb{E}_t \left(\frac{M_{t+1}}{M_t} \hat{V}_t^E \right) \right\} > 0$. Then, $\delta_t = 0$, and, since current investment decisions are not depending on the future, the levered firm investment policy is obtained as the solution of the following static program,

$$\operatorname{argmax}_{I_t \in [0,I]} \left\{ \left[-1 + \mathbb{E}_t \sum_{s=1}^{\infty} \frac{M_{t+s}}{M_t} y_{t+s}^{(t)} (1 - \delta_{t+s}) \right] I_t \right\}. \tag{2.3.12}$$

By anticipating future default decisions, the NPV from investing in date t project is lower than the unlevered case. As a consequence, we may frequently encounter projects with a positive NPV for the unlevered firm, but with negative NPV for shareholders in presence of leverage. Notably, the higher is debt relative to x_t, the higher is the chance that default will take place in the future. Hence, the effect of higher debt levels is that of increasing the threshold for $\mathbb{E}_t \sum_{s=1}^{\infty} \frac{M_{t+s}}{M_t} y_{t+s}^{(t)}$ which makes convenient for shareholders to invest in project t. Thus, the presence of debt may depress investments, especially when default is likely to occur in the near future. This effect is known as debt overhang, and it is frequently observed in distressed firms. Put differently, we observe a decoupling between the NPV of a project t cash flows, $\left[-1 + \mathbb{E}_t \sum_{s=1}^{\infty} \frac{M_{t+s}}{M_t} y_{t+s}^{(t)} \right] I_t$, and the NPV of the same project for shareholders, $\left[-1 + \mathbb{E}_t \sum_{s=1}^{\infty} \frac{M_{t+s}}{M_t} y_{t+s}^{(t)} (1 - \delta_{t+s}) \right] I_t$. As long as shareholders are in control of the firm, it is the latter that drives investment decisions.

2.3.3 *The Value of Corporate Governance*

In this section we depart from the general assumption that firms maximize shareholders value. The purpose of the discussion is to shed lights on some important factors explaining the value-oriented behaviors. Since we are not interested in the effects of debt financing, we let common stocks be the only class of securities in the firm's capital structure. In addition, the firm holds no cash on its balance sheet, and there are no transaction costs on financial markets. While the firm's *technology* is the same as in the previous section, we assume now that it is managed by a group of managers.

Suppose that shareholders can write a contract, that, other than being perfectly enforceable, it can specify the investment policy that must be followed by managers. If that was possible, shareholders would simply write their optimal investment policy in the corporate bylaws to obtain the unlevered firm value. However, real contracts are typically incomplete, as writing in a legally binding piece of paper the state-contingent prescriptions of an optimal dynamic program in not possible. For this reason, shareholders need to set up alternative governance mechanism that, hopefully, will align their interests with those of the managers in charge to manage the firm on their behalf, which is an example of *principal-agent* problem.

When contracts are incomplete, markets are also incomplete. While an equilibrium stochastic discount factor continues to exist for the purpose of valuing the firm and its securities consistently with Eq. (1.3.1), shareholders may no longer agree upon the objective of maximizing the value of the firm (see Sect. 1.3.2). This creates a second problem, as the controlling shareholder may be not interested in maximizing the cum-dividend value of equity. We exemplify the point in Sect. 2.3.3.2.

In Sect. 2.3.3.1, we consider a firm with a *perfectly dispersed* ownership. Since no one is in control and there are no externalities, we assume that each shareholder's utility function is monotone increasing in the cum-dividend market value of equity. As a consequence, shareholders would agree on proposing to the management a contract which requires them to maximize total shareholders value. However, because no one is in control, the private cost of monitoring managers will be generally too high, an argument we extend to shareholders meetings, in which a poor performing management could be replaced. Generally speaking, managers may be not acting in the best interest of shareholders. In the model, this possibility is introduced by assuming that investing in new projects requires managers to put additional effort in their jobs at the firm. This is not infrequent in the real world, which may be due to the lack of organizational capital, in the sense that top managers are typically time-constrained and may need to work several extra hours to complete a new project. In this regard, we denote by D the dollars equivalent value of the private detriment in which managers incur if working on a new investment project. As a result, if managers have a remuneration scheme independent from the firm's performance, and there is no threat of replacement, they will be always better-off by choosing to not invest in new projects. The relevant question is thus whether a *raider*, intended as a candidate controlling shareholders, may be successful to take control of the firm and replace the incumbent management team. Under a perfectly dispersed ownership, we show that this is not an easy task, despite the welfare loss caused by leaving on the ground valuable investment opportunities.

Instead, in Sect. 2.3.3.2 we assume the presence of a majority shareholder who is in the direct control of the firm. However, its objectives collides with the maximization of the total firm's value. In particular, *minority* shareholders will be harmed by the conflictual presence of the large shareholder. This applies for both the institutional and the private controlling shareholders, who can represent an holding company and an entrepreneur, respectively.

The models we present in this section are intentionally extreme. However, they provide food for thought. The message is that corporate governance and ownership structure are of utmost importance. Without a governance code able to ensure the total shareholders value maximization, firms may be managed in a very different fashion, and a corporate raid could be just a wishful thinking. Although in the remainder of the book we assume that firms are managed as to maximize shareholders value, we should keep in mind that this condition should be not always taken for granted.

2.3.3.1 Dispersed Ownership, Take-overs and Threat of Replacement

The model we introduce in this section is an adaptation of Grossman and Hart (1980). Specifically, we impose the following hypotheses:

(1) the firm is managed by its Board of Directors (BoD);
(2) the members of the BoD, or directors, are homogeneous and remunerated by a constant wage;
(3) all members have the same preferences and are all involved in the investment selection process for new projects;
(4) investing in a new project results in a private detriment $D > 0$ to each director;
(5) the BoD can be changed at the end of each date t with a majority vote at a shareholders meeting;
(6) the firm's ownership structure is perfectly dispersed (i.e. each shareholder is infinitesimal);
(7) replacing the BoD requires the payment of a search cost $C > 0$;
(8) a *raider* can bid a price to acquire the shares of the company, however incurring in legal and transaction costs equal to $c \geq 0$.

A perfectly dispersed ownership means that each shareholder holds an infinitesimal stake in the firm. While this is of course an abstraction, it aims at describing a situation in which the cost of each individual shareholder to participate actively in the firm's governance will exceed the corresponding benefits. To simplify the discussion, we use the terms tender and takeover interchangeably. Moreover, we move having in mind the equilibrium property for which the agents taking actions first are assumed to correctly anticipate the strategies of agents moving second (see also Sect. 1.3).

At each time t, the first mover is the BoD, as it is up to its member the decision to invest in the project t. Since the members of the BoD are homogeneous, they can be seen as a single individual, we simply define the *manager*. The second movers are in order the raider, and the incumbent shareholders. The virtual timing of events at each time t is thus the following.

(1) First, the manager decides whether to invest or not in project t.
(2) Second, the raider, once dividends are paid, decides whether to bid for the control of the company. In this regard, the raider will bid a price that ensures a non-negative NPV from the deal.
(3) Third, incumbent shareholders decide whether to participate to the tender-offer, or to remain within the firm.
(4) Fourth, if at least 50% of the shares outstanding are tendered to the raider, the takeover is completed and the raider gets in control of the firm.
(5) Fifth, shareholders convene at their period meeting and decide whether to replace the management or not. If a controlling shareholder exists within the ownership structure, she becomes automatically the new manager at no cost. As a result, there are three possible outcome: (i) the manager remains in charge, (ii) the manager is replaced by the incumbent shareholders, (iii) the manager is replaced by a raider that acquires the control of the firm with a tender offer.

We can then obtain the unique equilibrium of such a game with some logical observations. Suppose the incumbent manager predicts that she will be not replaced, regardless of her performance, which is the value creation from investing in positive NPV projects. If the threat of replacement is not credible, the manager will prefer not to invest in any project, independently from the NPV. In this way, she will not experience the private detriment related to the additional effort related to each project execution. Being unsatisfactory for this behavior, shareholders will be very much in the mood to fire the lazy manager, at the same time introducing a new remuneration policy to motivate the new management team to invest in projects with positive NPV.

We claim that there is no equilibrium in which a perfectly dispersed ownership is successful to remove the incumbent manager. The proof is as follows. In order to replace the incumbent manager, a coalition of shareholders must bear the search cost c to find a new management team and draft a bullet-proof contract for the newly hired. As is obvious, in case drafting a contract that aligns the incentive of managers to those of shareholders is not possible, there will be no reason for shareholders to bear the cost c and replace the manager. Consider now the alternative in which it is possible to align the incentives between the two stakeholders. Suppose that this is indeed the case. Since each shareholder is infinitesimal in the coalition, her incentive is that of abandoning the coalition and *free ride* the ending result. Since this argument holds for every member of the coalition, it follows that no coalition can be organized in the first place. It is the *tragedy of the commons*. Although replacing the incumbent manager would be collectively valuable, a perfect ownership dispersion generates such an extreme free-rider problem which prevents shareholders to coordinate with each other to improve the *corporate governance* of the firm.

Unless a change in the firm's ownership structure is possible, the manager would be right to conjecture that, regardless her behavior, she will remain in charge. In this regard, the striking implication of a perfectly dispersed ownership is that a tender-offer will never actually take place if $c > 0$. A a result, the incumbent manager will stay in power despite her poor performance, and there will be a net welfare loss for shareholders. To show this result, let V_t^E be the value of the firm's equity assuming a perfectly dispersed ownership. In this case, the BoD never invests in new projects and, consequently,

$$V_t^E = K_0 \mathbb{E}_t \sum_{j=1}^{\infty} M_{t,t+j} A_{t+j}. \tag{2.3.13}$$

In other words, with a dispersed ownership the value of growth opportunities is zero.[7] Now consider a *raider* that engages in a takeover bid. If the raider 's bid is accepted, she would get in control of the firm and become the new manager. Differently from incumbent shareholders, the raider does not incur in the search cost C, as she will manage the firm directly in her best interest.

Suppose that the investment projects that become available to the firm are not sources of externalities for the raider.[8] Then, the raider's choice to invest in projects with a negative NPV is suboptimal. However, since the new projects still require to put effort in the firm, the raider will directly experience the private detriment D. While minority shareholders would benefit from positive NPV projects, at the same time they will not share the costs of raider's effort in managing the firm. For this reason, we should expect that the raider will invest only in those projects that are worth the effort. Let θ be the raider stake in the firm, which we assume to remain constant in time.[9] As the raider keeps for itself only a fraction θ of the increase in the firm's value, she will put effort only in projects with an NPV at least equal to $\frac{1}{\theta}D > 0$. Hence, if the tender offer will be successful, the value of equity will be improved with $V_t' > V_t^E$,

$$V_t' = \underbrace{K_0 \mathbb{E}_t \sum_{j=1}^{\infty} M_{t,t+j} A_{t+j}}_{\text{Value of Assets in Place}} + \underbrace{\left[\begin{array}{c} I \sum_{j=1}^{\infty} M_{t,t+j} y_{t+j}^{(t)} \lambda_t + \mathbb{E}_t \sum_{i=1}^{\infty} M_{t,t+i} \\ \times \left[\sum_{j=1}^{\infty} M_{t+i,t+i+j} y_{t+i+j}^{(t+i)} - 1 \right] \lambda_{t+i} \end{array} \right]}_{\text{Value of Growth Opportunities}}, \tag{2.3.14}$$

where $\lambda_t := \mathbb{I}\left(\theta \mathbb{E}_t \sum_{s=1}^{\infty} M_{t,t+s} y_{t+s}^{(t)} \geq D\right)$ is an indicator function that denotes at which conditions it will be optimal for the rider to invest in new projects. While the presence of the raider does not entirely resolve the underinvestment problem, still it can improve total shareholders value, and the incumbent shareholders would benefit from its presence.

---

[7]Although the underlying economic mechanism is different, this result is not infrequent with this "kind" of investment opportunities. An example is the industry equilibrium is in Leahy (1993).

[8]An example is an individual investing in a factory right in front of her home. If engaging in a new project increases pollution, there is a negative externality for her.

[9]This is a very important assumption which we discuss at the end of Sect. 2.3.3.2.

To acquire the majority of the target company, the raider bids a price o_t at which the incumbent shareholders can tender their shares. Denoting by n_t the number of outstanding shares, the raider will bid only prices that are individually rational for her, in the sense that the deal has non-negative NPV,

$$V_t' - o_t n_{t+1} \geq c. \tag{2.3.15}$$

We are finally getting to the conclusion. From Eq. (2.3.15), the maximum offering price will be equal to $\frac{V_t^u - c}{n_{t+1}}$. Let s_t be the stock price at the end of date t. Suppose that the takeover is announced and there is a coalition of shareholders that adheres to the offer. Given this outcome, the equilibrium stock price aligns to its new fundamental value, which takes into account the change in corporate governance,

$$s_t = \frac{V_t'}{n_{t+1}}. \tag{2.3.16}$$

We can now compare for each shareholder the alternatives of either adhere to the tender offer or remain invested in the firm. If a shareholder decides to tender her shares, she gets $s_t - o_t$ per share. As the participation to the tender is voluntary, the offering price should be equal at least to the stock price, that is,

$$o_t \geq \frac{V_t'}{n_{t+1}}, \tag{2.3.17}$$

which is an *incentive compatibility* condition. Otherwise, the alternative of remaining invested in the firm would be preferred. If $c > 0$, the maximum offering price is $\frac{V_t' - c}{n_{t+1}}$, which does not induce any incumbent shareholder to adhere to the tender. Anticipating this outcome, the raider will refrain to bid for the company shares in the first place. In equilibrium, the manager predicts this, then guessing she will be not replaced at the end of each period, regardless her behavior. Hence, there will be no investments at all in the future, and the value of equity is given by Eq. (2.3.13). The value of the firm is lower than the value in case of a perfect corporate governance, as the manager foregoes all positive NPV projects.

The only case in which the tender may be successful is $c = 0$, as the maximum offering price in this case results equal to $\frac{V_t'}{n_{t+1}}$, although the raider will have no gain from the tender. In other words, if the raider is viewed as another company, the synergies of the merger, that are equal to the value of future growth options, will be completely transferred to the incumbent shareholders. It should be noticed that this depends on two crucial assumptions. The first is the atomistic dimension of each investor. The second instead, which is more subtle and common to all the models we presented, is the presence of perfect information between all the agents. While both are abstract assumptions, in many circumstances they are good approximation of what happens in reality. Nevertheless, there are solutions to resolve the free-rider problem; an example is the dilution mechanisms in favor of a raider that can be included in corporate bylaws.

2.3.3.2 Concentrated Ownership, Entrepreneurs and Minorities

Let assume that $c = 0$ and a large shareholder is in control of the firm. As commented in the previous section, the presence of a large shareholder does not fully solve the underinvestment problem. However, the value of the firm is improved by her presence, as "sufficiently" valuable investment projects will be selected. Nevertheless, the large shareholder may try to take advantage from the presence of minorities, as we show in the following two examples.

The first example features a parent company (HoldCo) as controlling shareholder and manager of the firm (SubCo). Let assume that HoldCo pays a fixed operating cost c in each period, which is covered by a revenue of equal amount. The majority stake in the SubCo is the only financial asset for simplicity. If a fraction $\alpha_t \in [0, \bar{\alpha} \leq 1]$ of the cost κ can be transferred to the SubCo, then the controlling shareholder has the interest in shifting as much costs as possible to SubCo. In this way, part of the HoldCo's original costs will be shared with SubCo's minorities. Unless specific provisions in the corporate bylaws, minority shareholders cannot oppose to this decision. One example is the case of excess headcount in one of the HoldCo's division. Instead of firing the employees in excess, which will be in any case costly, the HoldCo could renegotiate the contract with some of its employees, eventually finding an agreement for a new job at the SubCo.

In order to show the previous result in a more formal way, suppose that in each period the distribution of A_t is bounded below, and $A_t K_0 \geq \bar{\alpha} c$. Let $\theta > \frac{1}{2}$ the share of the HoldCo in the SubCo's capital, which is supposed to remain constant for the time being. For a given path $\{\alpha_t\}_{t \geq 0}$, the value of the HoldCo is equal to $\theta \left[\mathbb{E}_t \sum_{j=1}^{\infty} \frac{M_{t+s}}{M_t} \left(A_{t+s} K_0 - \alpha_{t+j-1} \kappa \right) + PVGO_t \right] - \mathbb{E}_t \sum_{j=1}^{\infty} \frac{M_{t+s}}{M_t} \left[y - \kappa \left(1 - \alpha_{t+j-1} \right) \right]$, where

$$PVGO_t := I \sum_{j=1}^{\infty} M_{t,t+j} y_{t+j}^{(t)} \lambda_t + \mathbb{E}_t \sum_{i=1}^{\infty} M_{t,t+i} \left[\sum_{j=1}^{\infty} M_{t+i,t+i+j} y_{t+i+j}^{(t+i)} - 1 \right] \lambda_{t+i}$$

is the value of SubCo's growth options.[10] The controlling shareholder chooses the *governance policy* $\{\alpha_t\}_{t \geq 0}$ which maximizes the holding's market value $\left(V_t^H\right)$,

$$V_t^H = \max_{\{\alpha_{t+s} \leq \bar{\alpha}\}_{s \geq 0}} \left\{ V_t^C + \theta \left[\mathbb{E}_t \sum_{j=1}^{\infty} \frac{M_{t+s}}{M_t} \left(A_{t+s} K_0 - \alpha_{t+j-1} \kappa \right) + PVGO_t \right] - \mathbb{E}_t \sum_{j=1}^{\infty} \frac{M_{t+s}}{M_t} \left[y - \kappa \left(1 - \alpha_{t+j-1} \right) \right] \right\} \tag{2.3.18}$$

[10]Notice that cost of shifting is agreed beforehand between HoldCo and SubCo, as α_t affects SubCo's costs for period $t + 1$.

which is equal to the equity value. Let W_t be the argument of the maximization problem described by the right hand side of the equation. Since the choice of each α_t is independent from the others $\alpha_{j \neq t}$, we have a sequence of static problems. Taking derivatives with respect to α_t, we obtain $\frac{\partial W_t}{\partial \alpha_t} = \frac{1-\theta}{1+r_{t+1}}\kappa > 0$. Therefore, in each period it is optimal for the HoldCo to transfer as much costs as possible to the SubCo, that is, $\alpha_t = \bar{\alpha}$, as originally claimed. As a result, the value of the SubCo (i.e. the firm in the original example of Sect. 2.3.3.1) is lowered by the NPV of the additional costs,

$$V_t^E = \mathbb{E}_t \sum_{j=1}^{\infty} \frac{M_{t+s}}{M_t} \left(A_{t+s} K_0 - \bar{\alpha}\kappa \right) + PVGO_t. \tag{2.3.19}$$

Notice that this is exactly the opposite of an *efficiency gain* for SubCo.[11] Put differently, the presence of a large shareholder may have a mixed effect on corporate governance. On the one hand, it resolves the managerial agency problem described in Sect. 2.3.3.1. On the other, it introduces other types of inefficiency, one of which could be the presence of intra-group costs shifting.

The message from this example is that minority shareholders may be hurt by the presence of an holding company controlling the firm's management. Nonetheless, this possibility effectively complicates further the possibility of successful tender offers. To see this point, suppose that t is the date at which HoldCo is bidding for SubCo's majority stake. For the success of the tender-offer, in Sect. 2.3.3.1 it was sufficient for the HoldCo to bid a price o_t at least equal to the post-announcement price conditional upon the occurrence of the tender. However, in doing this we implicitly assumed that the takeover improved the price per share. If that was not the case, the offer would be certainly unsuccessful, as the incumbent shareholders would have no reason to accept an offer which entails a certain loss in value. In the example above, this case corresponds to $PVGO_t < \mathbb{E}_t \sum_{j=1}^{\infty} \frac{M_{t+s}}{M_t} \bar{\alpha}\kappa$. In short, the NPV of intra-group cost shifting exceeds the value of replacing the incumbent manager.

As a second example, consider the case in which the controlling shareholder is an entrepreneur, who incurs in private expenses equal to κ in each period. Assume that a fraction $\alpha_t \in [0, \bar{\alpha} \leq 1]$ of these expenses can be transferred to the firm (e.g. luxury cars, private jet, hiring other relatives as employees to cover part of the enterpreneur's family cost). The fraction of private expenses transferred to the firm are called *perks*, and they are not that infrequent to observe in reality. It is immediate to verify that this setting is equivalent to that of the precedent example, where the controlling shareholder was instead another company. As such, all the previous conclusions remain unchanged. Hence, the presence of a large shareholders does not necessary to improve the governance of the firm.

As a technical aside, there is an important hypothesis in the analysis presented in this and the previous section which deserves an additional discussion.

[11] Efficiency gains are often advocated to promote M&A activities.

So far, we assumed that the large shareholder holds constant its stake in the firm. Suppose, instead, that as time goes by, its stake progressively declines. Consequently, the lower will be her stake, the less she will be motivated to put effort in the firm, as investing in a generic project t is rational for her provided that $\theta_t \mathbb{E}_t \sum_{s=1}^{\infty} M_{t,t+s} y_{t+s}^{(t)} \geq D$. Let t the date of the tender offer. For a given ownership path $\left\{\theta_j < \theta_t\right\}_{j>t}$, the tender may be no longer feasible, as the resulting value of future growth options could be insufficient. This example sheds lights on the importance of contractual provisions such as lock-up periods, in which the controlling shareholder is legally bind to hold constant its stake. Without a similar provision, the large shareholder may not be even able to commit to a static ownership policy, as DeMarzo and Urosevic (2006) show in a continuous time setting.

2.4 A General Expression for the Value of the Firm

The purpose of this section is to derive a general expression for the equilibrium value of the firm which is then valid for any arbitrary designed security and regardless the specific reasons underlying the corporate finance decisions, as well as the way through which an episode of default is resolved. At the same time, we wish to understand the restrictions imposed by the firm's budget constraint and the pricing kernel to the total market capitalization of the firm.

Our discussion is in three parts. First, we characterize the set of securities that are active at the end of each date t. Second, we give a general characterization of a bankruptcy procedure, in terms of resulting budget constraint which links the recovery rates associated to each class of security to the total available resources. Third, we show that Eq. (2.3.3) for the value of the firm is always valid. This result is of utmost importance, since it provides a very useful tool to think about the underlying drivers of value creation for the firm as a whole.

2.4.1 Abstract Securities

The concept of abstract securities is quite straightforward. A security is intended as a contract that entitles the holder to receive cash flows stream, and to benefit control rights (e.g. corporate governance rights in the case of shares). Cash flows are generelly called "fruits" for convenience, in the spirit of Lucas (1978). In our models, securities are all tradable on competitive markets. Notice that, from a legal perspective, not all tradable certificates, which are representative of a financial liability, are all considered as securities under different financial regulations.[12]

[12]The most important examples are leveraged loans in Europe.

However, as long as we conjecture that investors of firm's securities are price-taker, we can bypass such a complication and describe the firm's capital structure as a set of different types of corporate securities. We refer to the index s as a generic class of securities, or to a generic security in the same class.

At a certain time t, each class belongs to either one of the supergroups $\mathcal{O}_{t+1}$ and $\mathcal{M}_{t+1}$. Each set is defined at the end of each date t, consistently with the outstanding liabilities after that same period fruits have all been paid to incumbent security holders. Namely, $\mathcal{O}_{t+1}$ is the set of securities with maturity date $t+1$. If we let $\mathcal{S}_{t+1}$ the set of all class of securities at end of period t, the set $\mathcal{M}_{t+1}$ is defined as $\mathcal{M}_{t+1} = \mathcal{S}_{t+1} - \mathcal{O}_{t+1}$, that is, $\mathcal{M}_{t+1}$ is the set of outstanding securities in t with maturity date after $t+1$. Within each class s,[13] control rights are proportionally attributed based on the number of held securities. We denote by $n_{s,t+1}$ the number of outstanding securities of class s at the end of time t. Notably, n_{t+1} is not restricted to be an integer, and each class s is characterized by a specific time in which the class has started to exist, and possibly a second time coinciding with its expiry date. As in the previous sections, securities can be issued and traded at their ex-dividend, or *ex-fruit,* price.

As anticipated, control rights divide in *cash flows rights* and all the actions that each security holder may take individually, or jointly with other security holders, to protect its own interests in the firm. As an example is the right of debt holders to declare the firm bankrupt. For the moment, we need to keep track only of cash flows rights, which we represent as a stochastic process $\left\{\upsilon_{s,t}\right\}_{t\geq 0}$ such that $\upsilon_{s,j} = 0, \ \forall j : s \notin \mathcal{S}_j$. While the firm is solvent, we can therefore formulate its budget constraint as,

$$L_{t+1} - L_t = \left[\underbrace{\sum_{s\in\mathcal{M}_{t+1}} p_{s,t}\left(n_{s,t+1} - n_{s,t}\right) + \sum_{s\in\mathcal{O}_{t+1}} p_{s,t} n_{s,t+1} + L_t r_t}_{Capital\ Inflows} \right]$$
$$- \left[\underbrace{\sum_{s\in\mathcal{S}_t} \upsilon_{s,t} n_{s,t}}_{Capital\ Outflows} \right] + x_t + \pi_t - \sum_{s\in\mathcal{S}_t \cup \mathcal{S}_{t+1}} \Theta_{t,s}\left(1 - \tau_t\right), \tag{2.4.1}$$

[13]The index s is always sufficient to characterize all the relevant information pertaining to a certain type of securities in circulation. In particular, we do not need to keep track of the date at which a specific security was issued, as its maturity date, if any, will be equal to that of the other securities belonging to the same class.

where $\Theta_{t,s}$ is the amount of transaction costs to be paid relative to capital structure adjustments, or *corporate actions*, while τ_t is the effective corporate tax rate at time t. As usual, the value of the firm (V_t) is defined as the ex-fruits (ex-dividend) market value of all securities outstanding minus the available liquidity, that is,

$$V_t := \sum_{s \in \mathcal{S}_t} p_{s,t} n_{s,t+1} - L_{t+1}. \tag{2.4.2}$$

Without loss of generality, we can write $n_{s,t} = 0$ for all $s \notin \mathcal{S}_t$ and $p_{t,s} = 0$ for all $s \notin \mathcal{S}_{t+1}$. As a result, Eq. (2.4.1) can then be rearranged as follows,

$$\sum_{s \in \mathcal{S}_t} \left(p_{s,t} + \upsilon_{s,t}\right) n_{s,t} = L_t \left(1 + r_t\right) + V_{t+1} + x_t + \pi_t - \Theta_t \left(1 - \tau_t\right), \tag{2.4.3}$$

where $\Theta_t := \sum_{s \in \mathcal{S}_t \cup \mathcal{S}_{t+1}} \Theta_{t,s}$.

From Eq. (1.3.1), $\lim_{T\to\infty} \mathbb{E}_t \left(\frac{M_T}{M_t} \sum_{s \in \mathcal{S}_T} \left(p_{s,T} + \upsilon_{s,T}\right) n_{s,T}\right) = 0$. At the same time, Eq. (2.1.8) must be valid also in the general case, otherwise the SDF process would be not consistent with financial markets equilibrium. Consequently, the value of the firm must be always consistent with the following transversality condition,

$$\lim_{T\to\infty} \mathbb{E}_t \left(\frac{M_T}{M_t} V_T\right) = 0, \tag{2.4.4}$$

that eventually impose restrictions on the admissible investment and financing policies.

2.4.2 Restructuring, Renegotiation and Liquidation Procedures

Debt securities entail specific control rights which in case the firm violates certain contractual conditions could lead the firm to consider bankruptcy as the only resolutive action. The set of events that can trigger a default is not limited to missing interest or principal payments, but includes also to the violation of debt covenants or other provisions (e.g. a strong deterioration of collateral quality). To get general results, we need to model the outcome of a default event independently from the type of procedures, namely renegotiation, restructuring and liquidation (see Sect. 2.1.2). In this regard, we let $R_{s,t}$ be the recovery value of class s in case any of the previous events take place at time t.

Let t be the time when a debt restructuring occurs, and $\mathcal{R}_t \subseteq \mathcal{S}_t$ the set of securities involved in the restructuring process. Following Sect. 2.1.2 we have,

$$\sum_{s \in \mathcal{S}_t} \left(p_{s,t} + v_{s,t} \right) n_{s,t} = L_t \left(1 + r_t\right) + x_t + V_t + \pi_t - \Theta_t \left(1 - \tau_t\right) - bc_t, \qquad (2.4.5)$$

where $p_{s,t} = n_{s,t+1} = 0$ and $v_{s,t} n_{s,t} = R_{s,t}$ for each $s \in \mathcal{R}_t \subseteq \mathcal{S}_t$. Basically, the sum of recovery value and the cum-dividend market value of securities that are not involved in the restructuring process must be equal to the NPV of current and future free cash flows to the firm. Notice that, differently from the case in which a single type of bonds was present, the value of debt tax shield may be positive, as some debt holders may be not involved in the restructuring process. An example is the case in which secured debt holders are fully paid back, while unsecured bonds are swapped for ordinary shares. Besides, the same approach can be used to model the case of a renegotiation of the original debt contracts. In such a case, we would have $bc_t = 0$ and renegotiation costs, if any, being included in the transaction costs component Θ_t. Likewise, if t is a liquidation date, then, $p_{s,t} = 0 \ \forall s \in \mathcal{S}_t$ and the recovery value for each class is equal to $R_{s,t} = v_{s,t} n_{s,t}$. Hence, we have

$$\sum_{s \in \mathcal{S}_t} \left(p_{s,t} + v_{s,t} \right) n_{s,t} = L_t \left(1 + r_t\right) + x_t + V_t + \pi_t - \Theta_t \left(1 - \tau_t\right) - bc_t, \qquad (2.4.6)$$

as $V_t = 0$, and unlevered free cash flows, net of bankruptcy costs, are equal to the net proceeds from asset sales. In this regard, *fire-sales* may depress the second-hand market price of the firm's assets. Hence, in case of liquidation, bc_t includes the excess haircuts experienced in case of fire-sales.

Let δ_t be an indicator process which is equal to one in case of default or renegotiation at time t, or zero otherwise. Similarly, let l_t be an indicator process which takes the value of 1 in case the firm is liquidated at time t, or 0 otherwise. With this premise, the following *generalized budget* constraint is valid for every $t \in \mathbb{N}$

$$\sum_{s \in \mathcal{S}_t} \left(p_{s,t} + v_{s,t} \right) n_{s,t} = L_t \left(1 + r_t\right) + x_t + V_t + \pi_t - \Theta_t \left(1 - \tau_t\right) - bc_t \delta_t. \qquad (2.4.7)$$

Indeed, $\Pr\left(\delta_{j>i} = 0 | l_i = 1\right) = \Pr\left(l_{j>i} = 0 | l_i = 1\right) = 1$, as the firm ceases to exist after its liquidation.

2.4.3 *The Value of the Firm*

We are now ready to obtain a general expression for the value of the firm. In equilibrium, Eq. (1.3.1) holds for each class of security s in the capital structure $\mathcal{S}_t$.

Therefore,

$$\sum_{s\in\mathcal{S}_t}\left(p_{s,t}+v_{s,t}\right)n_{s,t}=\mathbb{E}\left\{\frac{M_{t+1}}{M_t}\left[\sum_{s\in\mathcal{S}_t}\left(p_{s,t+1}+v_{s,t+1}\right)n_{s,t+1}\right]\right\}. \tag{2.4.8}$$

Since Eq. (2.4.7) holds for each future date $t+j,\ j>0$, and $\frac{1}{1+r_{t+1}}=\mathbb{E}_t\left[\frac{M_{t+1}}{M_t}\right]$, we have

$$\begin{aligned}&\sum_{s\in\mathcal{S}_t}\left(p_{s,t}+v_{s,t}\right)n_{s,t}-L_{t+1}\\&\quad=\mathbb{E}_t\left\{\frac{M_{t+1}}{M_t}\left[x_{t+1}+V_{t+1}+\pi_{t+1}-\Theta_{t+1}\left(1-\tau_{t+1}\right)-bc_{t+1}\delta_{t+1}\right]\right\},\end{aligned} \tag{2.4.9}$$

that is,

$$V_t=\mathbb{E}_t\left\{\frac{M_{t+1}}{M_t}\left[x^*_{t+1}-\left(x_{t+1}-x^*_{t+1}\right)+\pi_{t+1}-\Theta_{t+1}\left(1-\tau_{t+1}\right)-bc_{t+1}\delta_{t+1}+V_{t+1}\right]\right\}. \tag{2.4.10}$$

where $\left\{x^*_t\right\}_{t\geq 0}$ is the unlevered free cash flows process with maximum NPV, that is, the one resulting from the investment decisions of the *unlevered firm* (see Sect. 2.3.1). Recalling Eq. (2.4.4), we can solve forward Eq. (2.4.10), then obtaining,

$$\begin{aligned}V_t=V^u_t&+\mathbb{E}_t\sum_{s=1}^{\infty}\frac{M_{t+s}}{M_t}\pi_{t+s}-\mathbb{E}_t\sum_{s=1}^{\infty}\frac{M_{t+s}}{M_t}\Theta_{t+s}\left(1-\tau_{t+s}\right)\\&-\mathbb{E}_t\sum_{s=1}^{\infty}\frac{M_{t+s}}{M_t}\left(x_{t+s}-x^*_{t+s}\right)-\mathbb{E}_t\sum_{s=1}^{\infty}\frac{M_{t+s}}{M_t}bc_{t+s}\delta_{t+s},\end{aligned} \tag{2.4.11}$$

where $V^u_t=\sum_{s=1}^{\infty}\frac{M_{t+s}}{M_t}x^*_{t+s}$ is the unlevered firm value. We can also write Eq. (2.4.11) in a more compact way as,

$$V_t=V^u_t+DTS_t-TC_t-AC_t-BC_t, \tag{2.4.12}$$

which states that the value of the firm, corresponding to the total market value of the outstanding securities net of the amount of cash reserves, is always equal to the sum of following 5 components:

- $V^u_t:=\sum_{s=1}^{\infty}\frac{M_{t+s}}{M_t}x^*_{t+s}$, the unlevered firm value;
- $DTS_t:=\mathbb{E}_t\sum_{s=1}^{\infty}\frac{M_{t+s}}{M_t}\pi_{t+s}$, the NPV of tax benefits from capital structure decisions (*tax shield* for short);

- $TC_t := \mathbb{E}_t \sum_{s=1}^{\infty} \frac{M_{t+s}}{M_t} \Theta_{t+s} (1 - \tau_{t+s})$, the NPV of transaction costs (*transaction costs* for short);
- $AC_t := \mathbb{E}_t \sum_{s=1}^{\infty} \frac{M_{t+s}}{M_t} \left(x_{t+s} - x^*_{t+s}\right)$, the NPV of agency costs (*agency costs* for short);
- $BC_t := \mathbb{E}_t \sum_{s=1}^{\infty} \frac{M_{t+s}}{M_t} bc_{t+s}\delta_{t+s}$, the NPV of bankruptcy costs (*bankruptcy costs* for short).

In equilibrium, the value of the firm is the net present value of the free cash flows generated by the firm's investment policy until default, plus the expected recovery value at the same date. Transaction costs, agency costs and capital structure effects drive the value of the firm apart from its unlevered benchmark, which is the maximum NPV of unlevered free cash flows. Once we have the firm's investment policy, which, in equilibrium, may be affected by financing decisions and other type of frictions, we can always obtain the value of the firm by looking at *asset side* dynamics only. Eventually, this is equivalent to forecast the total free cash flows generation process and its covariance with the SDF, which is the common estimation activity for equity analysts. On this regard, usually it is convenient to represent the value of the firm without explicit reference to agency costs, that is,

$$V_t = \mathbb{E}_t \sum_{s=1}^{\infty} \frac{M_{t+s}}{M_t} x_{t+s} + \mathbb{E}_t \sum_{s=1}^{\infty} \frac{M_{t+s}}{M_t} \pi_{t+s} - \mathbb{E}_t \sum_{s=1}^{\infty} \frac{M_{t+s}}{M_t} \Theta_{t+s} (1 - \tau_{t+s})$$
$$- \mathbb{E}_t \sum_{s=1}^{\infty} \frac{M_{t+s}}{M_t} bc_{t+s}\delta_{t+s}. \quad (2.4.13)$$

2.4.4 *Dividends, Buybacks and Expected Equity Returns*

We close this chapter with a practical example showing the importance of taking properly into account the firm's budget constraint. Consider an all-equity firm, with $L_t = 0$ and unlevered free cash flows evolving according to,

$$x_{t+1} = (1 + g)\, x_t e^{\varepsilon_{t+1} - \frac{1}{2}\sigma^2} \quad (2.4.14)$$

where g is a positive constant and $\varepsilon_t \sim_{i.i.d.} \mathcal{N}\left(0, \sigma^2\right)$ is a sequence of identically and independently distributed (i.i.d.) shocks. The stochastic discount factor evolves as,

$$M_{t+1} = (1 + r)^{-1} M_t e^{z_{t+1} - \frac{1}{2}\psi^2} \quad (2.4.15)$$

where r is the constant risk-free rate and $z_t \sim_{i.i.d.} \mathcal{N}\left(0, \psi^2\right)$ characterizes random variations in aggregate economic activity. While not strictly necessary, the correlation (ρ) between ε_t and z_t is assumed negative, consistent with a positive covariance between the firm's cash flows and the aggregate level of the economic activity. Under these hypotheses, the market value of equity is consistent with the classic Gordon (1959) model,

$$V_t^E = \mathbb{E}_t \sum_{j=1}^{\infty} \frac{M_{t+j}}{M_t} x_{t+j} =$$

$$x_t \mathbb{E}_t \sum_{j=1}^{\infty} \frac{e^{\sum_{k=1}^{j} z_k - \frac{1}{2}\psi^2}}{(1+r)^j} e^{\sum_{k=1}^{j} \varepsilon_k - \frac{1}{2}\sigma^2} = x_t \mathbb{E}_t \sum_{j=1}^{\infty} (1+g)^j \frac{e^{\sum_{k=1}^{j} z_k + \varepsilon_k - \frac{1}{2}\psi^2 - \frac{1}{2}\sigma^2}}{(1+r)^j}$$

$$x_t \mathbb{E}_t \sum_{j=1}^{\infty} (1+g)^j \frac{e^{\sum_{k=1}^{j} z_k + \varepsilon_k + \rho\sigma\psi - \rho\sigma\psi - \frac{1}{2}\psi^2 - \frac{1}{2}\sigma^2}}{(1+r)^j}$$

$$= x_t \sum_{j=1}^{\infty} (1+g)^j \frac{\prod_{k=1}^{j} e^{-|\rho|\sigma\psi} \mathbb{E}_t \left(e^{z_k + \varepsilon_k - \rho\sigma\psi - \frac{1}{2}\psi^2 - \frac{1}{2}\sigma^2} \right)}{(1+r)^j} =$$

$$x_t \sum_{j=1}^{\infty} \left[\frac{1+g}{(1+r)\, e^{|\rho|\sigma\psi}} \right]^j = \frac{x_t (1+g)}{\left[(1+r)\, e^{|\rho|\sigma\psi} - 1 \right] - g}, \tag{2.4.16}$$

as the variance of $z_t + \varepsilon_t$ is equal to $\sigma^2 + \psi^2 + 2\rho\sigma\psi$. It is easy to check that, as $\mathbb{E}_t (x_{t+1}) = (1+g)\, x_t$, and t $\mu := (1+r)\, e^{|\rho|\sigma\psi} - 1$ is the expected stock return, that is,

$$\mathbb{E}_t \left(r_{t+1}^E \right) = (1+r)\, e^{|\rho|\sigma\psi} - 1 \tag{2.4.17}$$

where $r_{t+1}^E := \frac{s_{t+1} + d_{t+1}}{s_t}$ is, indeed, the return on stocks.

Suppose we do not know $|\rho|\sigma\psi$ and we wish to compute the expected return of the stock having information on the firm's fundamentals (x_t, g). Then, by observing the stock market price s_t, we obtain the expected stocks' return as,

$$\mu = \underbrace{\frac{\frac{1}{n_{t+1}} \mathbb{E}_t (x_{t+1})}{s_t}}_{\text{Free cash flow yield}} + g \tag{2.4.18}$$

where n_{t+1} is the number of outstanding shares at the end of the trading date t. A common mistake in practice is to use expected *dividends per share* to proxy for $\frac{1}{n_{t+1}} \mathbb{E}_t (x_{t+1})$. However, if the firm delivers cash to its shareholders through share buybacks, $\frac{1}{n_t} \mathbb{E}_t (x_{t+1})$, instead of paying dividends, the use of the dividend per share will lead to substantial estimation errors.

To make an actual example, assume that the model is (statistically) valid for a large US industrial corporation with a global reach, and consider the following data points. The average long-run real growth rate for the GDP of OECD countries, which is a reasonable calibration for g, is estimated in the range 1.5–1.8%. Excluding buybacks, the dividend yield is about 2%. However dividends account for roughly one half of unlevered free cash flows, with the other half being used for share buybacks. Once we take into account the effects of buybacks, the unlevered free cash flows yield is equal to 4%, from which we obtain an expected real return in the range of 5.5–5.8%. Instead, if we wrongly assume $\frac{1}{n_{t+1}}\mathbb{E}_t(x_{t+1})$ equal to the expected dividend yield, we would underestimate the expected return by 2%, which is a quite substantial bias in a low yields environment.

The methodology we use to estimate the expected return of a stock is the *implied cost of capital*, which is very popular among practitioners. In general, the process is a bit more sophisticated. See, for e.g., Easton (2007), Hou et al. (2012), and Penman et al. (2019).

2.5 Related Literature

Sections 2.1–2.3 are the result of our own synthesis of a vast array of scattered results. The methodology we follow comes from Sargent (1987), DeMarzo (1988), Sethi et al. (1991, 1996), Sethi (1995), Amaro de Matos (2001) and Tirole (2005). To give an historical perspective, Merton Miller and Franco Modigliani originally examined the role of capital structure and dividends decisions in a deterministic partial equilibrium setting (Miller & Modigliani 1958, 1961, 1963). Stiglitz (1969) then extended their results introducing uncertainty in a general equilibrium model, although in its model debt is risk-free as debt holders could have been always paid back in full. One of the earliest extensions to the case of risky debt is Merton (1974, 1977), who adapts the Black–Scholes–Merton option pricing framework (Black and Scholes 1973; Merton 1973) to develop the first structural credit risk model. Hellwig (1981) introduces the possibility of default for investors that borrow to invest in the firm's securities, introducing for the first time financial market frictions. Implicitly, in our models we have ruled out this case as a byproduct of perfect secondary financial markets.

During the 1970s and early 1980s, there was a rich academic production in response to MM propositions. One example is debt overhang, we presented in Sect. 2.3.2, introduced in Myers (1977). Another related problem is the asset substitution (Jensen and Meckling 1976), in which shareholders have the incentive to increase cash flows risk as operating earnings falls and default becomes more enticing, the so-called "gamble for resurrection".[14] The *fil rouge* is an attempt

[14] In this regard, securities other than "plain vanilla" bonds and equity may be used to attenuate the diverging interests between share and debt holders, although not always with success. For instance,

to show that shareholders could create value through financing decisions, the latter being far from irrelevant. Interestingly, note that all of these results were obtained while dynamic general equilibrium theory was progressively developing, and its application to asset pricing problems was one of the research frontiers. This explains the fragmentation of several closely related results. In the 80s, the literature on equilibrium asset pricing was then sufficient to reduce the proof of MM propositions to an equilibrium asset pricing application. The incomplete markets general equilibrium extensions of MM results is in DeMarzo (1988).

Managerial agency conflicts are ubiquitous and have been largely analyzed in the literature. Hart (1995), Tirole (2001) and Tirole (2005) provide exhaustive reference to the subject. This raise the importance of corporate governance, and security design may be useful to align managerial interests with those of shareholders (Hart 1995; Dow and Raposo 2005). Furthermore, Zwiebel (1996) shows that managerial entrenchment, which is a type of agency conflict, may affect dynamic capital structure decisions. In particular, managers issue debt to credibly constrain their own future empire-building, with an impact on shareholders value. Similarly, Morellec et al. (2010) consider the case in which managers can capture part of the free cash flows to equity holders as private benefits, and have control over financing decisions. Using structural estimation, they quantify the size and impact of managerial agency costs to shareholders value.

References

Amaro de Matos, J. (2001). *Theoretical foundations of corporate finance*. Princeton University Press.

Black, F., & Scholes, M. (1973). The pricing of options and corporate liabilities. *Journal of Political Economy, 81*(3), 637–654.

DeMarzo, P. M. (1988). An extension of the Modigliani-Miller theorem to stochastic economies with incomplete markets and interdependent securities. *Journal of Economic Theory, 45*(2), 353–369.

DeMarzo, P. M., & Urosevic, B. (2006). Optimal trading and asset pricing with a large shareholder. *Journal of Political Economy, 114*(4), 774–815.

Dow, J., & Raposo, C. C. (2005). Ceo compensation, change, and corporate strategy. *The Journal of Finance, 60*(6), 2701–2727.

Easton, P. (2007). Estimating the cost of capital implied by market prices and accounting data. *Foundations and Trends® in Accounting,* 2(4), 241–364.

Gordon, M. J. (1959). Dividends, earnings, and stock prices. *The Review of Economics and Statistics, 41*(2), 99.

Grossman, S. J., & Hart, O. D. (1980). Takeover bids, the free-rider problem, and the theory of the corporation. *The Bell Journal of Economics, 11*(1), 42.

Hamada, R. S. (1972). The effect of the firm's capital structure on the systematic risk of common stocks. *The Journal of Finance, 27*(2), 435–452.

Hennessy and Tserlukevich (2004) shows that issuing warrants do not resolve the shareholders asset substitution problem in a dynamic setting, while it may exacerbate debt overhang.

Hart, O. D. (1995). *Firms, contracts, and financial structure*. Clarendon Press.
Hellwig, M. F. (1981). Bankruptcy, limited liability, and the Modigliani-Miller theorem. *The American Economic Review, 71*(1), 155–170.
Hennessy, C. A., & Tserlukevich, Y. (2004). Analyzing callable and convertible bonds when the Modigliani-Miller assumptions are violated. *SSRN Electronic Journal.*
Hou, K., van Dijk, M. A., & Zhang, Y. (2012). The implied cost of capital: A new approach. *Journal of Accounting and Economics, 53*(3), 504–526.
Jensen, M. C., & Meckling, W. H. (1976). Theory of the firm: Managerial behavior, agency costs and ownership structure. *Journal of Financial Economics, 3*(4), 305–360.
Leahy, J. V. (1993). Investment in competitive equilibrium: The optimality of myopic behavior. *The Quarterly Journal of Economics, 108*(4), 1105–1133.
Lucas, R. E. (1978). Asset prices in an exchange economy. *Econometrica, 46*(6), 1429.
Mella-Barral, P., & Perraudin, W. (1997). Strategic debt service. *The Journal of Finance, 52*(2), 531–556.
Merton, R. C. (1973). Theory of rational option pricing. *The Bell Journal of Economics and Management Science, 4*(1), 141.
Merton, R. C. (1974). On the pricing of corporate debt: The risk structure of interest rates. *The Journal of Finance, 29*, 449–470.
Merton, R. C. (1977). On the pricing of contingent claims and the Modigliani-Miller theorem. *Journal of Financial Economics, 5*(2), 241–249.
Miller, M., & Modigliani, F. (1958). The cost of capital, corporation finance and the theory of investment. *The American Economic Review, 48*(3), 261–297.
Miller, M. H., & Modigliani, F. (1961). Dividend policy, growth, and the valuation of shares. *The Journal of Business, 34*(4), 411.
Miller, M. H., & Modigliani, F. (1963). Corporate income taxes and the cost of capital: A correction. *The American Economic Review, 53*(3), 433–443.
Morellec, E., Nikolov, B., & Schurhoff, N. (2010). Corporate governance and capital structure dynamics. *The Journal of Finance, 67*(3), 803–848.
Myers, S. C. (1977). Determinants of corporate borrowing. *Journal of Financial Economics, 5*(2), 147–175.
Penman, S. H., Zhu, J., & Wang, H. (2019). The implied cost of capital: Accounting for growth. *SSRN Electronic Journal.*
Sargent, T. J. (1987). *Dynamic economic theory*. Harvard University Press.
Sethi, S. P., Derzko, N. A., & Lehoczky, J. P. (1991). A stochastic extension of the Miller-Modigliani framework. *Mathematical Finance, 1*(4), 57–76.
Sethi, P., Derzko, N. A., & Lehoczky, L. P. (1996). Erratum to "a stochastic extension of the Miller-Modigliani framework". *Mathematical Finance, 6*(4), 407–408.
Sethi, S. (1995). An extension of 'dividend policy, growth, and the valuation of shares' by Miller and Modigliani. *SSRN Electronic Journal.*
Shleifer, A., & Vishny, R. W. (1992). Liquidation values and debt capacity: A market equilibrium approach. *The Journal of Finance, 47*(4), 1343–1366.
Stiglitz, J. E. (1969). A re-examination of the Modigliani-Miller theorem. *The American Economic Review, 59*(5), 784–793.
Tirole, J. (2001). Corporate governance. *Econometrica, 69*(1), 1–35.
Tirole, J. (2005). *The theory of corporate finance*. Princeton University Press.
Zwiebel, J. (1996). Dynamic capital structure under managerial entrenchment. *The American Economic Review, 86*(5), 1197–1215.

Chapter 3
Borrowing Constraints, Debt Dynamics and Investment Decisions

This chapter deals with dynamic capital structure models with risk-free debt. This class of models is based on the presence of a *borrowing constraint* ensuring debt holders being always paid back in full. Namely, we consider the case of *secured* debt, in which a *collateral constraint* limits the amount of debt outstanding to the minimum resale price of the pledged assets, net of total interest expenses. Contrary to the case of unsecured debt, in which the firm borrows against cash flows, debt capacity is directly tight to the size of its balance sheet.

The use of collateral constraints is ubiquitous, as they are general enough to make the use of other types of borrowing constraints almost superfluous, especially from an empirical perspective. In principle, borrowing constraints that allows for risky debt are possible, as in Abel (2017). However, in several stock markets analyses, default losses for debt holders can be considered as a second-order problem, without substantial biases on empirical results. For this reason, it is customary to work with borrowing constraints that ensures that debt holders are always paid back in full. Besides, introducing transaction costs on primary markets, models with risk-free debt can still accommodate for a total cost of debt above the risk-free rate. On this point, Huang and Huang (2012) empirically document the existence of a substantial credit spread component that is unlikely to be related to default risk. This is not to say that corporate debt can be generally considered as risk-free, but rather that there might be situations in which this is a convenient working hypothesis. Chapter 5–7 focus on risky corporate debt.

The structure of the chapter is as follows. In Sect. 3.1 we introduce the concept of collateral constraint, and show that, under quite general hypothesis, it can be used to ensure that shareholders are never enticed by the alternative of default. One consequence is that the value of shareholders' default option is null and the ex-dividend equity market value is linearly decreasing with the face value of debt outstanding. Since there are no frictions for what concerns the issuance of new equity, holding liquidity is always costly to the firm because of the taxation on related interest income, and therefore free cash flows to equity holders are always

U. Sagliaschi, R. Savona, *Dynamical Corporate Finance*, Contributions to Finance and Accounting, https://doi.org/10.1007/978-3-030-77853-8_3

fully paid out as dividends or share buybacks. With linear taxes, the firm issues either the maximum amount of secured debt or no debt at all. Namely, the optimal capital structure trades off the tax benefits of debt, against the additional costs in which the firm incur because of the pledge. When the collateral constraint is binding, the book-leverage ratio is inversely related to the cost of debt, which is the sum of the risk-free interest rate plus the transaction cost per unit of debt issued. In Sect. 3.1 we also introduce the general notion of weighted average cost of capital (WACC), and we show the practitioners approach holds valid in equilibrium in presence of a collateral constraint ensuring that debt is risk-free.

Section 3.2 is dedicated to endogenous investment decisions. The model considers a firm operating with a constant returns to scale (CRS) technology in a perfectly competitive product market, subject to convex investment adjustment costs, in which shareholders choose the level of capital stock that maximizes the cum-dividend equity value. Although the equilibrium book-leverage is unaffected by introducing endogenous investment decisions, the collateral constraint makes investment and financing decisions mutually dependent, as long as issuing secured debt remains enticing for shareholders. In Sect. 3.3 we provide a first analysis of the relation between investment returns and securities returns, obtaining the basic version of the Investment CAPM (Zhang 2017). In Sect. 3.4 we reconsider the optimality conditions characterizing the levered firm's investment policy. When binding, the collateral constraint motivates shareholders to invest above the level which maximizes the NPV of unlevered free cash flows, because of the funding cost advantage of debt. This effect introduces investment agency costs in the model, which, in equilibrium, are more than offset by the difference between the NPV of tax benefits and that of transaction costs, consistent with Eq. (2.4.12) of the previous chapter.

3.1 Collateral Constraints and Optimal Capital Structure

3.1.1 Secured Debt and Flotation Costs

Firms can borrow money from investors essentially in two different ways, borrowing against cash flows or against assets. The first case links debt capacity directly to the free cash flows process; debt is *unsecured*, as lenders have no direct and exclusive right on any specific asset of the firm. In the second case, debt is protected by a lien written on one or more specific assets, which debt holders can seize and liquidate when default occurs. We say that debt is *secured* by a *pledged asset*, which serves as *collateral*. The activities required to originate and monitor secured debt contract are costly (e.g. legal expenses for writing the lien). For this reason, the pool of financial intermediaries, or *syndicate*, involved in the placement of a *new issue* will charge the firm with a flotation cost. Consistent with what frequently happen in practice, we assume that these transaction costs are proportional to the face value of the new issue. The syndicate eventually place the related debt securities[1] on the secondary market, in which *originators*, i.e. the members of the syndicate, and investors act both as price taker. Thus, the setting is equivalent to one in which the firm directly issues debt within a Walrasian secondary market, except that additional issuance costs must be considered in the firm's budget constraint.

We assume that secured debt instruments are issued with one period maturity, and coupon rate set at the risk-free rate (r_{t+1}). In this way, we can avoid price fluctuations related to change in interest rates. Pledge-able assets are restricted to the firm's capital stock, which is composed of K_t units of homogeneous capital goods. If the liquidation value of capital is strictly positive, there is always a maximum nominal amount of secured debt that can be issued as risk-free. Let φ_{t+1} be the flotation costs per unit of secured debt issued at time t, which we assume to be paid in $t+1$ (i.e. at maturity). The following *collateral constraint* implements a risk-free debt contract with face value $F_{t+1} > 0$ due at date $t+1$,

$$F_{t+1} \leq \frac{\underline{R}_{t+1} (1-\delta) K_{t+1}}{1 + r_{t+1} + \varphi_{t+1}}, \tag{3.1.1}$$

where $\delta \in [0, 1]$ is the depreciation rate of capital, while $\underline{R}_{t+1}$ is the lower bound for the support of the conditional distribution of the resale price of capital (R_{t+1}) in case of default and liquidation of the firm in $t+1$. Eq. (3.1.3) ensures that, even in case of default, debt holders and financial intermediaries are paid in full. For this reason it is also totally irrelevant assuming that transaction costs are paid at issuance or at maturity. When Eq. (3.1.3) holds valid, we speak of fully secured debt.

For ease of notation it is also common in corporate finance literature to set the price of new capital goods equal to one (*numeraire*). Besides, as long as liquidation frictions are not explicitly modeled, it is convenient to adopt the following working hypothesis,

$$\underline{R}_t = 1 - \alpha, \tag{3.1.2}$$

where $\alpha \in [0, 1]$ is a constant *haircut* rate. Notably, this haircut applies only in case the capital stock is sold by the lenders following an event of default. One of the possible interpretations is the presence of legal and execution costs. The collateral constraint resulting from Eq. (3.1.1–3.1.2),

$$F_{t+1} \leq \frac{(1-\alpha)(1-\delta) K_{t+1}}{1 + r_{t+1} + \varphi_{t+1}}. \tag{3.1.3}$$

[1] A security is transferrable by definition, as opposed to a standard banks loan which requires the prior consent of the borrower. In case the contract is originated as a loan, the contract must foresee a simple novation mechanism that ensures tradability without prior consent of the borrower (e.g. Transferable Loans Securities). An alternative mechanism is that of sub-participation, which is a form of securitization of the original debt contract. In a sub-participation agreement, one or more participants of the syndicate issue specific certificates that are backed by the original loan. Abstracting from counter-party risk (i.e. the intermediary may abscond cash from the vehicle/account dedicated to the sub-participation), both mechanisms are equivalent.

is assumed valid in the remainder of this chapter as well as in Chap. 4. In other words, in this and the following chapter the firm is assumed to be financed with equity and fully secured debt. As is evident, as the coupon rate is equal to r_{t+1}, secured debt trades always at *par value*,[2] that is,

$$V_t^B = F_{t+1}, \tag{3.1.4}$$

where V_t^B be the market value of debt outstanding at the end of time t (F_{t+1}).

A fully secured debt contract is risk-free. However, it is important to distinguish, at least in principle, the concepts of risk-free and default-free debt. Generally speaking, a security is risk-free if it entails deterministic payments. A defaultable debt instrument can be risk-free, provided that in case of default debt holders recover the NPV of residual coupons and principal payments. Under specific assumptions, Rampini and Viswanathan (2013) shows that a collateral constraint consistent with Eq. (3.1.1) ensures that default is never enticing for shareholders. Consequently, debt is default-free and not just risk-free, and dynamic capital structure models can be solved without considering explicitly the alternative of default. This is very convenient shortcut in several applications, and we are going to show under which mild conditions this approach can be effectively adopted in Sect. 3.1.2. However, if we allow for the presence of unsecured debt, results would be different, as we show in Sect. 7.1 of Chap. 7. Notice that the presence of a collateral constraint is a type of *financial friction*. However, this friction does not limit the ability of shareholders to infuse additional equity in the firm. In this regard, during the first decade of 2000s, several papers focus on this second issue; see, for e.g., Hennessy and Whited (2005) and Livdan et al. (2009). Here, we do not consider the presence of equity flotation costs or limits to outside equity, as the use of the model is primary intended for the case of listed companies that can easily issue additional shares at negligible costs. In the remainder of this section, as anticipated, we assume that the investment policy of the firm is exogenously given.

3.1.2 *Strict Individual Rationality and Absence of Default Risk*

As assumed in the previous chapter, when investment decisions are not explicitly modeled, we can characterize an investment policy through the resulting unlevered free cash flows process $\{x_t\}_{t\geq 0}$. However, as the hypothesis is that firm's capital stock is composed only of a single type of homogenous and perfectly divisible capital goods, then we can represent an investment policy more explicitly in terms of the capital stock process $\{K_{t+1}\}_{t\geq 0}$. Since there is no working capital for the

[2]The price per unit of debt's face value is equal to one.

moment,[3] operating cash flows are equal to after taxes operating earnings gross of depreciation expenses. In this regard, it is assumed that operating cash flows are non-negative for some capacity utilization level $u_t \leq K_t$. Hence, the following general relation between operating cash (y_t) and unlevered free cash flows (x_t) holds,

$$x_t = y_t - I_t = y\left(K_t, K_{t+1}, u_t, \mathbf{z}_t\right) - I_t, \tag{3.1.5}$$

where $I_t = K_{t+1} - \tilde{K}_t$ is total investment expenditure and $\mathbf{z}_t$ is the set of all other relevant state variables. The variable $\tilde{K}_t$ denotes the residual capital stock after the production takes place, while K_{t+1} is the capital stock available for production at time $t + 1$. For convenience, we also assume that the full capital stock available for production (K_t) depreciates regardless the firm is operating at maximum capacity or not. In other words, economic and accounting depreciation are equivalent.

At the beginning of every time t, the physical capital stock cannot be adjusted before production takes place, which is consistent with the investment dynamics. For this reason, shareholders can default only after the physical capital stock has depreciated, as in Hennessy and Whited (2005) and Garin (2015) amongst others. In other words, default may occur, say, only after production takes place.[4] Without such an assumption, default could be a strategic option to reduce the amount of capital stock before production occurs, which could contrast with the timing of investment decisions.

In the remainder of the chapter the tax shield on total interests expenses is characterized by a time-independent function π of the amount of liquidity and debt outstanding, $\pi_t = \pi\left(L_t, F_t, y_t, \mathbf{z}_t\right)$, $\pi_F \geq 0, \pi_L \leq 0$. The sign of its derivatives with respect to F_t, L_t highlights the fact that a positive interests income, such as interests on cash reserves, is always taxed, while the cost of debt financing may be tax deductible. Contextualizing the results discussed in Sect. 1.4 of the previous chapter in the case of a solvent firm, the budget constraint can be formulated as,

$$F_{t+1} + x_t + \pi_t + r_t L_t = D_t + \left(r_t + \varphi_t\right) F_t + \left(L_{t+1} - L_t\right), \tag{3.1.6}$$

where $D_t := d_t n_t + p_t\left(n_{t+1} - n_t\right)$ is the total cash outlays related to equity financing. Since there are neither equity flotation costs nor limits to outside equity injections, without loss of generality we can assume a constant number of shares. As a result, all payments will occur by means of dividends, which can be negative in case that shareholders need to recapitalize the firm. We then introduce a very useful concept under the hypothesis of an exogenous unlevered free cash flows process $\{x_t\}_{t \geq 0}$.

[3] In the next chapter we will add working capital to the model, with specific reference to inventories of intermediate production goods.

[4] Production may be null if this is the unique convenient alternative for the firm.

Definition 3.1 An investment policy $\{K_{t+1}\}_{t\geq 0}$ is strictly individually rational (SIR) if

$$\sum_{s=1}^{\infty} \frac{M_{t+s}}{M_t} x_{t+s}\left(K_{t+s}, K_{t+s+1}\right) \geq y\left(K_t, 0, \mathbf{z}_t\right) + (1-\delta) K_t. \tag{3.1.7}$$

A SIR investment policy has the property that it is never convenient for an all-equity firm to sell its capital stock and shut-down operations forever. The set of SIR policy is never empty, as $K_{t+1} = 0$ is SIR as $y_t \geq 0$. For the same reason, a SIR investment policy is also *individually rational* (see Sect. 2.1.1). In this regard, the firm's financing policy $\{F_{t+1}, L_{t+1}\}_{t\geq 0}$ is *individually rational* if $\pi_t \geq \varphi_t F_t$ in every period t. Otherwise, shareholders would incur a net loss by issuing secured debt. The following proposition clarifies the importance of these definitions.

Proposition 3.1 *Let $\{K_{+1}\}$ be a SIR investment policy and $\{F_{t+1}, L_{t+1}\}$ an individually rational financing policy. If there are no subsidies to investments in capital stock, that is $I_t = K_{t+1} - \tilde{K}_t$, then: (i) $K_{t+1} = 0$ is never strictly preferred for shareholders, and (ii) shareholders can credibly commit to repay debt in each period, as default is never strictly enticing.*

Proof Suppose the results of the proposition are valid. Using Eq. (2.4.11) we can write shareholders value as,

$$\hat{V}_t^E = L_t\left(1+r_t\right) + \sum_{j=0}^{\infty} \frac{M_{t+j}}{M_t} x_{t+j} - F_t + \sum_{j=0}^{\infty} \left(\pi_{t+j} - \varphi_{t+j} F_t\right). \tag{3.1.8}$$

Setting $K_{t+1} = 0$, shareholders obtain $L_t\left(1+r_t\right) + y\left(K_t, K_{t+1}, u_t, \mathbf{z}_t\right) + (1-\delta) K_t + \left[\pi_t - \left(1+c_t\right) F_t\right]$, which is never greater than the RHS of Eq. (3.1.8) by the SIR assumption and the fact that $\{F_{t+1}, L_{t+1}\}_{t\geq 0}$ is also assumed individually rational. Hence, $K_{t+1} = 0$ is never a strictly convenient alternative for shareholders if $\{K_{t+1}\}_{t\geq 0}$ is SIR. To prove the second part of the proposition, notice that the collateral constraint in Eq. (3.1.3) implies that $F_{t+1} \leq (1-\delta) K_{t+1}$. Consequently, if shareholders default and they do not continue to run the firm, they obtain at most $L_t\left(1+r_t\right) + y\left(K_t, K_{t+1}, u_t, \mathbf{z}_t\right) + (1-\delta) K_t - \left(1+c_t\right) F_t$, as $\alpha \geq 0$. As a result, an event of default followed by the termination of the firm's operations can be ruled out. It remains the case in which default takes place and, since the collateral constraint ensures debt holders are repaid in full, shareholders continue to run the firm. Holding the investment policy constant, default affects investment expenditure as a consequence of liquidation costs, that is,

$$I_t = K_{t+1} - \left[\underbrace{K_t (1-\delta) - F_t \frac{1 + r_t + \varphi_t}{1-\alpha}}_{\tilde{K}_t}\right]. \tag{3.1.9}$$

If $\alpha > 0$, the alternative of default has the effect of increasing the total investment expenditure required to implement the same investment policy. Furthermore, if shareholders switched to a different investment policy $\left\{K'_{t+1}\right\}_{t\geq 0}$, the total investment expenditure will be never reduced by the exercise of their default option. Finally, since in case that $\alpha = 0$ shareholders are indifferent to the alternative of default, we can conclude that they can credibly commit to never default in the future. □

The meaning of Proposition 3.1 is simple. When investment and financing decisions are exogenously given, mild regularity conditions are sufficient to exclude the case of default. These conditions however are not necessary once we take into account shareholders equilibrium behavior, as we show in the proof of the following proposition.

Proposition 3.2 *Let* $\chi = \left\{\chi_{t+1}\right\}_{t\geq 0} = \{\epsilon_t \in \{0,1\}, u_t \leq K_t, F_{t+1} \geq 0, K_{t+1} \geq 0, L_{t+1} \geq 0\}_{t\geq 0}$ *a state-contingent policy for the firm consistent with the budget constraint of the firm, where* $\epsilon_t = 1$ *corresponds to the choice of default. Suppose* $\exists\,(u_t, I_t, K_t):\ y_t \geq 0,\ \forall t \in \mathbb{N}$. *Let* χ^* *be the solution of shareholders' dynamic program characterizing the equilibrium behavior of the firm,*

$$
\begin{gathered}
\tilde{V}^E\left(F_t, K_t, L_t, \mathbf{z}_t\right) = \\
\max_{\chi_{t+1}}\left\{y_t + \pi_t - I_t - F_t\left(1+c_t\right)\left(1-\epsilon_t\right) + F_{t+1} + \mathbb{E}_t\left[M_{t,t+1}\tilde{V}^E\left(F_{t+1}, K_{t+1}, L_{t+1}, \mathbf{z}_{t+1}\right)\right]\right\} \\
s.t. \\
\chi_{t+1} = \{u_t \leq K_t, F_{t+1} \geq 0, K_{t+1} \geq 0, L_{t+1} \geq 0\} \\
I_t = K_{t+1} - (1-\delta)\tilde{K}_t \\
\tilde{K}_t = (1-\alpha)(1-\delta)K_{t+1}\epsilon_t + (1-\delta)K_{t+1}\left(1-\epsilon_t\right) \\
F_{t+1} \leq \frac{(1-\alpha)(1-\delta)K_{t+1}}{1+c_{t+1}} \\
y_t = f\left(u_t, I_t, K_t, \mathbf{z}_t\right) \\
\tilde{V}^E\left(F_t, K_t, L_t, \mathbf{z}_t\right) \geq 0,
\end{gathered}
\tag{3.1.10}
$$

where f *is the firm's technology, which may also include the results of optimal pricing decisions depending on the competitive landscape. Then, (i) shareholders can credibly commit to repay debt in future, as default is never enticing for them, that is,* $\epsilon_t^* = 0$ *for all dates* $t \in \mathbb{N}$, *and (ii)* χ^* *maximizes in each period the total value of the firm inclusive of the current free cash flows.*

Proof Suppose default is never optimal for shareholders. Since $\exists\,(u_t, I_t, K_t)$ such that $y_t \geq 0$, the problem in Eq. (3.1.10) is well posed as we can be sure there exists at least a policy χ such that shareholders value is non-negative, consistently with the individual rationality constraint. The value of the firm is equal to $V_t = V_t^E +$

$F_{t+1} = F_{t+1} + \mathbb{E}_t \left[M_{t,t+1} \tilde{V}^E \left(F_{t+1}, K_{t+1}, L_{t+1}, \mathbf{z}_{t+1} \right) \right]$. The term $-F_t \left(1 + c_t\right)$ is independent from the choice of control variables, and therefore can be taken out of the maximization problem. Since there is no alternative policy that can strictly improve shareholders value, $\hat{V}^E \left(F_t, K_t, L_t, \mathbf{z}_t\right) + F_t \left(1 + r_t\right)$ is the maximum value of the firm before any payment is made or received. Hence, as $y_t + \pi_t - \varphi_t F_t - I_t$ denotes the total free cash flows to the firm (fcf_t), shareholders optimization problem is equivalent to,

$$\max_{\{u_t \le K_t, F_{t+1} \ge 0, K_{t+1} \ge 0, L_{t+1} \ge 0\}} \left\{ fcf_t + V_t \left(F_{t+1}, K_{t+1}, L_{t+1}, \mathbf{z}_t \right) \right\}$$

$$\begin{aligned} & s.t. \\ I_t &= K_{t+1} - (1 - \delta) K_t \\ F_{t+1} &\le \frac{(1 - \alpha)(1 - \delta) K_{t+1}}{1 + r_{t+1} + \varphi_{t+1}} \\ y_t &= f\left(u_t, I_t, K_t, \mathbf{z}_t\right) \\ fcf_t &= y_t + \pi_t - \varphi_t F_t - I_t, \end{aligned} \tag{3.1.11}$$

thereby completing the proof of the second part of the proposition. Thus, we remain to show that default is never enticing for shareholders. From the definition of $\tilde{K}_t$, it is immediate to see that the only effects of default is to reduce dividends by $\alpha (1 - \delta) K_t \ge 0$. As a result, shareholders never profit from the exercise of their default option and, consequently, they can credibly commit to repay debt in the future. □

Proposition 3.2 holds independently from the specific technology and competitive landscape we consider. The advantage is that it allows to formulate shareholders problem without taking into account the alternative of default, which would complicate further the analysis. Moreover, the same problem can be formulated in terms of maximization of the cum-dividend value of the firm, which is sometimes a more convenient way of proceeding.

3.1.3 The Value of the Firm, Optimal Capital Structure and The Weighted Average Cost of Capital

Differently from interest expenses, transaction costs related to the issuance of secured debt are not paid to any of the firm's investors. Thus, they are equivalent to operating expenses, such as wages or other cost items, as opposed to coupons, which instead are part of debt holders' remuneration. However, for accounting purpose, transaction costs paid on securities issued by the firm are included in interest expenses. Besides, as we pointed out in Sect. 2.2.3, total interests expenses, which in this case amounts to $(r_t + \varphi_t) F_t$, are considered as cost items for tax purpose. Consistent with the tax law interpretation of interests expenses, we define cost of debt (c_t) as the sum of the coupon rate plus the transaction cost per unit of debt's notional, that is $c_t := r_t + \varphi_t$. In this regard, it is convenient to separate the tax shield on interests expenses from the taxation of interests earned on liquidity reserves, adopting the following representation,

$$\pi_t = \pi^{(F)}\left(F_t, L_t, \mathbf{z}_t\right) - \pi^{(L)}\left(F_t, L_t, \mathbf{z}_t\right). \tag{3.1.12}$$

Hence, applying Eq. (2.4.13) to this specific context, the value of the firm (V_t) can be obtained according to the following expression,

$$V_t = \mathbb{E}_t \sum_{s=1}^{\infty} \frac{M_{t+s}}{M_t} x_{t+s} + \underbrace{\mathbb{E}_t \sum_{s=1}^{\infty} \frac{M_{t+s}}{M_t} \left[\pi^{(F)}\left(F_{t+s}, \mathbf{z}_{t+s}\right) - \pi^{(L)}\left(L_{t+s}, \mathbf{z}_{t+s}\right)\right]}_{DTS_t} - \underbrace{\mathbb{E}_t \sum_{s=1}^{\infty} \frac{M_{t+s}}{M_t} \varphi_{t+s} F_{t+s}}_{TC_t}, \tag{3.1.13}$$

where DTS_t is the value of debt tax shield, net of the effect of interest income related to the presence of liquidity, while TC_t is the net present value of debt's transaction costs. Accordingly, debt financing improves the value of the firm through the fiscal deduction of interest charges, although transaction costs paid to financial intermediaries operate in the opposite direction.

In order to derive more precise quantitative results, we adopt a linear tax structure,

$$\begin{cases} \pi^{(F)}\left(F_t, \mathbf{z}_t\right) = \tau\left(r_t + \varphi_t\right) F_t & \text{tax shield on interests expenses,} \\ \pi^{(L)}\left(L_t, \mathbf{z}_t\right) = \tau r_t L_t & \text{taxation of interest income,} \end{cases} \tag{3.1.14}$$

where $\tau \geq 0$ is the corporate tax rate. This is a very common working hypothesis in the literature, which we will use again. With linear taxes, the expression for the value of the firm becomes even more intuitive,

$$V_t = \mathbb{E}_t \sum_{s=1}^{\infty} \frac{M_{t+s}}{M_t} x_{t+s} + \underbrace{\mathbb{E}_t \sum_{s=1}^{\infty} \frac{M_{t+s}}{M_t} \left[\tau\left(r_{t+s} + \varphi_{t+s}\right) F_{t+s}\right]}_{\text{Tax benefits of Debt}} - \underbrace{\mathbb{E}_t \sum_{s=1}^{\infty} \frac{M_{t+s}}{M_t} \left[\tau r_{t+s} L_{t+s}\right]}_{\text{Cost of Liquidity}} - \underbrace{\mathbb{E}_t \sum_{s=1}^{\infty} \frac{M_{t+s}}{M_t} \varphi_{t+s} F_{t+s}}_{\text{Transaction Costs}}. \tag{3.1.15}$$

In equilibrium, shareholders never hold cash reserves, because of the next loss from the taxation of interest income, that is, the term $\mathbb{E}_t \sum_{s=1}^{\infty} \frac{M_{t+s}}{M_t} [\tau r_{t+s} L_{t+s}]$ in Eq. (3.1.15) above. Hence, without loss of generality we can assume that liquidity reserves are always null, since it is never rational for shareholders to incur the related cost. Notice that this is correct as long as shareholders are free to inject new equity in the firm without costs. Let $\gamma_{t+1} := \frac{(1-\alpha)(1-\delta)}{1+c_{t+1}}$ the maximum book-leverage consistent with the collateral constraint; with an exogenous investment policy, the optimal capital structure of the firm is obtained in each period as the solution of the following static linear program,

$$\max_{F_{t+1} \in [0; \gamma_{t+1} K_{t+1}]} [\tau c_{t+1} - \varphi_{t+1}] F_{t+1}, \tag{3.1.16}$$

as the choice of F_{t+1} at time t does not affect that of F_{j+1} at each future date $j > t$. In this problem, the net marginal benefit of a unit of debt is constant and equal to $\tau c_{t+1} - \varphi_{t+1}$. Whenever this quantity is equal to zero, shareholders's value is independent from the choice of F_{t+1}, that is, any $F_{t+1} \in [0, \gamma_t K_{t+1}]$ is equally optimal. Conversely, when $\tau c_{t+1} > \varphi_{t+1}$, shareholders are better-off by borrowing the largest amount of debt possible, that is,

$$F_{t+1} = \gamma_{t+} K_{t+1}, \tag{3.1.17}$$

while $F_{t+1} = 0$ is the optimal choice for the case $\tau c_{t+1} < \varphi_{t+1}$. Notably, when issuing debt is convenient for the firm, the book-leverage ratio $\left(\frac{F_{t+1}}{K_{t+1}}\right)$ is inversely related to the cost of debt (c_{t+1}),

$$\frac{F_{t+1}}{K_{t+1}} = \frac{(1-\alpha)(1-\delta)}{1+c_{t+1}} = \gamma_{t+1}, \tag{3.1.18}$$

which is a very interesting result of the model, we can also test empirically. Besides, this result remains valid in presence of endogenous investment decisions (we discuss this point later).

Regardless how investment decisions are taken, the presence of the collateral constraint provides an equilibrium foundation to the *practice* of the weighted average cost of capital (WACC) in *security analysis*. Generally speaking, the firm's WACC is defined as a stochastic process $\{wacc_{t,t+1}\}_{t=0}^{\infty}$ such that, for each date $t \in \mathbb{N}$, the following equation holds,

$$V_t = \frac{\mathbb{E}_t (x_{t+1} + V_{t+1})}{1 + wacc_{t,t+1}}. \tag{3.1.19}$$

Let $r_{t+1}^E := \frac{D_{t+1} + V_{t+1}^E}{V_t^E}$ the stock returns, and assume that $L_{t+1} = 0$ consistently with the sub-optimality of liquidity reserves. As an application of the budget constraint, i.e. Eq. (3.1.6), and Propositions 3.1–3.2, which rule out the possibility of default, the following equation is valid for each time $t \in \mathbb{N}$,

$$F_{t+2} + x_{t+1} = D_{t+1} + F_{t+1} \left[1 + (1 - \tau)\, \tau c_{t+1}\right]. \qquad (3.1.20)$$

Adding V_{t+1}^{E} to both sides of the previous expression, we obtain,

$$V_{t+1} + x_{t+1} = V_{t+1}^{E} + D_{t+1} + F_{t+1} \left[1 + (1 - \tau)\, \tau c_{t+1}\right]. \qquad (3.1.21)$$

Substituting Eqs. (3.1.21) in (3.1.19), the weighted average cost of capital can be eventually obtained as,

$$wacc_{t,t+1} = \mathbb{E}_t \left\{ \frac{V_{t+1}^{E} + D_{t+1}}{V_t^{E}} \frac{V_t^{E}}{V_t} + \frac{F_{t+1} \left[1 + (1 - \tau)\, \tau c_{t+1}\right]}{V_t} \right\} - 1, \qquad (3.1.22)$$

that is,

$$wacc_{t,t+1} = \frac{V_t^{E}}{V_t} \mathbb{E}_t \left(r_{t+1}^{E} \right) + \frac{F_{t,t+1}}{V_t} c_{t+1} (1 - \tau), \qquad (3.1.23)$$

where $c_{t+1} = r_{t+1} + \varphi_{t+1}$ is the *cost of deb*t. Equation (3.1.23) is the standard WACC formula used by practitioners in security analysis, which can be found on every introductory corporate finance textbook. The model presented in this section provides an equilibrium foundation of this practice. In particular, the practitioners' approach is consistent with equilibrium pricing only if debt trades at par on the secondary market, and the "credit spread" charged to the firm can be entirely attributed to a transaction cost component. This could be a convenient approximation in several applications, even in absence of an explicit borrowing or collateral constraint (see Sect. 7.4.3).

3.2 Perfect Product Market Competition and Optimal investment-Financing Decisions

The structure of the competitive landscape, or *industrial organization*, affects shareholders' production and investment decisions. In this section, we introduce endogenous investment decisions by considering the case of *perfect product market competition*. In other words, it is assumed that the firm is able to sell any amount of its produced goods at the market price, which is taken as given by all the competitors in the same industry. Another element that influences investment decisions is the production technology available to the firm, which we model in a quasi-reduced form way. Namely, the following relation between the capacity used in the production process ($u_t \leq K_t$) and operating cash flows (y_t) is assumed valid,

$$y_t = A_t u_t (1 - \tau) + \tau \delta K_t, \tag{3.2.1}$$

where A_t is a strictly positive exogenous stochastic process characterizing the firm's profitability, while $\phi(K_{t+1}, K_t) \geq 0$ are investment adjustment costs. The latter are equal to zero iff $K_{t+1} = (1 - \delta) K_t$, that is, if there are neither acquisition or disposal of new assets. The technical motivation for the presence of $\phi(K_{t+1}, K_t)$ will be clear later in our discussion. The term $\tau \delta K_t$ is instead the *investment tax shield*, that is the tax savings on accounting depreciations.

Since operating cash flows are monotone increasing in u_t, in equilibrium we necessary have $u_t = K_t$. Thus, we can reformulate Eq. (3.2.1) as,

$$y_t = [A_t K_t - \phi(K_{t+1}, K_t)](1 - \tau) + \tau \delta K_t, \tag{3.2.2}$$

without loss of generality. Furthermore, Proposition 3.2 allows us to rule out from the analysis the case of default. Therefore, the evolution of capital stock is always governed by following difference equation,

$$K_{t+1} = K_t (1 - \delta) + I_t. \tag{3.2.3}$$

Besides, from the analysis of the previous section, there is no need to consider financing policies allowing for a non-zero liquidity balance. Therefore, we can assume without loss of generality $L_{t+1} = 0$, obtaining a substantial simplification of the notation required to set up the shareholders optimization problem.

Investment adjustment costs assume different meanings depending on the sign of I_t. When new capital stock is added ($I_t > 0$), the term $\phi(K_{t+1}, K_t)$ should be generally interpreted as additional operating expenses in which the firm incur to install new equipments. On the other hand, when the firm is selling part of its assets ($I_t < 0$), the term $\phi(K_{t+1}, K_t)$ could capture irreversibility costs, such as second-hand market frictions (e.g. haircuts to the resale price of capital goods). In applied works, adjustment costs are usually modeled in the following way,

$$\phi(K_{t+1}, K_t) = \frac{\theta(I_t)}{2} \left(\frac{I_t}{K_t}\right)^2 K_t = \begin{cases} \frac{\theta^+}{2} \left(\frac{I_t}{K_t}\right)^2 K_t & I_t \geq 0 \\ \frac{\theta^-}{2} \left(\frac{I_t}{K_t}\right)^2 K_t & I_t < 0 \end{cases} \tag{3.2.4}$$

which has the advantage of being differentiable at the *separation threshold* $I_t = 0$.[5]

[5]The proof of this claim is straightforward: $\frac{\partial \phi_t}{\partial I_t^-}|_{,t=0} = \theta^- \frac{I_t}{K_t}|_{I_t=0} = 0$ and $\frac{\partial \phi_t}{\partial I_{i,t}^+}|_{I_t=0} = \theta^+ \frac{I_t}{K_t}|_{,t=0} = 0$.

3.2.1 The Value of the Unlevered Firm

Consider the case of an all-equity firm, i.e. for some exogenous reason shareholders cannot issue securities other than common stocks. Shareholders of the firms act in their own best interest, and, consequently, their investment decisions are the solution of the following dynamic program,

$$\hat{V}_t^E(K_t, z_t) =$$

$$\max_{K_{t+1}} \left\{ \underbrace{\left[\begin{array}{l} \underbrace{A_t K_t (1-\tau) + \delta\tau K_t - \phi(K_{t+1}, K_t)(1-\tau) - [K_{t+1} - (1-\delta) K_t]}_{x_t(K_t, K_{t+1})} \\ +\mathbb{E}_t \left[M_{t,t+1} \hat{V}_{t+1}^E (K_{t+1}, z_t) \right] \end{array} \right]}_{W_t} \right\}, \tag{3.2.5}$$

The solution of the previous optimization problem can be obtained from the following conditions,

$$\begin{cases} \frac{\partial W_t}{\partial K_{t+1}} = 0 \implies 1 + \theta(I_t) \frac{I_t}{K_t} (1-\tau) = \mathbb{E}_t \left(\frac{M_{t+1}}{M_t} \frac{\partial \hat{V}_{t+1}^E}{\partial K_{t+1}} \right) \\ \dfrac{\partial \hat{V}^E(K_t, z_t)}{\partial K_t} = A_t(1-\tau) + \delta\tau + \dfrac{\theta(I_t)}{2} \left(\dfrac{I_t}{K_t} \right)^2 (1-\tau) + (1-\delta) \left[1 + (1-\tau)\theta(I_t) \left(\dfrac{I_t}{K_t} \right) \right] \end{cases} \tag{3.2.6}$$

which are based on the implicit assumption that the value function $\hat{V}_t^E(K_t, z_t)$ is differentiable in K_t. Starting from the top, $\frac{\partial W_t}{\partial K_{t+1}} = 0$ is the necessary FOC for an optimum. Applying the *envelope theorem* we can show that $\frac{\partial \hat{V}^E(K_t, z_t)}{\partial K_t}$ is equal to the marginal operating cash flows, $A_t(1-\tau) + \delta\tau + \frac{\theta(I_t)}{2}\left(\frac{I_t}{K_t}\right)^2 (1-\tau) + (1-\delta)\left[1 + (1-\tau)\theta(I_t)\left(\frac{I_t}{K_t}\right)\right]$. Putting together, these conditions can be used to obtain the following *Euler equation*, which must be valid along optimal investment path,

$$\underbrace{1+\theta\left(I_t\right)\frac{I_t}{K_t}(1-\tau)=}_{\text{Marginal Cost of Investment}}$$

$$\mathbb{E}_t\left\{\frac{M_{t+1}}{M_t}\left[\underbrace{\left[\begin{array}{l}A_t(1-\tau)+\delta\tau+\frac{\theta(I_{t+1})}{2}\left(\frac{I_{t+1}}{K_{t+1}}\right)^2(1-\tau)\\+(1-\delta)\left[1+(1-\tau)\theta\left(I_{t+1}\right)\left(\frac{I_{t+1}}{K_{t+1}}\right)\right]\end{array}\right]}_{\text{Marginal Benefit of Investment}}\right]\right\}. \tag{3.2.7}$$

Equation (3.2.7) is a restatement of the positive NPV rule in capital budgeting. Namely, the firm should invest until the marginal net present value of an additional investment unit is null. In fact, we can multiply both sides of the FOC in Eq. (3.2.8) times an infinitesimal investment dI,

$$\mathbb{E}_t\left(\frac{M_{t+1}}{M_t}\frac{\partial\hat{V}_{t+1}^E}{\partial K_{t+1}}dI\right)-\left[1+\theta\left(I_t\right)\frac{I_t}{K_t}(1-\tau)\right]dI=0. \tag{3.2.8}$$

At the margin, the term $\left[1+\theta\left(I_t\right)\frac{I_t}{K_{t-1}}(1-\tau)\right]dI$ is the total expense for installing dI units of capital, while $\mathbb{E}_t\left(\frac{M_{t+1}}{M_t}\frac{\partial\hat{V}_{t+1}^E}{\partial K_{t+1}}dI\right)$ is the change in the (ex-dividend) equity value. At an optimum, shareholders must gain nothing from this infinitesimal adjustment.

The value of the firm is equal to,

$$V_t=V_t^u=\mathbb{E}_t\sum_{s=1}^{\infty}M_{t,t+s}x_{t+s}^* \tag{3.2.9}$$

where x_t^* is the unlevered free cash flows process resulting from Eq. (3.2.7) and the necessary transversality condition for optimality $\lim_{T\to\infty}\mathbb{E}\left\{\frac{M_T}{M_t}\partial\hat{V}_K^E\left(K_T\right)K_T\right\}=0$ (see Miao 2020, Chapter 7). Notice that, by definition $V_t^u=\mathbb{E}_t\sum_{s=0}^{\infty}M_{t,t+s}x_{t+s}^*\geq\mathbb{E}_t\sum_{s=0}^{\infty}M_{t,t+s}x_{t+s}$, for any admissible$\{x_t\}_{t\geq 0}$. For ease of notation, in the remainder of this section we will suppress the asterisk $(*)$ and write $V_t^u=\mathbb{E}_t\sum_{s=1}^{\infty}M_{t,t+s}x_{t+s}$, implicitly assuming $x_t^*=x_t$.

Hence, we are left with the final task of looking for a more eloquent expression for V_t^u. To accomplish this, we start with multiplying both sides of Eq. (3.2.7) by K_t, observing that,

$$\left[\theta_{t+1}\frac{I_{t+1}}{K_{t+1}}(1-\delta)+\frac{\theta_{t+1}}{2}\left(\frac{I_{t+1}}{K_{t+1}}\right)^2\right]K_{t+1}=$$
$$\theta_{t+1}I_{t+1}\left[1-\delta+\frac{I_{t+1}}{K_{t+1}}\right]-\frac{\theta_{t+1}}{2}\left(\frac{I_{t+1}}{K_{t+1}}\right)^2=\theta_{t+1}\left(\frac{I_{t+1}}{K_{t+1}}\right)K_{t+2}. \tag{3.2.10}$$

Then, rearranging the resulting expression in order to have $\mathbb{E}_t\left\{M_{t,t+1}x_{t+1}\right\}$ on the LHS, we eventually obtain,

$$\mathbb{E}_t\left\{M_{t,t+1}x_{t+1}\right\}=$$
$$\mathbb{E}_t\left\{M_{t,t+1}\left[A_{t+1}(1-\tau)K_{t+1}+\delta\tau K_{t+1}-\frac{\theta(I_{t+1})}{2}\left(\frac{I_{t+1}}{K_t}\right)^2K_{t+1}(1-\tau)-I_{t+1}\right]\right\}=$$
$$K_{t+1}+(1-\tau)\theta(I_t)\left(\frac{I_t}{K_t}\right)K_{t+1}-\mathbb{E}\left\{M_{t,t+1}\left[K_{t+2}+(1-\tau)\theta(I_{t+1})\left(\frac{I_{t+1}}{K_{t+1}}\right)K_{t+2}\right]\right\}. \tag{3.2.11}$$

Substituting the previous expression recursively in Eq. (3.2.15), it takes just few simple algebraic steps to conclude that,

$$V_t=V_t^u=\left[1+(1-\tau)\theta(I_t)\left(\frac{I_t}{K_t}\right)\right]K_{t+1}. \tag{3.2.12}$$

Finally, the ratio between the market value of the firm (V_t) and the book-value of its capital stock (K_t) is defined as Tobin's Q (Q_t),

$$Q_t:=\frac{V_t}{K_{t+1}}, \tag{3.2.13}$$

and it is equal in this case to $1+(1-\tau)\theta(I_t)\left(\frac{I_t}{K_t}\right)$. Notice that, Q_t is increasing in the magnitude of investment adjustment costs. We will come back again on this very important, and, to some extent, controversial, aspect of the model.

3.2.2 Optimal Investment and Financing Decisions

In this section we allow the firm to issue secured debt, subject to the collateral constraint provided by Eq. (3.1.3). Shareholders' problem therefore modifies as follows,

$$\hat{V}_t^E(F_t, K_t, z_t) =$$
$$\max_{F_{t+1}\geq 0, K_{t+1}\geq 0} \left\{[A_t K_t - \phi(K_t, K_{t+1}) - (1+c_t)F_t](1-\tau) + \tau\delta K_t - I_t + F_{t+1} + \mathbb{E}_t\left(M_{t,t+1}\hat{V}_{t+1}^E\right)\right\}$$
$$s.t.$$
$$K_{t+1} = K_t(1-\delta) + I_t$$
$$F_{t+1}(1+c_{t+1}) \leq (1-\alpha)K_t. \tag{3.2.14}$$

Starting with the optimal debt policy, suppose the collateral constraint is never binding in equilibrium. In such a case, the first order condition for optimal investment would be the same of the previous section, and being agency costs absent, shareholders value will be equal to,

$$[A_t K_t - \phi(K_t, K_{t+1}) - (1+c_t)F_t](1-\tau) + \tau\delta K_t - I_t$$
$$+ \underbrace{\left[1 + (1-\tau)\theta(I_t)\left(\frac{I_t}{K_t}\right)\right]K_{t+1}}_{V_t^u} + DTS_t - TC_t \tag{3.2.15}$$

where,

$$\begin{cases} DTS_t = \frac{\tau c_{t+1}F_{t+1}}{1+r_{t+1}} + \mathbb{E}_t \sum_{s=2}^{\infty} \frac{M_{t+s}}{M_t}\tau c_{t+s}F_{t+s} & \text{Value of debt tax shield,} \\ TC_t = \frac{\varphi_{t+1}F_{t+1}}{1+r_{t+1}} + \mathbb{E}_t \sum_{s=2}^{\infty} \frac{M_{t+s}}{M_t}\varphi_{t+s}F_{t+s} & \text{NPV debt transaction costs.} \end{cases} \tag{3.2.16}$$

If $\tau c_{t+1} > \varphi_{t+1}$, shareholders could improve their equity value by issuing additional debt up to the maximum allowed by the collateral constraint. Hence, in this case the collateral constraint cannot be slack at an optimum. Furthermore, if the collateral constraint is binding, the marginal value of an additional unit of capital would be greater than zero if shareholders invest according the unlevered firm's investment policy. The reason is because by increasing further the capital stock, shareholders would be able to issue additional debt and capture the associated net benefit $\left(\tau c_{t,t+1} - \varphi_{t,t+1} > 0\right)$. Hence, whenever $\tau r_{t,t+1} > \varphi(1-\tau)$, shareholders are always better off by issuing as much as debt as possible, and investment decisions are distorted by the net benefits of debt financing. Equivalently, there is a funding cost advantage of debt financing, which will be more evident when will consider the relation between the firm's WACC and expected investment returns in Sect. 3.4. Conversely, in case $\tau r_{t,t+1} = \varphi(1-\tau)$ shareholders are indifferent to any level of debt which is compatible with the collateral constraint, while $\tau r_{t,t+1} < \varphi(1-\tau)$ implies that $F_t = 0$ is strictly optimal for shareholders.

At this point, we can now reformulate shareholders' problem in Eq. (3.2.14) as,

$$\begin{cases} \hat{V}^E(F_t, K_t, \mathbf{z}_t) = \max_{K_{t+1}} \{[A_t K_t - \delta K_t - c_t F_t - \phi(K_t, K_{t+1})](1-\tau) + K_t - K_{t+1} \\ \quad +\gamma_{t+1} K_{t+1} - F_t + \mathbb{E}_t\left[\frac{M_{t+1}}{M_t}\hat{V}^E(F_{t+1} = \gamma_{t+1}K_{t+1}, K_{t+1}, \mathbf{z}_t)\right]\} & \tau c_{t+1} \geq \varphi_{t+1} \\ \hat{V}^E(F_t, K_t, \mathbf{z}_t) = \max_{K_{t+1}} \{[A_t K_t - \delta K_t - c_t F_t - \phi(K_t, K_{t+1})](1-\tau) + K_t - K_{t+1} \\ \quad -F_t + \mathbb{E}_t\left[\frac{M_{t+1}}{M_t}\hat{V}^E(F_{t+1} = 0, K_{t+1}, \mathbf{z}_t)\right]\} & \tau c_{t+1} < \varphi_{t+1} \end{cases} \tag{3.2.17}$$

where $\gamma_{t+1} = \frac{(1-\alpha)(1-\delta)}{1+c_{t+1}}$. As a consequence, the following optimality conditions are necessary to characterize shareholders' equilibrium behavior,

$$\begin{cases} 1 + \theta(I_t)\frac{I_t}{K_t}(1-\tau) + \gamma_{t+1} = \mathbb{E}_t\left[\frac{M_{t+1}}{M_t}x_{t+1}\left(\lambda_{t+1}\frac{\partial \hat{V}^E_{t+1}}{\partial F_{t+1}} + \frac{\partial \hat{V}^E_{t+1}}{\partial K_{t+1}}\right)\right] \\ \lambda_{t+1} := \gamma_{t+1}\mathbb{I}(\tau c_{t+1} \geq \varphi_{t+1}) \\ \frac{\partial \hat{V}^E_{t+1}}{\partial F_{t+1}} = -[1 + c_{t+1}(1-\tau)] \\ \frac{\partial \hat{V}^E_{t+1}}{\partial K_{t+1}} = A_{t+1}(1-\tau) + \delta\tau + \frac{\theta(I_{t+1})}{2}\left(\frac{I_{t+1}}{K_{t+1}}\right)^2(1-\tau) + (1-\delta) \\ \qquad \times\left[1 + (1-\tau)\theta(I_{t+1})\left(\frac{I_{t+1}}{K_{t+1}}\right)\right] \\ F_{t+1} = \lambda_{t+1}K_{t+1} \end{cases} . \tag{3.2.18}$$

Proceeding from the top to the bottom, Eq. (3.2.18) includes the first order conditions for K_{t+1} and F_{t+1}, the related envelope conditions and the collateral constraint. From the first four conditions, we obtain the following investment Euler equation, which, jointly with the transversality condition

$\lim_{T\to\infty}\mathbb{E}\left\{\frac{M_T}{M_t}\frac{\partial \hat{V}_T^E}{\partial K_T}K_T\right\} = 0$, characterizes the optimal investment strategy for the firm,

$$\underbrace{1+\theta\left(I_t\right)\frac{I_t}{K_t}(1-\tau)}_{\text{Marginal Cost of Investment}}=\mathbb{E}_t\left\{\frac{M_{t+1}}{M_t}x_{t+1}\left[\underbrace{A_{t+1}(1-\tau)+\delta\tau+\frac{\theta\left(I_{t+1}\right)}{2}\left(\frac{I_{t+1}}{K_{t+1}}\right)^2(1-\tau)}_{\text{Marginal Change in Operating Cash Flows}}\right.\right.$$

$$\left.\left.\underbrace{+(1-\delta)\left[1+(1-\tau)\theta\left(I_{t+1}\right)\left(\frac{I_{t+1}}{K_{t+1}}\right)\right]}_{\text{Marginal Change in Operating Cash Flowse}}+\underbrace{\lambda_{t+1}\left(\tau c_{t+1}-\varphi_{t+1}\right)}_{\text{Marginal Net Tax Benefit of Debt Financing}}\right]\right\}. \tag{3.2.19}$$

Notice that Eq. (3.2.19) is again representative of the positive NPV rule in capital budgeting. However, the presence of debt introduces a potential misalignment between the marginal levered and unlevered NPV of an additional unit of capital stock, as a consequence of the optimal use of secured debt ($F_{t+1} = \lambda_{t+1}K_{t+1}$). This difference relates to the presence of the tax shield on interest expenses, which, when in excess of flotation costs, improves the total free cash flows to the firm.

Interestingly, we can show that Tobin's Q is characterized by the same expression as in the unlevered case, that is,

$$Q_t = 1+(1-\tau)\theta\left(I_t\right)\left(\frac{I_t}{K_t}\right), \tag{3.2.20}$$

albeit I_t will be higher compared to the unlevered case when the collateral constraint is binding, as a consequence of the optimal use of secured debt financing which, in turns, improves the value of the firm above V_t^u. To prove this claim, it is sufficient to note that, as a corollary to Proposition 3.2, we necessary have $V_t \geq V_t^u$. Then, we can rewrite Eq. (3.2.19) as,

$$\mathbb{E}_t\left(\frac{M_{t+1}}{M_t}x_{t+1}\right)=$$

$$\mathbb{E}_t\left\{\frac{M_{t+1}}{M_t}\left[A_{t+1}(1-\tau)K_{t+1}+\delta\tau K_{t+1}-\frac{\theta\left(I_{t+1}\right)}{2}\left(\frac{I_{t+1}}{K_{t+1}}\right)^2K_{t+1}(1-\tau)-I_{t+1}\right]\right\}=$$

$$K_{t+1}+(1-\tau)\theta\left(I_t\right)\left(\frac{I_t}{K_t}\right)K_{t+1}-\mathbb{E}\left\{\frac{M_{t+1}}{M_t}\left[K_{t+1}+(1-\tau)\theta\left(I_{t+1}\right)\left(\frac{I_{t+1}}{K_{t+1}}\right)K_{t+1}\right]\right\}-$$

$$\mathbb{E}_t\left\{M_{t,t+1}\lambda_{t+1}\left(\tau c_{t+1}-\varphi_{t+1}\right)K_t\right\}. \tag{3.2.21}$$

and, repeating the same steps as in the previous section, the general expression for the value of the firm,

$$V_t = \mathbb{E}_t \sum_{s=1}^{\infty} \frac{M_{t+1s}}{M_t} \left[x_{t+s} + \gamma_{t+s} F_{t+s} \left(\tau c_{t+s} - \varphi_{t+s}\right)\right], \tag{3.2.22}$$

simplifies to,

$$V_t = \left[1 + (1-\tau)\,\theta\,(I_t)\left(\frac{I_t}{K_t}\right)\right] K_{t+1}. \tag{3.2.23}$$

Finally, the fact that investment is higher in the levered case follows from comparing Eq. (3.2.19) for the cases in which $\gamma_{t+1} = 0$ and $\gamma_{t+1} = \gamma > 0$, respectively. The economic intuition is straightforward. Because the net benefit of debt financing is linear in the capital stock, the firm has incentive to deviate from the unlevered investment policy until the marginal loss in terms of NPV of unlevered free cash flows is equal to $\tau c_{t+1} - \varphi_{t+1}$. This is a form of agency cost, as we clarify in Sect. 3.4. Instead, next section discusses the relation between investment returns and securities returns.

3.3 Financial Returns and the Investment CAPM

The model developed in the previous section provides the theoretical framework for several related topics:

(1) the relation between the firm's fundamentals and securities returns;
(2) the use of WACC in capital budgeting decisions;
(3) the relation between levered and unlevered expected equity returns (Hamada 1972);
(4) an "efficient markets" explanation of the observed excess returns for portfolios of stocks with high (expected) profitability and low investment-to-assets ratios (Liu et al. 2009; Li and Zhang 2010; Zhang 2017; Hou et al. 2021)

3.3.1 Fundamentals and Securities Returns

Starting from the relation between securities returns and fundamentals, as an application of the firm's budget constraint, the following equation holds for every time $t \in \mathbb{N}$,

$$\frac{V_t^E}{V_t}\left(1 + r_{t+1}^E\right) + \frac{F_{t+1}}{V_t}\left(1 + r_{t+1}\right) = \frac{x_{t+1} + V_{t+1}}{V_t}. \tag{3.3.1}$$

By considering the equilibrium behavior of the firm, the equation is equivalent to

$$\frac{V_t^E}{V_t}\left(1+r_{t+1}^E\right)+\frac{F_{t+1}}{V_t}\left(1+r_{t+1}\right)=$$
$$\frac{V_{t+1}+A_{t+1}\left(1-\tau\right)K_{t+1}+\delta\tau K_{t+1}-\frac{\theta(I_{t+1})}{2}\left(\frac{I_{t+1}}{K_{t+1}}\right)^2K_{t+1}\left(1-\tau\right)-I_{t+1}+\left(\tau c_{t+1}-\varphi_{t+1}\right)F_{t+1}}{\left[1+\left(1-\tau\right)\theta\left(I_t\right)\left(\frac{I_t}{K_t}\right)\right]K_{t+1}}. \tag{3.3.2}$$

With few algebraic manipulations, we obtain a more compact formulation of Eq. (3.3.3):

$$\frac{V_t^E}{V_t}r_{t+1}^E+\frac{F_{t+1}}{V_t}c_{t+1}\left(1-\tau\right)=\frac{\left[A_{t+1}+\left(1-\delta\right)\frac{\theta(I_{t+1})}{2}\left(\frac{I_{t+1}}{K_{t+1}}\right)^2-\delta\right]\left(1-\tau\right)}{\left[1+\left(1-\tau\right)\theta\left(I_t\right)\left(\frac{I_t}{K_t}\right)\right]}. \tag{3.3.3}$$

Now, let us re-examine the envelope condition in Eq. (3.2.18),

$$\frac{\partial \hat{V}_{t+1}^E}{\partial K_{t+1}}=\frac{\partial fcf_{t+1}}{\partial K_{t+1}}+\mathbb{E}_t\left(\frac{\partial \hat{V}_{t+1}^E}{\partial K_{t+1}}\frac{\partial K_{t+2}}{\partial K_{t+1}}\right)=\frac{\partial fcf_{t+1}}{\partial K_{t+1}}=\frac{\partial y_{t+1}}{\partial K_{t+1}}-\frac{\partial fcf_{t+1}}{\partial K_{t+1}}$$
$$\left[A_{t+1}+\frac{\theta\left(I_{t+1}\right)}{2}\left(\frac{I_{t+1}}{K_{t+1}}\right)^2\right]\left(1-\tau\right)+\delta\tau+\left(1-\delta\right)\left(1-\tau\right)\theta\left(I_{t+1}\right)\left(\frac{I_{t+1}}{K_{t+1}}\right)+\left(1-\delta\right)=$$
$$\left[A_{t+1}+\left(1-\delta\right)\frac{\theta\left(I_{t+1}\right)}{2}\left(\frac{I_{t+1}}{K_{t+1}}\right)^2-\delta\right]\left(1-\tau\right)+1+\left(1-\tau\right)\theta\left(I_t\right)\left(\frac{I_t}{K_t}\right). \tag{3.3.4}$$

It is now immediate to notice that the numerator of the fraction at RHS side of Eq. (3.3.4) is equal to $\frac{\partial(y_{t+1}-\delta(1-\tau)K_{t+1})}{\partial K_{t+1}}$. The expression $y_{t+1}-\delta\left(1-\tau\right)K_{t+1}$ corresponds to the firm's NOPaT, that is EbIT minus taxes on operating earnings, which includes investment adjustment costs. At the same time, $1+\left(1-\tau\right)\theta\left(I_t\right)\left(\frac{I_t}{K_t}\right)$ is the marginal cost of a unit of capital. Therefore, the RHS of Eq. (3.3.4) is the ratio between the marginal NOPaT and the marginal cost of investment, which can be interpreted as the marginal after-tax return of invested capital. Hence, the weighted average returns of the firm's securities is equal to the marginal returns from investments. This result is originally due to Cochrane (1991), and later became the backbone of investment-based asset pricing models. In particular, the relation presented here is the one characterizing Zhang's Investment CAPM (Zhang 2017). Furthermore, a simple manipulation of Eq. (3.3.4) reveals that stock returns are equal to the ratio between the marginal net income

$\left(\frac{\partial}{\partial K_{t+1}}\left[y_{t+1}-\delta\left(1-\tau\right)K_{t+1}-F_{t+1}c_{t+1}\left(1-\tau\right)\right]\right)$ and the marginal cost for shareholders to invest in additional capital stock $\left(1+\theta\left(I_t\right)\left(\frac{I_t}{K_t}\right)-\lambda_{t+1}\right)$

$$r^E_{t+1}=\frac{\underbrace{\left[A_{t+1}+\left(1-\delta\right)\frac{\theta\left(I_{t+1}\right)}{2}\left(\frac{I_{t+1}}{K_{t+1}}\right)^2-\delta-c_{t+1}\lambda_{t+1}\right]\left(1-\tau\right)}_{\text{Marginal Net Income}}}{\underbrace{1+\theta\left(I_t\right)\left(\frac{I_t}{K_t}\right)-\lambda_{t+1}}_{\text{Marginal Change in Equity Book Value}}}, \tag{3.3.5}$$

which can be interpreted as the marginal return on equity book value. Indeed, $1+\theta\left(I_t\right)\left(\frac{I_t}{K_t}\right)-\lambda_{t+1}$ carries the interpretation of the marginal change in current dividends to fund an additional unit of capital stock.

3.3.2 Capital Budgeting and WACC

A common capital budgeting approach used by practitioners is to select and invest in all projects with an expected return greater than the WACC, which is the so-called "IRR" rule (Bierman 1993; Graham & Harvey 2001). In the model, this rule turns out to be consistent with the Euler equation characterizing the firm's equilibrium investment policy. Indeed, recalling from Sect. 3.1.3 that,

$$wacc_{t,t+1}=\frac{V^E_t}{V_t}\mathbb{E}_t\left(r^E_{t+1}\right)+\frac{F_{t+1}}{V_t}c_{t+1}\left(1-\tau\right), \tag{3.3.6}$$

if we take expectations on both sides of Eq. (3.3.3), we obtain,

$$wacc_{t,t+1}=\frac{\left[A_{t+1}+\left(1-\delta\right)\frac{\theta\left(I_{t+1}\right)}{2}\left(\frac{I_{t+1}}{K_{t+1}}\right)^2-\delta\right]\left(1-\tau\right)}{\left[1+\left(1-\tau\right)\theta\left(I_t\right)\left(\frac{I_t}{K_t}\right)\right]}. \tag{3.3.7}$$

Hence, in equilibrium shareholders invest until the expected marginal return of investments is equal to the weighted average cost of capital, which is indeed the formal statement of the IRR rule. However, this result is not very robust, and the optimality of the IRR rule should not be taken for granted in all circumstances. Nevertheless, it is interesting to note that Eq. (3.3.7) explicitly reveals the funding cost advantage of debt, as the debt is issued whenever it lowers the weighted average cost of capital, thereby boosting investments.

3.3.3 The Hamada Equation

Provided that $\tau c_{t+1} \leq \varphi_{t+1}$ for all time $t \in \mathbb{N}$, the expected equity returns are consistent with the Hamada's equation (Hamada 1972). In such a case the free cash flows and unlevered free cash flows to the firm are equivalent, and the investment policy is the same as in the unlevered case. Consequently, by defining $r_{t+1}^{u} := \frac{x_{t+1}+V_{t+1}^{u}}{V_{t+1}^{u}}$, we have:

$$\frac{V_t^E}{V_t}\mathbb{E}_t\left(r_{t+1}^{E}\right)+\frac{F_{t+1}}{V_t}r_{t+1}=\mathbb{E}_t\left(r_{t+1}^{u}\right). \tag{3.3.8}$$

As a result, we obtain the following relation for *levered* stock returns,

$$\mathbb{E}_t\left(r_{t+1}^{E}\right)=r_{t+1}+\left(1+\frac{F_{t+1}}{V_t^E}\right)\left[\mathbb{E}_t\left(r_{t+1}^{u}\right)-r_{t+1}\right] \tag{3.3.9}$$

which is the classic Hamada's formula when debt's financing is irrelevant for investment decisions (cf. Grinblatt and Titman 2011). It is important to acknowledge that the same result cannot be extended to the more general case in which $\tau c_{t+1} > \varphi_{t,t+1}$. Indeed, as debt becomes *value relevant*, the firm's investment policy is no longer the same as in the unlevered case, due to the presence of the collateral constraint. Nevertheless, we may use Eq. (3.3.6) to write,

$$\mathbb{E}_t\left(r_{t+1}^{E}\right)=r_{t+1}+\left(1+\frac{F_{t+1}}{V_t^E}\right)\left[wacc_{t,t+1}-r_{t+1}\right]. \tag{3.3.10}$$

which is valid in general, and, in absence of debt, $wacc_{t,t+1}=\mathbb{E}_t\left(r_{t+1}^{u}\right)$. Notably, the weighted average cost of capital can be computed directly from the firm's real characteristics, consistent with Eq. (3.3.5). In the financial practice, if the model is empirically sound and robust, this could be a very convenient way to avoid the estimation of conditional beta coefficients, which is a rather complicated task.

3.3.4 The Investment CAPM and the Cross-Section of Equity Returns

As the model can be used to relate the firm's real characteristics with expected stock returns, it is natural to ask whether it can compete with the standard Fama and French (1993) regression for the cross-section of stock returns. It turns out that it does (Li et al. 2009; Hou et al. 2021), in the sense that it very well explains the excess returns of portfolios that (systematically) invest in firms with lower investment-to-assets ratios and higher expected profitability. To understand why the model empirically explains such a relation, consider for simplicity the unlevered case, in which $\mathbb{E}_t\left(r_{t+1}^E\right) = wacc_{t,t+1}$. From Eq. (3.3.7), firms with higher $\mathbb{E}_t\left(A_{t+1}\right)$ and lower $\left(\frac{I_t}{K_t}\right)$ either face higher adjustment costs or a higher cost of capital. The latter case is equivalent to higher conditional expected stock returns. As is obvious, a similar circumstance can survive in general equilibrium only if the dividends resulting from the firm's optimized investment decisions are "riskier" to investors. Nevertheless, the model suggests that the firm's *characteristics* are sufficient statistics for predicting expected returns, just as conditional beta coefficients and equity risk premia do in traditional demand-side asset pricing models such as the consumption CAPM (Rubinstein 1976; Lucas 1978; Breeden 1979, amongst others). In other words, once controlling for firm's characteristics, *covariances* should have no additional power in explaining the cross-sectional returns. However, which characteristics should be included depends on the model we choose. As the consumption CAPM, the investment CAPM holds with reference to the equilibrium outcome of a specific artificial economy. Although Eq. (3.3.7) is not rejected by the data (Zhang 2017), the hypothesis of perfect competition entails some quantitative limitations which we discuss in the next chapter.

3.4 Debt Agency Costs and the Trade-off Theory

Although Tobin's Q has the same analytical expression in both the levered and unlevered case,

$$Q_t = 1 + (1-\tau)\,\theta\left(I_t\right)\left(\frac{I_t}{K_t}\right), \tag{3.4.1}$$

the firm invests more when $\tau c_{t+1} > \varphi_{t+1}$ as a result of the funding cost advantage of debt. However, higher investment relative to the unlevered case result in a lower NPV of unlevered free cash flows. As the value of the firm is higher, this loss is more than offset by the value of the debt tax shield net of that of transaction costs. In other words, the tax benefits of debt financing have a distortionary effect on the firm's investment policy, which is overall beneficial thanks to the presence of the tax shield on interest expenses. Let x_t^{**} be the unlevered free cash flows process generated by the levered firm's investment policy. Then, using Eq. (2.4.13), the following expression characterizes the value of the firm.

$$V_t = V_t^u - \left(\underbrace{\mathbb{E}_t \sum_{s=1}^{\infty} \frac{M_{t+s}}{M_t} x_{t+s}^{*} - \mathbb{E}_t \sum_{s=1}^{\infty} \frac{M_{t+s}}{M_t} x_{t+s}^{**}}_{AC_t} \right) + \underbrace{\mathbb{E}_t \sum_{s=1}^{\infty} \frac{M_{t+s}}{M_t} \lambda_{t+s} \left(\tau c_{t+s} - \varphi_{t+s}\right) \gamma_{t+s} K_{t+1}}_{DTS_t - TC_t} \tag{3.4.2}$$

Notably, the quantity $AC_t := \mathbb{E}_t \sum_{s=1}^{\infty} \frac{M_{t+s}}{M_t} x_{t+s}^{*} - \mathbb{E}_t \sum_{s=1}^{\infty} \frac{M_{t+s}}{M_t} x_{t+s}$ corresponds to the agency costs of debt, although their presence have no-effect on debt holders welfare, since the latter are always paid back in full.

Despite its simplicity, the model provides interesting insights for dynamic capital structure patterns. Firstly, it provides an equilibrium explanation to "pecking-order" theories (Myers & Majluf 1984; Frank et al. 2020), in the sense that firms prefer to issue as much debt as possible to fund new investments, in order to capture the value of debt tax shield. Secondly, holding α to be constant, which carries also the interpretation of the fraction of assets that can be pledged as collateral, firms prefer either $F_{t+1} = 0$ or to keep their book-leverage $\left(\frac{F_{t+1}}{K_t}\right)$ equal to $\frac{(1-\alpha)(1-\delta)}{(1+c_{t+1})}$, depending on the relative convenience of debt's financing (i.e. $\tau c_{t+1} \gtreqless \varphi_{t+1}$). The former case provides a potential explanation of the zero leverage puzzle (Strebulaev & Yang 2013), namely, the existence of firms that do not make use of debt even when interest expenses may be tax deductible. In particular, firms that find credit very expensive (high values for φ_{t+1}), will remain unlevered. In the latter case, instead, we observe the existence of an optimal book-leverage ratio, which is inversely related to the cost of debt financing. On the one hand, this means that firms should borrow more when the cost of debt is lower. On the other, in periods when interests rates are stable, the book-leverage of the firm should fluctuates around a target value. This prediction is actually consistent with the empirical findings of DeAngelo and Roll (2015). Furthermore, the market-leverage $\frac{F_{t+1}}{V_t}$,

$$\frac{F_{t+1}}{V_t} = \frac{1}{1 + (1-\tau)\,\theta\left(I_t\right)\left(\frac{I_t}{K_t}\right)} \frac{(1-\alpha)}{(1+c_{t+1})}, \tag{3.4.3}$$

may vary across time, but should be often *mean-reverting* around a target value, consistently with the findings of Fama and French (2002). Hence, the model shows a good performance in explaining several patterns observed empirically, although firms do not issue only secured debt, and in some cases they do not issue secured debt at all. A potential explanation for this conundrum is because several debt contracts are designed to avoid the default of the issuer. However, there might be other reasons, which can be attributed to the existence of long-run lending relationships in which share and debt holders coordinate on very specific equilibria (see Sect. 7.4).

The model also contributes in explaining why default rates tend to be low for listed companies, as well as the limited use of leverage for firms with mostly intangibles assets ($\alpha \approx 1$), contrary to the case of capital intensive sectors, which typically feature high book-leverage ratios. Examples are technology and energy stocks, where the former usually do not make use of debt as opposed to the latter. However, from this example we also understand that the transaction costs argument to explain non-zero credit spreads may be fragile, as there have been several episodes of default in the energy sector. In this regard, the model predicts that the equity value function is linearly decreasing in the amount of debt outstanding, as shareholders' option to default never gets strictly in-the-money. As we document in the following chapters, with unsecured debt, default might be enticing for shareholders, then generating a strictly convex relation between the value of equity and the amount of debt outstanding, as in the structural credit risk model of Merton (1973). Empirically, Eisdorfer et al. (2019) documents the importance of correctly assessing the value of the equity default option for distressed firms. According to their analysis, the market seems to underestimate the value of this option, as it was erroneously adopting the model developed in this section to value companies with high default probability. Yet, the model does a pretty good job in its simplicity to explain several stylized facts and it also provides a very good starting point for equity valuation models (Belo et al. 2013). On this point, the next chapter deals with imperfect industry competition, which is a necessary assumption for a more realistic model, as we discuss in Sect. 4.1.

3.5 Related Literature

Borrowing constraints are pervasive in the corporate finance literature. Notable examples are Holmstrom and Tirole (1997) and Kiyotaki and Moore (1997). Tangential to our framework, the main references are Cochrane (1991), Hennessy and Whited (2005), Liu et al. (2009), Livdan et al. (2009) and Zhang (2017). One application we have not discussed is the presence of equity flotation costs and limits to outside equity injections. With financially constrained firms, as in Livdan et al. (2009), holding liquidity reserves could be strategic as to avoid costly recapitalization or, in the worst case, an undesired event of default. Whited (1992) provides indirect empirical evidences supporting the existence of financing constraints on shareholders side. However, for large sized companies these results appear a bit blurred. In particular, once we introduce imperfect competition in the firm's product market (see Chap. 4), there is no evidence supporting the role of financial constraints to explain the relationship between investment and profitability (Cooper & Ejarque 2003). Besides, there are evidence that seasoned equity offerings

(SEO) discounts and direct transactions costs are mostly affected by the accounting quality of the issuer (Lee & Masulis 2009), which we ruled out in our framework having assumed perfect information (see Sect. 1.3.2). In other words, unless we allow for a tangible information asymmetry between investors and firms, the high competition between financial intermediaries should result in very limited equity issuance costs. The model we presented in this section is based on this hypothesis, which we maintain in the following chapters.

Although the Investment CAPM does a quite good job in explaining the cross-section of equity returns, one major drawback is the consistency of structural estimates for the parameters characterizing investment adjustment costs (Liu et al. 2009). Despite investment adjustment costs are relevant (Bai et al. 2019), especially in terms of investment irreversibility, they cannot fully explain the difference between expected profitability and stock market returns (Hall 2004). The reason is because it is quite counterfactual to connect profitability with costly investment adjustments. Rather, profitability stems from the firm's ability to charge a mark-up on its average production cost, a feature that is absent in models which are characterized by perfect industry competition. For this reason, in the next chapter we are going to discuss the effects of imperfect competition and *market power*.

It is interesting to note that the Investment CAPM is nothing but the supply-side of financial markets competitive equilibrium, and, in general equilibrium, necessary entails the same prediction of demand side models such as the Consumption CAPM. However, the latter typically suffer from several empirical limitations (Mehra and Prescott 1985; Weil 1989), mostly as a consequence of aggregation problems (see Sect. 1.3.3). The Investment CAPM partly overcome these issues. Besides, it also comes with a higher degree of realism. In fact, several surveys show that the majority of listed companies follow a capital budgeting process consistent with the positive NPV rule and its potential refinements (Bierman, 1993; Graham & Harvey 2001; Jagannathan et al. 2011; McDonald 2006; Brunzell et al. 2013).

A major limitation of the model is the presence of fully secured debt as the only alternative to equity financing. In Sect. 7.1.1 we remove this assumption and introduce risky unsecured debt. As risky secured debt can be well approximated as a mix of fully secured and risky unsecured debt, the model we present in Sect. 7.1.1 can be used for quantitative-oriented analysis. Nevertheless, in several circumstances it is not entirely wrong to assume a simple capital structure as the one presented in this chapter, which is tantamount to approximate corporate debt as a risk-free bond (see Sect. 7.4). In this regard, Graham (2000, 2001, 2003, 2005 and Kemsley and Nissim (2002) are examples of empirical papers estimating the value relevance of debt tax shield in a way which is similar to the model presented in this section.

References

Abel, A. B. (2017). Optimal debt and profitability in the trade-off theory. *The Journal of Finance, 73*(1), 95–143.

Bai, H., Li, E. X. N., Xue, C., & Zhang, L. (2019). Does costly reversibility matter for U.S. public firms? *SSRN Electronic Journal*.

Belo, F., Xue, C., & Zhang, L. (2013). A supply approach to valuation. *Review of Financial Studies, 26*(12), 3029–3067.

Bierman, H. (1993). Capital budgeting in 1992: A survey. *Financial Management, 22*(3). https://doi.org/10.2307/3665921

Breeden, D. T. (1979). An intertemporal asset pricing model with stochastic consumption and investment opportunities. *Journal of Financial Economics, 7*(3), 265–296.

Brunzell, T., Liljeblom, E., and Vaihekoski, M. (2013). Determinants of capital budgeting methods and hurdle rates in nordic firms. *Accounting and Finance, 53*(1), 85–110.

Cochrane, J. H. (1991). Production-based asset pricing and the link between stock returns and economic fluctuations. *The Journal of Finance, 46*(1), 209–237.

Cooper, R., & Ejarque, J. (2003). Financial frictions and investment: requiem in Q. *Review of Economic Dynamics, 6*(4), 710–728.

DeAngelo, H., & Roll, R. (2015). How stable are corporate capital structures? *The Journal of Finance, 70*(1), 373–418.

Eisdorfer, A., Goyal, A., & Zhdanov, A. (2019). Equity misvaluation and default options. *The Journal of Finance, 74*(2), 845–898.

Fama, E. F., & French, K. R. (1993). Common risk factors in the returns on stocks and bonds. *Journal of Financial Economics, 33*(1), 3–56.

Fama, E. F., & French, K. R. (2002). Testing trade-off and pecking order predictions about dividends and debt. *Review of Financial Studies, 15*(1), 1–33.

Frank, M. Z., Goyal, V. K., & Shen, T. (2020). The pecking order theory of capital structure: Where do we stand? *Oxford Research Encylopedia of Economics and Finance*.

Garin, J. (2015). Borrowing constraints, collateral fluctuations, and the labor market. *Journal of Economic Dynamics and Control, 57*, 112–130.

Graham, J. R. (2000). How big are the tax benefits of debt? *The Journal of Finance, 55*(5), 1901–1941.

Graham, J. R. (2001). Estimating the tax benefits of debt. *Journal of Applied Corporate Finance, 14*(1), 42–54.

Graham, J. R. (2003). Taxes and corporate finance: A review. *Taxes and Corporate Finance: A Review John R. Graham The Review of Financial Studies, 16*(4), 1075–1129.

Graham, J. R. (2005). A review of taxes and corporate finance. *Foundations and Trends® in Finance, 1*(7), 573–691.

Graham, J. R., & Harvey, C. R. (2001). The theory and practice of corporate finance: Evidence from the field. *Journal of Financial Economics, 60*(2–3), 187–243.

Grinblatt, M., & Titman, S. (2011). *Financial markets and corporate strategy*. McGraw-Hill Higher Education.

Hall, R. E. (2004). Measuring factor adjustment costs. *The Quarterly Journal of Economics, 119*(3), 899–927.

Hamada, R. S. (1972). The effect of the firm's capital structure on the systematic risk of common stocks. *The Journal of Finance, 27*(2), 435–452.

Hennessy, C. A., & Whited, T. M. (2005). Debt dynamics. *The Journal of Finance, 60*(3), 1129–1165.

Holmstrom, B., & Tirole, J. (1997). Financial intermediation, loanable funds, and the real sector. *The Quarterly Journal of Economics, 112*(3), 663–691.

Hou, K., Mo, H., Xue, C., & Zhang, L. (2021). An augmented q-factor model with expected growth. *Review of Finance*, 25(1), 1–41.

Huang, J.-Z., & Huang, M. (2012). How much of the corporate-treasury yield spread is due to credit risk? *Review of Asset Pricing Studies, 2*(2), 153–202.
Jagannathan, R., Meier, I., & Tarhan, V. (2011). The cross section of hurdle rates for capital budgeting: An empirical analysis of survey data. *NBER Working Papers*, w16770.
Kemsley, D., & Nissim, D. (2002). Valuation of the debt tax shield. *The Journal of Finance, 57*(5), 2045–2073.
Kiyotaki, N., & Moore, J. (1997). Credit cycles. *Journal of Political Economy, 105*(2), 211–248.
Lee, G., & Masulis, R. W. (2009). Seasoned equity offerings: Quality of accounting information and expected flotation costs? *Journal of Financial Economics, 92*(3), 443–469.
Li, E. X. N., Livdan, D., & Zhang, L. (2009). Anomalies. *Review of Financial Studies, 22*(11), 4301–4334.
Li, D., & Zhang, L. (2010). Does q-theory with investment frictions explain anomalies in the cross section of returns? *Journal of Financial Economics, 98*(2), 297–314.
Liu, L., Whited, T., & Zhang, L. (2009). Investment-based expected stock returns. *Journal of Political Economy, 117*(6), 1105–1139.
Livdan, D., Sapriza, H., & Zhang, L. (2009). Financially constrained stock returns. *The Journal of Finance, 64*(4), 1827–1862.
Lucas, R. E. (1978). Asset prices in an exchange economy. *Econometrica, 46*(6), 1429.
McDonald, R. L. (2006). The role of real options in capital budgeting: Theory and practice. *Journal of Applied Corporate Finance, 18*(2), 28–39.
Mehra, R., & Prescott, E. C. (1985). The equity premium: A puzzle. *Journal of Monetary Economics, 15*(2), 145–161.
Merton, R. C. (1973). Theory of rational option pricing. *The Bell Journal of Economics and Management Science, 4*(1), 141.
Miao, J. (2020). *Economic dynamics in discrete time*. MIT Press.
Myers, S. C., & Majluf, N. S. (1984). Corporate financing and investment decisions when firms have information that investors do not have. *Journal of Financial Economics, 13*(2), 187–221.
Rampini, A. A., & Viswanathan, S. (2013). Collateral and capital structure. *Journal of Financial Economics, 109*(2), 466–492.
Rubinstein, M. (1976). The valuation of uncertain income streams and the pricing of options. *The Bell Journal of Economics, 7*(2), 407.
Strebulaev, I. A., & Yang, B. (2013). The mystery of zero-leverage firms. *Journal of Financial Economics, 109*(1), 1–23.
Weil, P. (1989). The equity premium puzzle and the risk-free rate puzzle. *Journal of Monetary Economics, 24*(3), 401–421.
Whited, T. M. (1992). Debt, liquidity constraints, and corporate investment: Evidence from panel data. *The Journal of Finance, 47*(4), 1425–1460.
Zhang, L. (2017). The investment CAPM. *European Financial Management, 23*(4), 545–603.

Chapter 4
Imperfect Competition, Working Capital and Tobin's Q

In the previous chapter we studied equilibrium investment and financing decisions in the case of perfect competition in the firm's product market. A counterfactual result of the model is that the wedge between the expected firm's profitability and the cost of capital is entirely driven by the size of investment adjustment costs. Namely, the larger $||\theta(I_t)||$, the wider is the spread between the return on invested capital (RoIC), which is the ratio between operating earnings and the total capital stock, and the firm's WACC, holding everything else constant. However, it is well known from *industrial organization* that profitability is inherently related to the market power of the firm (Tirole 1988). In other words, although investment adjustment costs may be important to characterize several features, such as *investment irreversibility* in capital intensive industries, they cannot fully explain the cost of capital for highly profitable industries.

To make an example, consider a luxury car maker (L) and a small car producer (S), both employing the same technology to manufacture their vehicles. Although the reference sector is the same, the two firms operate in very different industries. It is reasonable to expect that L has few competitors, and a certain degree of market power which comes as a consequence of the brand, design and performance of its cars. Instead, the small car producer is likely to be almost price-taker, due to the presence of several competing brands making its product as almost perfect substitute. Thus, it is natural to expect that L will obtain on average much higher operating margins than S. In the basic Investment CAPM of Chap. 3, this is equivalent to $\mathbb{E}_t\left(A^L_{t+1}\right) >> \mathbb{E}_t\left(A^S_{t+1}\right)$. As θ^+ and θ^- are unlikely to be significantly different between the two firms, according to Eq. (3.3.7) in Sect. 3.3, the luxury car producer should have a cost of capital much higher than the small car producer, holding everything else constant.

Although not impossible from a theoretical perspective, a similar result would be equivalent to asserting that the luxury car industry is much riskier than the small car industry, which is not necessarily the case. Rather, the demand for high-end products may be more resilient during recessions. Besides, the quantitative prediction of the

U. Sagliaschi, R. Savona, *Dynamical Corporate Finance*, Contributions to Finance and Accounting, https://doi.org/10.1007/978-3-030-77853-8_4

model are definitely a bit of extreme. To see the point, suppose $\delta = \tau = \theta^+ = \theta^- = 0$ and let $r_{t+1}^{E,L}$ be the returns of the luxury car makers' stocks. If L has an expected RoIC of 50%, i.e. $\mathbb{E}_t\left(A_{t+1}^L\right) = 0.5$, then $\mathbb{E}_t\left(r_{t+1}^{E,L}\right)$ should be also equal to 50%, which is a rather implausible number for the cost of capital of an healthy company. The problem is that, with perfect competition in the firm's product market, holding the cost of capital constant, profitability is increasing in the size of adjustment costs.

Unless these are extremely high, the model cannot explain the substantial difference between profitability and expected stock returns. Section 4.1 clarifies this in a more formal way. Moreover, in Sect. 4.2 we present a model of imperfect market competition, in which every firm within the same industry is monopolist of its own brand of products. Intentionally, investment adjustment costs have been left out from the analysis, in order to isolate the effect of market power.[1] However, to add realism, we introduce the (potential) presence of working capital, in terms of inventories of intermediate production goods. Instead, we do not consider trade receivables and payables, as they can be viewed as a specific form of secured debt financing, unless we allow for counterparty risk in trade financing. To simplify the discussion, additional production expenses are left for Sect. 7.1.1. However, it turns out that this simplification has no impact on our results, once we keep in mind that profitability should be intended as the after-tax return on invested capital (i.e. NOPaT over the invested capital). Thus, the results of the model we present in this chapter can be directly tested empirically. In this regard, the introduction of working capital is crucial, as *inventory days* can be an important determinant of free cash flows.

The introduction of market power does not alter equilibrium financing decisions, in that the collateral constraint remains always binding whenever $\tau c_{t+1} \geq \varphi_{t+1}$. However, even with a CRS technology, there are decreasing returns to scale in total revenues. Since the optimal investment level remains characterized by the positive NPV rule, the average return from investment exceeds its marginal level in equilibrium. In a nutshell, the less a brand can be substituted in the same industry, the higher will be the expected profitability of the firm owner of the same brand. In Sect. 4.3, we discuss the relationship between securities returns and the firm's fundamental in equilibrium, and we suggest a possible empirical validation test. Finally, in Sect. 4.4 we discuss a more refined empirical strategy which could be more suitable for security analysis.

4.1 The Limits of Perfect Product Markets Competition

The Investment CAPM extends to the inclusion of product market settings other than perfect competition. By product market, we mean the trading arrangement in which the firm is able to sell its products or services. Despite perfect competition

[1] As they might be relevant in several cases, we reintroduce investment adjustment costs in Sect. 7.1, in which we refine the model introduced in this chapter.

remains a pillar of neoclassical equilibrium models, it is not suitable to describe how firms are able to generate returns above their cost of capital in equilibrium. Indeed, in any (interior) equilibrium without adjustment costs, Tobin's Q is equal to one and expected profitability is equal to the weighted average cost of capital of the firm. Hence, with negligible investment adjustment costs, either because the firm is not investing or $||\theta(I_t)|| \approx 0$, we could obtain wrong predictions, as in the example of the luxury car producer.

Formally, we can show the previous result setting $\theta(I_t) = 0$ in the model discussed in Chap. 3. The first implication is that, both the unlevered and levered firm have a Tobin's Q which is equal to one in equilibrium,

$$\frac{V_t^u}{K_{t+1}^u} = \frac{V_t}{K_{t+1}} = 1. \tag{4.1.1}$$

At first, we would tempted to claim that, despite this equivalence, the levered firm will capitalize more as a consequence of a higher equilibrium capital stock, i.e. $K_{t+1} > K_{t+1}^u$. However, this turns out to be a wrong conclusion with no adjustments costs. Consider the Euler equation characterizing the optimal investment level for the unlevered case,

$$1 = \mathbb{E}_t \left\{ \frac{M_{t+1}}{M_t} \left[A_{t+1}(1-\tau) + \delta\tau + (1-\delta) \right] \right\}, \tag{4.1.2}$$

and the one for the levered case,

$$1 = \mathbb{E}_t \left\{ \frac{M_{t+1}}{M_t} \left[A_{t+1}(1-\tau) + \delta\tau + (1-\delta) + \lambda_t (\tau c_{t+1} - \varphi_{t+1}) \right] \right\}. \tag{4.1.3}$$

As is evident, the two conditions cannot hold simultaneously, unless $\tau c_{t+1} = \varphi_{t+1}$ or $\alpha = 1$. Firstly, this means that one of the two optimization has not an interior solution, that is, the optimal capital stock is either zero or unbounded in one of the two cases. Secondly, both conditions impose a restriction on the dynamics of the (before-tax) return on invested capital A_t, which means that investments, and, consequently, the firm's capital stock, are undetermined. Without investment adjustment costs, the firm's objective function is linear in the capital stock. Therefore, all investment policies should generate the same value for shareholders. Otherwise, the problem is unbounded, and therefore inconsistent with the demand side of the economy, or shareholders find it optimal to set capital $K_{t+1} = 0$. Hence, an interior equilibrium exists only if shareholders are indifferent to any value for K_{t+1}.

To better understand this result, consider the static model of perfect competition in which the firm operates with a linear technology. The optimization problem faced by the firm features a linear objective function (profits), subject to a linear equality constraint (technology). Suppose that the market price of the produced good, taken as given by the firm, is greater than or equal to the marginal cost of production, so that the firm has a weak incentive to operate. Then, we may have two opposite cases, of which only one can actually survive in equilibrium. Either the producer is indifferent to any production plan, as the market price is equal to the marginal cost of production, or the optimal production level is unbounded, in case the market price exceeds the marginal cost. As is natural, an equilibrium cannot support an unbounded production level, as resources are necessary scarce in any "reasonable" model economy. Therefore, the only possibility we have is that firms make zero profits in equilibrium.

Going back to our model, which is stochastic and dynamic, investments at time t generate profits only at time $t + 1$, subject to a certain degree of randomness. As such, instead of making zero profits, absent any other frictions, expected profitability $\mathbb{E}_t\left[(A_{t+1} - \delta)(1 - \tau)\right]$ must be aligned to an appropriate discount rate, which stems from the SDF of the economy and its covariance with the stochastic process $\{A_t\}_{t\geq 0}$. Indeed, if $\theta(I_t) = 0$, Eq. (3.3.7) requires that,

$$wacc_{t,t+1} = \mathbb{E}_t\left[(A_{t+1} - \delta)(1 - \tau)\right], \tag{4.1.4}$$

where $(A_{t+1} - \delta)(1 - \tau)$ is the after-tax return on invested capital.

The previous analysis shows the prominent role of adjustment costs in the basic Investment CAPM. Without them, there would be little chance to reconcile stock returns with firms' fundamentals. This is certainly an issue which cannot be ignored. On the one hand, despite some evidence of costly investment reversibility (Bai et al. 2019), Hall (2004) argues that investment adjustment costs are too small to play such an important role in jointly explaining profitability and fluctuations in the market value of securities. On the other, Cooper and Ejarque (2003) documents empirically that market power largely explains the relation between investment and profitability, consistent with the earlier findings of Lindenberg and Ross (1981). The rationale of this result is essentially the same of the example of car producers, which opens up to the possibility that in many circumstances investment adjustment costs may be statistically relevant just as a consequence of abstracting from market power. For this reason, the remainder of the chapter extends the basic Investment CAPM to the case of imperfect competition, assuming that each firm within its reference industry is monopolist of its own branded products. This is a quite nice description of several industries, and includes perfect competition as a limiting case. We show that, in order to maximize shareholders value, firms must adjust their output capacity in response to expected shifts in the demand schedule for their products, which is no longer flat, contrary to the case of perfect competition. This will enable us to obtain a more realistic link between profitability and expected equity returns.

4.2 Monopolistic Competition and Market Power

Let assume that each industry corresponds to the market for a certain type of products, which is available through different *brands*, or *varieties*. Within a given industry, each firm is monopolist of its own *brand*, which means that, given the demand schedule for its *variety*, a firm can unilaterally fix the price at which consumers will be able to buy its products. The higher the degree of substitutability between different brands within the same industry, the more the latter is competitive, and, in the limit case of perfect substitutability, we get back to the case of perfect competition. Thus, the model is general enough to include the basic version of the Investment CAPM.

For simplicity, we will assume that each firm produces a single type of non-storable and non-durable goods. Both hypotheses serve to abstract from decisions on the convenience of inventories of finished products, as well as *intertemporal pricing* issues, such as the Coase conjecture for durable goods producers (Coase 1972; Gul et al. 1986).[2] As anticipated, investment adjustment costs will be left out of the analysis in the first place, although we will reintroduce later in Sect. 7.1, when considering a more general version of the model.

As for the firm's capital structure, the model setting is the same as the one used in the previous chapter. There are neither limits to equity injections nor equity flotation costs. Equity and secured debt are the only means of financing, and we assume the presence of a collateral constraint in the usual form $F_{t+1}(1 + c_{t+1}) \leq (1 - \alpha) K_{t+1}$. Debt matures in each period, and the coupon rate is equal to r_{t+1}. The issuance of new debt securities is subject to flotation costs equal to φ_{t+1} per dollar of debt issued. As a result, $c_{t+1} = r_{t+1} + \varphi_{t+1}$ is the cost of debt. Furthermore, as Proposition 3.2 remains valid, firms will never default in the model. Accordingly, we can directly exclude the case of default from the analysis. Besides, as holding cash remains suboptimal due to linear corporate taxes, we can also exclude liquidity without loss of generality.

4.2.1 *Timing of Decisions and Optimal Price Setting*

The model is in discrete time and each date $t \in \mathbb{N}$ is a point on the real line all having the same temporal distance one each other. However, things occur according to a virtual sequence at each date which we now turn to describe. Before doing this it is important to observe that Proposition 3.2 remains valid as there are no fixed production costs except for depreciation expenses, as its results are independent from the firm's technology and the industrial organization setting. Hence, we do not need to take into account the alternative of default, and the maximization of shareholders value is equivalent to maximize the NPV of total free cash flows.

Given the capital stock K_t, at time t the firm decides first how much to produce and the price at which consumers will be able to purchase its goods. The price is set before consumers can actually come and buy the firm's products at the same date.

[2]See also Sects. 6.2 and 6.3. The reader should get acquainted with the literature on the Coase conjecture. Tirole (1988) is a very good and accessible reference. A basic knowledge of the Coase conjecture is essential to understand the effects of shareholders inability to commit to a static capital structure policy in the dynamic capital structure model presented in Chap. 6.

Furthermore, there is *no price discrimination*, in that, once the firm has decided a price p_t, the same price is applied irreversibly to all trades taking place at time t. In this regard, the firm can freely adjust the price of its products in each period.

The capital stock is not the only input of the production process. We assume that at time $t-1$, the firm had to spend κK_t dollars for intermediate production goods to be used at time t, independently from the effective capacity in use at the same date ($u_t \leq A_t K_t$). This mechanism allows to introduce *working capital* in the model, as the firm incurs the payment of expenses before the items purchased become cost elements in the P&L statement. In this regard, intermediate inputs are assumed to depreciate completely if the firm does not run at full capacity, in which case inventories are fully exhausted.

Let u_t be the quantity of goods produced at time t, which denotes the actual capacity in use. The production process described so far then results in the following expression for the firm's operating cash flows (y_t),

$$y_t = \underbrace{(p_t s_t - \kappa K_t - \delta K_t)(1-\tau) + \delta K_t}_{\text{Net Operating Cash Flows After Taxes}} - \underbrace{\kappa (K_{t+1} - K_t)}_{\text{Change in Working Capital}} \tag{4.2.1}$$

given the following *technology constraint* for u_t,

$$s_t \leq u_t \leq A_t K_t, \tag{4.2.2}$$

where s_t is the quantity of goods sold, which can be at most equal to the production in the same period (u_t),[3] while $A_t \in \mathbf{z}_t$ is now a strictly positive exogenous stochastic process which reveals the firm's *capital efficiency*.

From the perspective of the firm's *balance sheet statement*, at time $t-1$ the expense kK_t, which corresponds to the end-of-period value of intermediate inputs inventories, is a *current asset*. At time t inventories are used to produce the firm's final goods, or perish. As such, they become an economic cost, that is, an item of the *Profit and Loss statement*, and therefore the original expense κK_{t-1} eventually becomes tax deductible. In other words, since revenues are collected only in t, but inventories are purchased in $t-1$, the firm's has a fixed *operating cycle* of one period. As in Chap. 3, the fixed capital stock K_t depreciates at the constant rate $\delta \in [0, 1]$, and there is no difference between economic and accounting depreciation.

We let $q(p = p_t, \mathbf{z} = \mathbf{z}_t)$ be the demand schedule for the firms' products, which is assumed to be strictly decreasing in p_t and perfectly known by the firm. Notice that a perfect knowledge of the demand stems from a perfect knowledge of consumer tastes, as the outcome of the exogenous random vector $\mathbf{z}_t$ is revealed at the "beginning" of each date t. As is common in industrial organization, the demand schedule is the maximum amount of goods that consumers will buy at the prices set by the firm right before trades take place at a certain date. In other words, unless the firm unilaterally decides to rationing one or more consumers, $q(p = p_t, \mathbf{z} = \mathbf{z}_t)$ is

[3] Recall the assumption of non-storability and non-durability of the goods produced by the firm.

the quantity sold at price p_t. Since the firm can freely adjust the price for its goods at each date t, and such a decision has no effect on future revenues,[4] we can analyze the optimal capacity and pricing problem in isolation, that is, independently from optimal investment and financing decisions. Notably, this is actually possible as we are preserving the hypothesis that economic and accounting depreciation coincides, so that the fixed capital stock (K_t) depreciates independently from the capacity in use.[5] Thus, in each period shareholders solve the following subprogram,

$$
\begin{gathered}
\max_{p_t, s_t} y_t \\
y_t = (p_t s_t - \kappa K_t - \delta K_t)(1-\tau) + \delta K_t - \kappa (K_{t+1} - K_t) \\
s.t. \\
u_t \leq A_t K_t \text{ (Output Capacity)} \\
s_t \leq u_t \text{ (Sales Capacity)} \\
s_t \leq q(p = p_t, \mathbf{z} = \mathbf{z}_t) \text{ (Demand Schedule)}.
\end{gathered}
\tag{4.2.3}
$$

Before proceeding with the solution of the previous problem, we recall the definition of *price elasticity of demand* (η_t), or *elasticity* for short,

$$
\eta_t := -\frac{\partial q(p = p_t, \mathbf{z} = \mathbf{z}_t)}{\partial p} \frac{p_t}{q(p = p_t, \mathbf{z} = \mathbf{z}_t)}. \tag{4.2.4}
$$

We assume $\eta_t \geq 1$, holding with equality only in the limiting case of perfect competition, which for the moment will be left out of the analysis.

We claim that, in equilibrium, the three constraints in Eq. (4.2.3) must be binding. Starting from the bottom, it is never convenient for the firm to sell less than $q(p = p_t, \mathbf{z} = \mathbf{z}_t)$ for a given choice of $p_t > 0$, as $\frac{\partial y_t}{\partial s_t} = p_t > 0$. Hence, $s_t = q(p = p_t, \mathbf{z} = \mathbf{z}_t)$ always, and the sales capacity constraint becomes $q(p = p_t, \mathbf{z} = \mathbf{z}_t) \leq u_t$. Since $\eta_t > 1$, it follows that revenues, that are equal to $p_t q(p = p_t, \mathbf{z} = \mathbf{z}_t)$, are strictly decreasing in p_t, or equivalently, strictly increasing in the quantity sold $s_t = q(p = p_t, \mathbf{z} = \mathbf{z}_t)$. As a consequence, if p_t is such that $q(p = p_t, \mathbf{z} = \mathbf{z}_t) < u_t$, operating cash flows can be improved by lowering p_t until $u_t = q(p = p_t, \mathbf{z} = \mathbf{z}_t)$. Hence, it is never convenient for the firm to set a price resulting in a slack sales capacity constraint, that is $s_t = q(p = p_t, \mathbf{z} = \mathbf{z}_t) = u_t$

[4] This is true as long as the firm produces non-durable goods, otherwise the Coase conjecture may be a serious obstacle (see also Sect. 6.2.2.). The result can be extended to the case of a durable good producer, provided that the firm is able to commit to sell in each period a different vintage of its products. For example, a smartphone producer must be able develop a different version of its devices in each period, and commit not to sell additional units of the current available version in future.

[5] Otherwise, investments will be affected by capacity and pricing decisions, as the latter are linked to the former by $q(p = p_t, \mathbf{z} = \mathbf{z}_t)$ and the technology constraint in Eq. (4.2.2).

is always valid. In the same way, it is never convenient for the firm to operate below capacity, i.e. setting p_t such that $q\left(p = p_t, \mathbf{z} = \mathbf{z}_t\right) < A_t K_t$. As before, operating cash flows can be improved by lowering p_t until $q\left(p = p_t, \mathbf{z} = \mathbf{z}_t\right) < A_t K_t$. Hence, in equilibrium it must be the case that $s_t = q\left(p = p_t, \mathbf{z} = \mathbf{z}_t\right) = u_t = A_t K_t$. As a consequence, the optimal capacity-pricing problem described by Eq. (4.2.3) is equivalent to choosing a price p_t which allows the firm to sell the maximum amount of goods that can be produced in each period, that is,

$$p_t \in \mathbb{R}^+ : \; A_t K_t = q\left(p = p_t, \mathbf{z} = \mathbf{z}_t\right). \tag{4.2.5}$$

To this purpose, it is often convenient to define the equilibrium inverse demand schedule as

$$p_t = q_t^{-1}\left(A_t K_t\right), \tag{4.2.6}$$

where $q_t\left(p\right) = q\left(p, \mathbf{z} = \mathbf{z}_t\right)$.

4.2.2 Optimal Investment and Financing Decisions

Shareholders maximize the cum-dividend equity value in each period. As current dividends are strictly increasing in operating cash flows, it is optimal for shareholders to choose the amount of produced good and its selling price in order to maximize y_t, consistently with the analysis presented in the previous section. In particular, this requires the firm to operate at its maximum capacity and set a price at which all goods produced are sold, that is, $A_t K_t = q\left(p = p_t, \mathbf{z} = \mathbf{z}_t\right)$. Consequently, shareholders' optimal investment and financing decisions are the solution of the following intertemporal optimization problem,

$$\begin{aligned}
\hat{V}_t^E &= \max_{F_{t+1} \geq 0, K_{t+1} \geq 0} \left\{ D_t + \mathbb{E}_t\left(\frac{M_{t+1}}{M_t}\hat{V}_{t+1}^E\right)\right\} \\
& \qquad s.t \\
D_t &= \left[q_t^{-1}\left(A_t K_t\right) A_t K_t - c_t F_t\right]\left(1-\tau\right) + \tau\kappa K_t - \kappa K_{t+1} + \tau\delta K_t - I_t - F_t + F_{t+1} \\
I_t &= K_{t+1} - K_t\left(1-\delta\right), \\
F_{t+1} &\leq \frac{\left(1-\alpha\right)}{\left(1+c_{t+1}\right)} K_{t+1},
\end{aligned} \tag{4.2.7}$$

We can use the same argument followed in Sect. 3.2.2 to show that, if $\tau c_{t+1} \geq \varphi_{t+1}$, then $F_{t+1} = \frac{(1-\alpha)}{(1+c_{t+1})} K_{t+1}$ without loss of generality,[6] while $F_{t+1} = 0$ holds in the opposite case. Thus, we can formulate the Problem (4.2.7) in a more convenient way as follows,

$$\hat{V}_t^E (A_t, F_t, K_t, \mathbf{z}_t) = \max_{K_{t+1}} \Big\{ \Big[q_t^{-1} (A_t K_t) A_t K_t - \delta K_t - c_t F_t \Big] (1 - \tau) + \tau \kappa K_t + K_t$$
$$- (1 + \kappa) K_{t+1} + \lambda_{t+1} K_{t+1} - F_t + \mathbb{E}_t \left[\frac{M_{t+1}}{M_t} \hat{V}_t^E (A_{t+1}, F_{t+1} = \lambda_{t+1} K_{t+1}, K_{t+1}, \mathbf{z}_t) \right] \Big\} \tag{4.2.8}$$

where $\lambda_{t+1} := \gamma_{t+1} \mathbb{I}\left(\tau c_{t,t+1} \geq \varphi_{t,t+1}\right)$, $\gamma_{t+1} := \frac{(1-\alpha)(1-\delta)}{1+c_{t+1}}$ and $F_{t+1} = \lambda_{t+1} K_{t+1}$. Assuming that $\hat{V}_t^E$ is differentiable, the first order conditions necessary to characterize the optimal investment policy are:

$$\begin{cases} 1 + \kappa = \mathbb{E}_t \left[\dfrac{M_{t+1}}{M_t} \left(\gamma_t \dfrac{\partial \widetilde{V}_{t+1}^E}{\partial F_{t+1}} \mathbb{I} \left(\tau c_{t+1} \geq \varphi_{t+1} \right) + \dfrac{\partial \widetilde{V}_{t+1}^E}{\partial K_{t+1}} \right) \right] & \text{First Order Condition,} \\ \dfrac{\partial \widetilde{V}_{t+1}^E}{\partial F_{t+1}} = -1 - r_{t+1} - \varphi_{t+1} + \tau c_{t+1} & \text{Envelope Condition } F_{t+1}, \\ \dfrac{\partial V_{t+1}^E}{\partial K_{t+1}} = \left(1 - \dfrac{1}{\eta_{t+1}} \right) p_{t+1} A_{t+1} (1 - \tau) + \tau \kappa + \tau \delta + (1 - \delta) & \text{Envelope Condition } K_{t+1}. \end{cases} \tag{4.2.9}$$

Putting together, the previous conditions require the optimal investment strategy for the firm to satisfy the following Euler equation,

$$1 = \mathbb{E}_t \left\{ \frac{M_{t+1}}{M_t} \left[\underbrace{ \begin{bmatrix} \underbrace{\left(p_{t+1} A_{t+1} \left(1 - \eta_{t+1}^{-1} \right) - \delta \right) (1 - \tau) + 1 - \delta + \kappa \tau}_{\text{Marginal Cash Return on Capital Stock}} \\ - \underbrace{\kappa \left(1 + r_{t+1} \right)}_{\text{Cost of Op. Cycle}} + \underbrace{\lambda_{t+1} \left(\tau c_{t+1} - \varphi_{t+1} \right)}_{\text{Debt's funding advantage}} \end{bmatrix} }_{\text{Investment Returns}} \right] \right\}, \tag{4.2.10}$$

as well as the transversality condition $\lim_{T \to \infty} \mathbb{E} \left\{ \frac{M_T}{M_t} \frac{\partial \hat{V}_T^E}{\partial K_T} K_T \right\} = 0$ (see Miao 2020, Chapter 7). On the LHS of Eq. (4.2.10) we have the price paid for a unit of capital goods, while on the RHS its expected marginal benefit. In equilibrium,

[6] When the previous inequality holds as equality, shareholders are indifferent to any $F_{t+1} \in \left[0, \frac{(1-\alpha)}{(1+c_{t+1})} K_{t+1}\right]$. Without loss of generality we can assume $F_{t+1} = \frac{(1-\alpha)}{(1+c_{t+1})} K_{t+1}$, as the presence of debt will be not affect investment decisions in this case.

shareholders invest until the NPV of adding an infinitesimal amount of capital dI_t is null, which is again the positive NPV rule in capital budgeting. Nevertheless, what has changed from Sect. 3.2.2, is that investment returns depend on the demand elasticity, rather than the size of adjustment costs. Therefore, once an additional amount of capital dI_t is purchased in t, the price of goods sold in $t+1$ will be "depressed" by an amount equal to $-\frac{1}{\eta_t}\frac{p_t}{q_t}dI_t$, otherwise the additional quantity produced $A_{t+1}dI_t$ would remain unsold. Hence, in equilibrium firms with higher market power, thanks to a more rigid demand schedule, will face a higher marginal cost to expand their output capacity. However, a lower elasticity of demand results also in higher expected profitability.

Furthermore, note that Eq. (4.2.10) can be solved for the optimal fixed capital stock without knowing $K_{t\pm s}$, $s > 1$. Hence, it is optimal for shareholders to solve a sequence of *static* problems. Put differently, the model predicts an *myopic* equilibrium behavior for the firm. In intertemporal decision problems, a behavioral rule is said to be myopic if it is based on the optimization of short-term objectives. Since dynamic programs are in general hard to solve, this type of behavior is actually more consistent with the way in which firms are managed in reality, which certainly favors the model.

4.2.3 Constant Price Elasticity of Demand and the Value of the Firm

In corporate finance applications, it is convenient to consider a demand function characterized by a constant price elasticity, and a single state variable. Thus, in the rest of the chapter we will adopt the following working hypothesis,

$$q_t(p) = Y_t p^{-\eta}, \ \eta > 1, \tag{4.2.11}$$

where Y_t denotes the industry aggregate demand, which each firm in the same industry is supposed to take as given.[7] As a result, optimal price setting requires that,

$$p_t = \left(\frac{A_t K_t}{Y_t}\right)^{-\frac{1}{\eta}}, \tag{4.2.12}$$

[7]This is a very important aspect from a game-theoretic perspective. If we let i be a generic firm, by aggregate consistency, $\sum_i A_{i,t}K_{i,t} = Y_t$ in general equilibrium.

and, consequently, Eq. (4.2.10) becomes equivalent to,

$$\frac{1}{\eta}\mathbb{E}_t\left\{\frac{M_{t+1}}{M_t}p_{t+1}A_{t+1}K_{t+1}\right\} =$$
$$\frac{1}{\eta-1}\frac{1}{1-\tau}\left\{\kappa+\frac{r_{t+1}+\delta-\left[\tau\left(\kappa+\delta\right)+\lambda_{t+1}\left(\varphi_{t+1}-\tau c_{t+1}\right)\right]}{1+r_{t+1}}\right\}K_{t+1}. \tag{4.2.13}$$

The RHS of the equation is equal to the NPV of additional profits compared to the case of perfect competition (*monopoly rents*), which is consequential to the firm's market power. To see this point, notice that, in the limiting case of perfect competition, Eq. (4.2.13) is equivalent to,

$$\lim_{\eta\to\infty}\mathbb{E}_t\left\{\frac{M_{t+1}}{M_t}p_{t+1}A_{t+1}K_{t+1}\right\}$$
$$=\frac{1}{1-\tau}\left\{\kappa+\frac{r_{t+1}+\delta-\left[\tau\left(\kappa+\delta\right)+\lambda_{t+1}\left(\varphi_{t+1}-\tau c_{t+1}\right)\right]}{1+r_{t+1}}\right\}K_{t+1}. \tag{4.2.14}$$

This is a key point in this chapter, as it contains all the economic intuitions required to understand the relationship between stock returns and profitability.

By following the same logic we used in Sect. 3.3.2, the Euler equation with respect to unlevered free cash flows (x_t) is,

$$\mathbb{E}_t\left\{M_{t,t+1}\left[x_{t+1}+\lambda_{t+1}\left(\tau c_{t+1}-\varphi_{t+1}\right)F_{t+1}\right]\right\} =$$
$$K_{t+1}\left(1+\kappa\right)-\mathbb{E}_t\left[M_{t+1}K_{t+2}\left(1+\kappa\right)\right]+\frac{1}{\eta}\mathbb{E}_t\left[M_{t+1}p_{t+1}A_{t+1}K_{t+1}\left(1-\tau\right)\right]. \tag{4.2.15}$$

From the application of Eq. (2.4.13), the value of the firm is equal to,

$$V_t=\mathbb{E}_t\sum_{s=1}^{\infty}\frac{M_{t+s}}{M_t}\left[x_{t+s}+\lambda_{t+s}\left(\tau c_{t+s}-\varphi_{t+s}\right)F_{t+s}\right], \tag{4.2.16}$$

and, recursively substituting Eq. (4.2.15) into Eq. (4.2.16), we eventually obtain,

$$V_t=\underbrace{K_{t+1}\left(1+\kappa\right)}_{\text{Invested Capital}}+\underbrace{\frac{1-\tau}{\eta}\mathbb{E}_t\sum_{s=1}^{\infty}\frac{M_{t+s}}{M_t}p_{t+s}A_{t+s}K_{t+s}}_{\text{NPV Monopoly Rents}}. \tag{4.2.17}$$

The RHS of Eq. (4.2.17) carries a simple and intuitive economic interpretation. By definition, the sum of the accounting book-value of fixed assets (K_{t+1}) and working capital (κK_{t+1}) is the firm's total invested capital (IC_{t+1}), $IC_{t+1} = K_{t+1} + \kappa K_{t+1}$. If there was perfect product market competition (i.e. $\eta \rightarrow \infty$), the value of the firm would be equal to its total after-tax invested capital, that is, $V_t = K_{t+1}(1+\kappa)$, which is consistent with what we discussed in Sect. 4.1. Imperfect competition attributes market power to the firm, and consequently, the achieved extra-profitability improves its total market value by the NPV of monopoly rents $\left(\frac{1-\tau}{\eta}\mathbb{E}_t \sum_{s=1}^{\infty} M_{t,t+s} p_{t+s} A_{t+s} K_{t+s}\right)$. Namely, the lower the η, the higher the firm's market power and consequently the NPV of monopoly rents (NPVMR).

4.3 Imperfect Competition and the Cross-Section of Stock Returns

4.3.1 Tobin's Q, Expected Stock Returns and Residual Income

Tobin's Q (Q_t) is defined more generally as,

$$Q_t := \frac{V_t}{IC_{t+1}} \tag{4.3.1}$$

where $IC_{t+1} = (1+\kappa) K_{t+1}$ is the firm invested capital. Notice that Tobin's Q is always greater than one with imperfect competition. However, the source of "extra-value" is the firm's market power, which is far more reasonable than investment adjustment costs. Furthermore, since there are decreasing returns to scale in the firm's revenues and operating cash flows, average profitability always exceeds marginal profitability. This observation suggests the following analysis on the relationship between profitability and security returns, which is based on Balvers et al. (2017).

Let $\Theta_t := V_t - K_{t+1} = \frac{1-\tau}{\eta}\mathbb{E}_t \sum_{s=1}^{\infty} M_{t,t+s} p_{t+s} A_{t+s} K_{t+s}$ be the NPV of monopoly rents (NPVMR), and $\rho_{t+1} := \frac{\Theta_{t+1}}{\Theta_t} - 1$ be the related growth rate. Following the same routine developed in Sect. 3.3, we can use the firm's budget constraint to write the following equation,

$$\begin{aligned} &\frac{V_t^E}{V_t}\left(1 + r_{t+1}^E\right) + \frac{F_{t+1}}{V_t}\left[1 + c_{t+1}(1-\tau)\right] \\ &= \frac{(p_{t+1}A_{t+1} - \kappa - \delta)(1-\tau) K_{t+1} + (1+\kappa) K_{t+1} + \Theta_{t+1}}{V_t}. \end{aligned} \tag{4.3.2}$$

With the following algebraic steps,

$$\frac{(p_{t+1}A_{t+1}-\kappa-\delta)(1-\tau)K_{t+1}+(1+\kappa)K_{t+1}+\Theta_{t+1}}{V_t}=$$

$$\frac{(p_{t+1}A_{t+1}-\kappa-\delta)(1-\tau)K_{t+1}+V_t+\Theta_{t+1}-\Theta_t}{V_t}=$$

$$1+\frac{(p_{t+1}A_{t+1}-\kappa-\delta)(1-\tau)K_{t+1}}{V_t}+\frac{\Theta_t\rho_{t+1}}{V_t},$$

the RHS of Eq. (4.3.2) can be simplified as $1+\frac{\frac{1}{1+\kappa}(p_{t+1}A_{t+1}-\kappa-\delta)(1-\tau)}{Q_t}+\frac{[V_t-K_{t+1}(1+\kappa)]\rho_{t+1}}{V_t}$, eventually obtaining the following equilibrium relationship,

$$\frac{V_t^E}{V_t}\left(1+r_{t+1}^E\right)+\frac{F_{t+1}}{V_t}\left[1+c_{t+1}(1-\tau)\right]=1+\frac{\Pi_{t+1}(1-\tau)}{Q_t}+\left(1-\frac{1}{Q_t}\right)\rho_{t+1}, \tag{4.3.3}$$

where $\Pi_{t+1}:=\frac{p_{t+1}A_{t+1}-\kappa-\delta}{1+\kappa}$ is the before-tax *return on invested capital* (RoIC). Notice the presence of the dilution factor $\frac{1}{1+\kappa}$, which is due to the presence of working capital. Taking expectations on both sides of Eq. (4.3.3), we conclude that the firm's WACC, which is equal to $\frac{V_t^E}{V_t}\mathbb{E}_t\left(r_{t+1}^E\right)+\frac{F_{t+1}}{V_t}c_{t+1}$ (see Sect. 3.1.3), is a weighted average of the firm's expected profitability ($\Pi_{t+1}(1-\tau)$) and growth rate of NPVMR, that is,

$$wacc_{t,t+1}=\frac{1}{Q_t}\left[\mathbb{E}_t(\Pi_{t+1})(1-\tau)\right]+\left(1-\frac{1}{Q_t}\right)\mathbb{E}_t(\rho_{t+1}). \tag{4.3.4}$$

To better express $\mathbb{E}_t\left(r_{t+1}^E\right)$, let BV_{t+1} be the book-value of equity at date t, $BV_{t+1}:=IC_{t+1}-F_{t+1}$. Observing that the firm's net income (NI_{t+1}) is equal to $[\Pi_{t+1}IC_{t+1}-c_{t+1}F_{t+1}](1-\tau)$, Eq. (4.3.4) can be rearranged in order to have $\mathbb{E}_t\left(r_{t+1}^E\right)$ on the LHS,

$$\frac{V_t^E}{V_t}\mathbb{E}_t\left(r_{t,t+1}^E\right)+\frac{F_{t+1}}{V_t}c_{t,t+1}(1-\tau)=\frac{1}{Q_t}\left[\mathbb{E}_t(\Pi_{t+1})(1-\tau)\right]+\left(1-\frac{1}{Q_t}\right)\mathbb{E}_t(\rho_{t+1}),$$

$$\mathbb{E}_t\left(r_{t,t+1}^E\right)+\frac{F_{t+1}}{V_t^E}c_{t,t+1}(1-\tau)=\frac{IC_{t+1}}{V_{t+1}^E}\left[\mathbb{E}_t(\Pi_{t+1})(1-\tau)\right]+\left(\frac{V_t-IC_{t+1}}{V_t^E}\right)\mathbb{E}_t(\rho_{t+1}),$$

$$\mathbb{E}_t\left(r_{t,t+1}^E\right)=\frac{\mathbb{E}_t(NI_{t+1})}{V_{t+1}^E}+\left(\frac{V_t^E+F_{t+1}-(F_{t+1}+BV_{t+1})}{V_t^E}\right)\mathbb{E}_t(\rho_{t+1})$$

eventually obtaining,

$$\mathbb{E}_t\left(r_{t+1}^E\right) = \frac{BV_{t+1}}{V_t^E}\frac{\mathbb{E}_t\left[\Pi_{t+1}(1-\tau) - c_{t+1}F_{t+1}\right]}{BV_{t+1}} + \left(1 - \frac{BV_{t+1}}{V_t^E}\right)\mathbb{E}_t\left(\rho_{t+1}\right). \tag{4.3.5}$$

In equilibrium, expected stock returns are equal to the weighted average of the expected *return on equity* (RoE), $\frac{\mathbb{E}_t[\Pi_{t+1}(1-\tau)-c_{t+1}F_{t+1}]}{BV_{t+1}}$, and expected growth in NPVMR, with weights equal to the book-to-price ratio, $\frac{BV_{t+1}}{V_t^E}$, and $1 - \frac{BV_{t+1}}{V_t^E}$ respectively. In other words, with imperfect competition, stock returns are a weighted average of expected profitability and growth, with weights depending on the book-to-price ratio (BB). In this regard, Novy-Marx (2013) finds that RoE and BP have separate explanatory power in the cross-section of stock returns, while Hou et al. (2020) shows the predictive power of the sales growth rate, which is a good proxy for ρ_{t+1}.

Holding expected profitability, leverage and $\mathbb{E}_t\left(\rho_{t+1}\right)$ all constant, a lower Tobin's Q implies higher expected stock returns. The market however is *efficient*, in that a lower *multiple* must be consistent with higher cash flows risk, as it appears evident from a simple probabilistic manipulation of the expression for NPVMR,

$$\Theta_t = \frac{1-\tau}{\eta}\mathbb{E}_t\sum_{s=1}^{\infty} M_{t,t+s}p_{t+s}A_{t+s}K_{t+s} =$$

$$\frac{1-\tau}{\eta}\mathbb{E}_t\sum_{s=1}^{\infty}\left\{\mathbb{E}_t\left(\frac{M_{t+s}}{M_t}\right)\mathbb{E}_t\left(p_{t+s}A_{t+s}K_{t+s}\right) + \mathbb{COV}_t\left(\frac{M_{t+s}}{M_t}, p_{t+s}A_{t+s}K_{t+s}\right)\right\}. \tag{4.3.6}$$

Hence, higher expected stock returns come as a consequence of higher systematic risk of the firm's extra-profits, as in the classic conditional CAPM.[8] Put differently, if the expected RoE and $\mathbb{E}_t\left(\rho_{t+1}\right)$ are the same across different firms, Tobin's Q is a sufficient statistic for stock returns, as in Berk et al. (1999).[9] Similarly, holding Tobin's Q and $\mathbb{E}_t\left(\rho_{t+1}\right)$ constant, higher expected profitability implies higher expected returns, as in the Investment CAPM of Sect. 3.3.

Finally, the expression for the value of the firm provides a micro-foundation for residual income valuation models, which suggest to value the firm as the sum of its accounting book-value plus the NPV of the operating income generated in excess of $wacc_{t,t+1}IC_{t+1}$[10] (Peasnell 1982; Edwards & Bell 1995; Feltham & Ohlson 1995;

[8] See Cochrane (2009).

[9] More precisely, in Berk et al. (1999), holding constant the "weight" and the "size" of growth options, the book-to-price ratio is a sufficient statistic for expected stocks' returns.

[10] This quantity corresponds to the dollar-valued cost of capital of the firm.

Ohlson 1995). In fact, writing Eq. (4.3.4) with respect Q_t on the LHS, we obtain,

$$Q_t = \frac{\mathbb{E}_t \left\{ \Pi_{t+1} \left[(1-\tau) - \frac{\rho_{t+1}}{\Pi_{t+1}} \right] \right\}}{wacc_{t,t+1} - \mathbb{E}_t(\rho_{t+1})}, \quad (4.3.7)$$

that is,

$$V_t = IC_{t+1} + \frac{\left\{ \mathbb{E}_t \left[\Pi_{t+1}(1-\tau) \right] - wacc_{t,t+1} \right\} IC_{t+1}}{wacc_{t,t+1} - \mathbb{E}_t(\rho_{t+1})}. \quad (4.3.8)$$

4.3.2 Empirical Considerations

A more convenient way to express Eq. (4.3.5) is perhaps the following,

$$\mathbb{E}_t\left(r_{t+1}^E\right) = \frac{\mathbb{E}_t\left[\Pi_{t+1}(1-\tau) - c_{t+1}F_{t+1}\right]}{V_{t+1}^E} + \left(1 - \frac{BV_{t+1}}{V_t^E}\right)\mathbb{E}_t(\rho_{t+1}), \quad (4.3.9)$$

in which we recognize the firm's expected earnings yield,[11] $\frac{\mathbb{E}_t\left[\Pi_{t+1}(1-\tau) - c_{t+1}F_{t+1}\right]}{V_{t+1}^E}$. It is not infrequent to see practitioners estimating the expected return of a stock, or an index, by considering its expected earning yield. As suggested by Eq. (4.3.9), this approach is likely to fail most of the times, unless $\mathbb{E}_t(\rho_{t+1}) = 0$ or $\eta \to \infty$. In other words, expected earnings yields can be used as a proxy for expected stock returns only when competition is high enough that monopoly rents are actually irrelevant. Notably, a similar situation is reflected in a Tobin's Q close to one, so we may say that for stocks with $Q_t \approx 1$, the expected earnings yield is indeed a good proxy for expected returns.

In general, Eq. (4.3.9) can be tested empirically and also giving a way to measure conditional expected stock returns. Let us assume to have at our disposal a *panel dataset* with yearly observations of market, fundamentals and consensus estimates[12] data for a given universe of listed companies.

Our first task is to implement Eq. (4.3.9) for each stock in the cross-section given the available public informational set. Since we observe the equity market value, expected earnings can be proxied by considering, at each time t, the consensus estimate for the next 12 months (NTM) earnings.[13] As a result, we obtain the

---

[11] The expected earnings yield is the inverse of the Price-to-Earnings ratio, computed with respect to expected net income.

[12] By consensus estimates we mean the median of sell-side forecasts for future fundamentals.

[13] Here, by earnings we intend the firm's net income.

forward earnings yield, we denotes by $EY_{i,t}^{NTM}$. Likewise, $\frac{BV_{t+1}}{V_{t+1}^E}$ can be proxied by considering the forward (NTM) or last reported book-to-price ratio. The choice depends essentially on the relationship between imminent capital expenditures and NTM earnings. If the former contributes to the latter, we should always use the forward book-to-price ratio, which we denotes with $BP_{i,t}^{NTM}$. This is actually the most frequent case, and we use $BP_{i,t}^{NTM}$ as an additional empirical hypothesis.

We can proxy $\mathbb{E}_t(\rho_{t+1})$ by the consensus industry growth rate for the second-twelve months (STM), $g_t^{STM} := \frac{\mathbb{E}_t(Y_{t+2})-\mathbb{E}_t(Y_{t+1})}{\mathbb{E}_t(Y_{t+1})}$. To motivate this approach, notice that, as $p_{t+1}A_{t+1}K_{t+1} \propto Y_{t+1}$, we can reasonably introduce the stochastic process $\Gamma_t = \frac{\Theta_t}{\mathbb{E}_t(Y_{t+1})}$. Consequently, for values of ρ_{t+1} that are not too large, we can approximate $\mathbb{E}_t(\rho_{t+1})$ as follows,

$$\mathbb{E}_t(\rho_{t+1}) \approx \frac{\mathbb{E}_t(Y_{t+2}) - \mathbb{E}_t(Y_{t+1})}{\mathbb{E}_t(Y_{t+1})} + \frac{\mathbb{E}_t(\Gamma_{t+1}) - \mathbb{E}_t(\Gamma_t)}{\mathbb{E}_t(\Gamma_t)} = g_t^{STM} + \varepsilon_t. \tag{4.3.10}$$

where $\varepsilon_t := \frac{\mathbb{E}_t(\Gamma_{t+1})-\mathbb{E}_t(\Gamma_t)}{\mathbb{E}_t(\Gamma_t)}$ can be considered as a disturbance term. Within the sample, for each stock i, the conditional expected returns are expressed as,

$$\mathbb{E}_t\left(r_{i,t+1}^E\right) = EY_{i,t}^{NTM} + \left(1 - BP_{i,t}^{NTM}\right) g_{i,t}^{STM} + \varepsilon_{i,t}. \tag{4.3.11}$$

At this point, we need to introduce specific statistical assumptions on the distribution of the disturbance term $\varepsilon_{i,t}$. To this purpose, we assume that $\mathbb{E}_t\left(\varepsilon_{i,t}\right) = 0$. This condition could be motivated observing that $\varepsilon_{i,t}$ is the expected change of the multiple $\frac{\Theta_{i,t}}{\mathbb{E}_t(Y_{i,t+1})}$, and change in stock market multiples are not so easy to predict. Notice that by introducing these additional hypothesis, our model for expected stock returns becomes,

$$\begin{cases} \mathbb{E}_t\left(r_{i,t+1}^E\right) = EY_{i,t}^{NTM} + \left(1 - BP_{i,t}^{NTM}\right) g_{i,t}^{STM} + \varepsilon_{i,t} \\ \mathbb{E}_t\left(\varepsilon_{i,t}\right) = 0 \end{cases}, \tag{4.3.12}$$

which is far more restrictive than the original version in Eq. (4.3.9). For this reason, Eq. (4.3.12) may be not suitable to fit the data not because Eq. (4.3.9) is not valid but, rather, because the way in which we model the NPVMR growth is not valid.

If the model in Eq. (4.3.12) is correct, which is our null hypothesis (H_0), the pricing error,

$$\epsilon_{i,t} = r_{i,t}^E - \left[EY_{i,t}^{NTM} + \left(1 - BP_{i,t}^{NTM}\right) g_{i,t}^{STM}\right] - \varepsilon_{i,t} \tag{4.3.13}$$

should be unpredictable using fundamental and market-based variables. Namely, if H_0 is true, for every firm characteristic s, and including the constant $h_{i,t}^{(s)} = 1$, the following moment condition must be verified,

$$\mathbb{E}\left\{\left[r_i^E - EY_i^{NTM} - \left(1 - BP_i^{NTM}\right) g_i^{STM}\right] h_i^{(s)}\right\} = 0. \tag{4.3.14}$$

If T is the number of observations, N the number of stocks, and n the number of characteristics, except the constant $\left(h_{i,t}^{(s=1)} = 1\right)$, we have a total of $N \times (n+1)$ different moment conditions. The LHS of each of these conditions can be estimated as,

$$\Psi_{i,s}(T) = \sum_{t=1}^{T} \left[r_{i,t}^E - EY_{i,t}^{NTM} - \left(1 - BP_{i,t}^{NTM}\right) g_{i,t}^{STM}\right] h_{i,t}^{(s)}. \tag{4.3.15}$$

If the model is correctly specified, the $N \times (K+1)$ estimates for $\Psi_{i,s}(T)$ should not be jointly different from zero. More formally, by letting $\mathbf{h}_{i,t} := \left(h_{i,t}^{(s)}\right)_{s=1}^{n+1}$, under appropriate regularity conditions for the distribution of $X = \left[\left(\mathbf{h}_{i,t}\right)_{i=1}^{N}\right]_{t=1}^{T}$, and given a consistent estimator $\hat{S}$ for the variance of $\boldsymbol{\Psi} = \left(\Psi_{i,s}(T)\right)$, the statistic,

$$W := T \cdot \left(\boldsymbol{\Psi}^{\top} \hat{S}^{-1} \boldsymbol{\Psi}\right) \rightarrow_{p|H_0} \chi^2_{N \times (n+1)}, \tag{4.3.16}$$

is asymptotically distributed as a Chi-squared with $N \times (K+1)$ degrees of freedoms under the null hypothesis $H_0 : \mathbb{E}\left\{\left[r_i^E - EY_i^{NTM} - \left(1 - BP_i^{NTM}\right) g_i^{STM}\right] x_i^{(s)}\right\} = 0,\ \forall (s, i)$.

Hence, we can test for the validity of the model comparing the estimate obtained for the statistic W with an appropriate quantile of its asymptotic distribution. The procedure is the well-known Wald test and relies on the central limit theorem, we assume to be valid for X. The Wald test can be seen as a more primitive version of the *overindentifying restriction test* which is used in conjunction with the Generalized Methods of Moments (GMM) in structural econometrics (cf. Sect. 7.3.3). The difference with the case of GMM is that W is independent on the structural parameters of the model. When instead W depends on a set $\boldsymbol{\alpha}$ of structural parameters, the GMM estimates the parameters of the model in order to shrink W as much as possible, consistently with the null hypothesis. As a result, we obtain a statistic (J) which is the minimum value of $W(\boldsymbol{\alpha})$ for the sample. While J remains asymptotically distributed as a Chi-squared under appropriate regularity conditions, the degrees of freedom are reduced by the number of the estimated parameters. In case the degrees of freedom are equal to zero, $J = 0$ and there is nothing to test. For this reason, models in which the number of (independent) moment conditions are equal to the number of structural parameters to be estimated are said *just identified*. Only models in which we have a number of moment conditions greater than the number of parameters to be estimated are structurally testable. Models of this type are said *overindentified*. An example is the basic version of the Investment CAPM, where $\boldsymbol{\theta} = \{\theta^-, \theta^+\}$ must be estimated from at least three moments conditions. When the Wald test can be directly applied, the model being tested is always overidentified, in that $J = W$ regardless the structural parameters of the model. This is a very nice property of the model proposed in this section, which requires no investment adjustment costs. In this regard, if H_0 is not rejected, we can also conclude that investment adjustment costs may be not so important to explain the cross-section of stock returns.

In this context, a major drawback of structural methods is that, unless the case of small investible universe, it is usually an hard task obtaining a good estimate for $\hat{S}$ that can be inverted with sufficient precisions. Besides, some firms may exist only at certain dates, as in the case of IPOs, mergers and acquisitions or delistings, thereby resulting in an unbalanced panel data. To handle this problem, we can focus on portfolios of stocks operating in the same reference industry, or in the same industry and geographic area if we wish, rather than individual firms. By following a uniform weighting scheme within each portfolio, the procedure can then be easily implemented. Once finding no statistical evidence to reject H_0, we can next measure expected returns from the systematic component of Eq. (4.3.11), that is,

$$\mathbb{E}\left(r_{i,t+1}^E | X_{i,t}\right) = EY_{i,t}^{NTM} + \left(1 - BP_{i,t}^{NTM}\right) g_{i,t}^{STM}, \tag{4.3.17}$$

where $X_{i,t}$ is the set of all the public informational set. Notice that, within the model economy, $\mathbb{E}\left(r_{i,t+1}^E | X_{i,t}\right) \neq \mathbb{E}_t\left(r_{i,t+1}^E\right)$, as the agents have perfect knowledge of $\mathbb{E}_t\left(\rho_{t+1}\right)$. However, without additional hypothesis we cannot say anything about ε_t, and therefore Eq. (4.3.16) is the best measure of conditional expected returns we can get in practice. In the next section we see how we can improve the analysis by introducing some mild hypothesis for the exogenous stochastic process $\{A_t, M_t, Y_t\}_{t \geq 0}$. The problem with the model actually comes with situations in which, when using accounting data, we empirically observe $BP_{i,t}^{NTM} > 1$. Often it is possible to save the model also in this case, assuming that the consensus estimate for the equity book-value is misrepresented for some reason, and "prudentially" setting $BP_{i,t}^{NTM} = 1$. This approach is a good approximation for firms operating in highly competitive industries that recently experienced a sharp deterioration in their assets quality, which is not an infrequent case when $BP_{i,t}^{NTM} > 1$.[14]

[14]Needless to say, it must be the case that such a deterioration is is not yet included in $BP_{i,t}^{NTM}$, otherwise we would incur in a double counting.

4.4 Equilibrium Models and Security Analysis

4.4.1 A Simple Quantitative Model

The framework we introduced so far is a useful tool for *security analysis*, and specifically for estimating the firm's key profitability indicators (KPIs) then obtaining a *target equity value*. As we stressed in Sect. 1.3, equilibria are properties for model economies, not for the real world. Therefore, models should be first tested, through structural estimation methods, in order to very whether they can be assumed as approximately valid to describe the real world of corporate finance. If this is the case, then the model can be used to forecast the firm's key profitability indicators (KPIs) and eventually understand whether stock mispricings are statistically significant. In order to improve the empirical analysis of Sect. 4.3.2, we introduce the following hypotheses regarding the exogenous stochastic processes involved in the general version of the model:

(1) $A_t = A$;
(2) $\varepsilon_t \sim_{i.i.d} \mathcal{N}\left(0, \sigma_\varepsilon^2\right)$;
(3) $\varphi_t = \varphi \geq 0$;
(4) $M_{t,t+1} = \frac{1}{1+r} e^{\mu_t - \frac{1}{2}\sigma_\mu^2}$, $\mu_t \sim_{i.i.d.} \mathcal{N}\left(0, \sigma_\mu^2\right)$;
(5) $Y_t = Y_{t-1} e^{\ln G_{t-1} + \varepsilon_t - \frac{1}{2}\sigma_\varepsilon^2}$, $\varepsilon_t \sim_{i.i.d.} \mathcal{N}\left(0, \sigma_\varepsilon^2\right)$;
(6) G_t is a strictly positive exogenous stochastic process, independent from any other random variable in the model;
(7) the joint distribution of (ε_t, μ_t) is strongly stationary.

Some comments before proceeding to the analysis are useful. First, the stochastic process $g_t := G_t - 1$ is the conditional expected growth in industry demand (Y_t), $g_t = \mathbb{E}_t\left(\frac{Y_{t+1}}{Y_t}\right) - 1$. Second, the cost of debt is constant and equal to $c = r + \varphi$, where $r > 0$ is the risk-free rate, and, consequently, if $\tau c \geq \varphi$, the book-leverage is constant and equal to,

$$\frac{F_{t+1}}{K_{t+1}} = \frac{(1-\alpha)(1-\delta)}{1+c}. \tag{4.4.1}$$

Third, with reference to the notation introduced in the previous section, we have $\lambda_{t+1} = \lambda = \frac{(1-\alpha)(1-\delta)}{1+c}\mathbb{I}(\tau c \geq \varphi)$ and $F_{t+1} = \lambda K_{t+1} \geq 0$. As a result, the equilibrium capital stock (K_{t+1}) is the solution of the following equation,

$$(1+\kappa) = \mathbb{E}_t\left\{\frac{e^{\mu_{t+1}-\frac{1}{2}\sigma_\mu^2}}{1+r}\left[\begin{array}{c}\frac{\eta-1}{\eta}\left(\frac{AK_{t+1}}{Y_{t+1}}\right)^{-\frac{1}{\eta}}(1-\tau) - \tau\kappa \\ +\lambda(\tau c - \varphi) + 1 - \delta(1-\tau)\end{array}\right]\right\}. \tag{4.4.2}$$

4.4.2 Expected Fundamentals

The first task in security analysis is obtaining consistent forecasts for the firm's KPIs. To do so, we may start from the capital stock, and, rearranging Eq. (4.4.2) in order to have K_{t+1} on the LHS, we obtain the following expression,

$$K_{t+1}=\left\{\frac{\mathbb{E}_t\left[e^{\mu_{t+1}-\frac{1}{2}\sigma_\mu^2}e^{\frac{1}{\eta}\left(\varepsilon_{t+1}-\frac{1}{2}\sigma_\varepsilon^2\right)}\right]}{\frac{\eta}{\eta-1}\frac{A^{\frac{1}{\eta}}}{1-\tau}\left\{(1+r)(1+\kappa)-1+\delta(1-\tau)-\lambda(\tau c-\varphi)\right\}}\right\}^{\eta}G_tY_t. \tag{4.4.3}$$

Notice that the effect of financial leverage, which is consistent with the over-investment problem described in Sect. 3.4 of the previous chapter. Since the shocks (ε_t,μ_t) are strongly stationary, we can introduce the constant $C_0 := \mathbb{E}_t\left[e^{\mu_{t+1}-\frac{1}{2}\sigma_\mu^2}e^{\frac{1}{\eta}\left(\varepsilon_{t+1}-\frac{1}{2}\sigma_\varepsilon^2\right)}\right]=\mathbb{E}\left[e^{\mu_t-\frac{1}{2}\sigma_\mu^2}e^{\frac{1}{\eta}\left(\varepsilon_t-\frac{1}{2}\sigma_\varepsilon^2\right)}\right]$, which can be computed thanks to the multivariate lognormal random distribution properties. We can also define another constant (C_1),

$$C_1:=\left[\frac{C_0}{\frac{\eta}{\eta-1}\frac{A^{\frac{1}{\eta}}}{1-\tau}\left\{(1+r)(1+\kappa)-1+\delta(1-\tau)-\lambda(\tau c-\varphi)\right\}}\right]^{\eta}, \tag{4.4.4}$$

which allows us to conclude that K_{t+1} is always proportional to the expected industry demand,

$$K_{t+1}=C_1\underbrace{G_tY_t}_{\mathbb{E}_t(Y_{t+1})}. \tag{4.4.5}$$

One important effect is that, the expected ratio between revenues and invested capital (*Sales-to-Capital Employed* ratio) is constant. To prove this claim, recall that sales are equal to $p_{t+1}AK_{t+1}=\left(\frac{AK_{t+1}}{Y_{t+1}}\right)^{-\eta}AK_{t+1}$; therefore,

$$p_{t+1}AK_{t+1}=e^{\frac{1}{\eta}\left(\varepsilon_{t+1}-\frac{1}{2}\sigma_\varepsilon^2\right)}\left(\frac{AC_1G_tY_t}{G_tY_t}\right)^{-\eta}AK_{t+1}, \tag{4.4.6}$$

and the ratio between revenues and invested capital is equal to,

$$\frac{p_{t+1}q_{t+1}}{IC_{t+1}}=\frac{p_{t+1}A}{1+\kappa}=\frac{A^{1-\eta}C_1^{-\eta}}{1+\kappa}e^{\frac{1}{\eta}\left(\varepsilon_{t+1}-\frac{1}{2}\sigma_\varepsilon^2\right)}. \tag{4.4.7}$$

Taking expectations, we obtain,

$$\frac{\mathbb{E}_t\left(p_{t+1}q_{t+1}\right)}{IC_{t+1}} = C_4, \tag{4.4.8}$$

where $C_4 := \frac{A^{1-\eta}C_1^{-\eta}C_3}{1+\kappa}$ and $C_3 := \mathbb{E}\left[e^{\frac{1}{\eta}\left(\varepsilon-\frac{1}{2}\sigma_\varepsilon^2\right)}\right]$ are two positive constants.

Another interesting implication is that the firm operates with a constant expected operating margin, the latter being defined as the ratio between earnings before interests and taxes ($EbIT_t$) and revenues ($p_{t+s}q_{t+s}$). At time $t+1$, total costs are equal to $\kappa K_{t+1} + \delta K_{t+1}$, where κK_{t+1} are representing the intermediate inputs purchased in t (cf. *cost of goods sold* in accounting). As a result, it is immediate to show that,

$$\mathbb{E}_t\left[\frac{EbIT_{t+1}}{p_{t+1}q_{t+1}}\right] = 1 - \frac{\kappa+\delta}{C_4}, \tag{4.4.9}$$

as we claimed before. Let $\Pi_{t+1} := \frac{EbIT_{t+1}}{IC_{t+1}}$ be the before-tax return on invested capital. Then, based on previous results, its expected value is also constant,

$$\mathbb{E}_t\left(RoIC_{t+1}\right) = \frac{\left(1-\frac{\kappa+\delta}{C_4}\right)\mathbb{E}_t\left(p_{t+1}q_{t+1}\right)}{IC_{t+1}} = C_4 - (\kappa+\delta) > 0. \tag{4.4.10}$$

Hence, the model provides an equilibrium foundation on two very common assumptions in practice, namely, a constant expected RoIC and a constant expected operating margin.

Denoting by Π the expected value of the before tax return on invested capital, $\Pi := C_4 - (\kappa+\delta)$, unlevered free cash flows (x_t) are given by,

$$x_{t+1} = \left(\underbrace{p_{t+1}q_{t+1} - \delta K_{t+1} - \kappa K_{t+1}}_{\text{Earnings before Interests and Taxes}}\right)(1-\tau) - \left[\underbrace{(1+\kappa)K_{t+2} - (1+\kappa)K_{t+1}}_{\text{Change in Invested Capital}}\right]. \tag{4.4.11}$$

With the following algebraic steps,

$$\begin{gathered}
\mathbb{E}_t\left(x_{t+1}\right) = \Pi\left(1-\tau\right)IC_{t+1} - (1+\kappa)\,\mathbb{E}_t\left(K_{t+2}-K_{t+1}\right) \\
\Pi\left(1-\tau\right)IC_{t+1} - (1+\kappa)\,C_1\mathbb{E}_t\left(Y_{t+2}-Y_{t+1}\right) = \\
\Pi\left(1-\tau\right)IC_{t+1} - (1+\kappa)\,C_1\mathbb{E}_t\left(Y_{t+1}\left(1+g_{t+1}\right)e^{\mu_{t+2}-\frac{1}{2}\sigma_\mu^2} - Y_{t+1}\right) = \\
\Pi\left(1-\tau\right)IC_{t+1} - (1+\kappa)\,C_1\mathbb{E}_t\left(Y_{t+1}\right)\mathbb{E}_t\left(g_{t+1}\right),
\end{gathered}$$

we eventually obtain the following relation,

$$\mathbb{E}_t\left(x_{t+1}\right)=\mathbb{E}_t\left(EbIT_{t+1}\right)\left[(1-\tau)-\frac{\mathbb{E}_t\left(g_{t+1}\right)}{\Pi}\right]. \tag{4.4.12}$$

where $\mathbb{E}_t\left(EbIT_{t+1}\right)=\Pi\cdot IC_{t+1}$.

Equation (4.4.12) is very popular among practitioners in order to predict unlevered free cash flows. The term $\frac{\mathbb{E}_t(g_{t+1})}{\Pi}$ is commonly referred as plowback ratio, and corresponds to the fraction of EbIT that must be reinvested according to the expected industry growth rate. By applying the law of iterated expectations, we can also generalize this result to any future date,

$$\mathbb{E}_t\left(x_{t+s}\right)=\left[\Pi\cdot\mathbb{E}_t\left(IC_{t+s}\right)\right]\left[(1-\tau)-\frac{\mathbb{E}_t\left(g_{t+s}\right)}{\Pi}\right], \tag{4.4.13}$$

where $\mathbb{E}_t\left(IC_{t+s}\right)$ obtained from Eq. (4.4.5) and the dynamics of G_t,

$$\mathbb{E}_t\left(IC_{t+s}\right)=C_1\mathbb{E}_t\left(Y_{t+s}\right)=C_1Y_t\prod_{j=0}^{s-1}\left[1+\mathbb{E}_t\left(g_{t+j}\right)\right]. \tag{4.4.14}$$

4.4.3 Stock Market Multiples and Valuation Models

It would be tempting to obtain the value of the firm by discounting the expected unlevered free cash flows at a constant weighted average cost of capital. However, this approach may be inconsistent with equilibrium asset pricing. Let $\mathbb{C}_t$ be the conditional covariance operator. Recalling that,

$$V_t=\mathbb{E}_t\sum_{s=1}^{\infty}\frac{M_{t+s}}{M_t}\left[x_{t+s}+\lambda\left(\tau C-\varphi\right)K_{t+s}\right], \tag{4.4.15}$$

we obtain a specific version of the fundamental equilibrium valuation formula,

$$V_t=\sum_{s=1}^{\infty}\frac{OM\left[(1-\tau)-\frac{\mathbb{E}_t(g_{t+s})}{\Pi}+\frac{\lambda(\tau c-\varphi)}{1+\kappa}\right]+\mathbb{C}_t\left(x_{t+s},e^{\sum_{j=1}^{s}\mu_{t+j}-\frac{1}{2}\sigma_\mu^2}\right)}{(1+r)^s}, \tag{4.4.16}$$

as in Christensen and Feltham (2009). However, it is usually more convenient to exploit the properties of the model, and make use Eq. (4.2.17) to obtain the equilibrium value of the firm,

$$V_t = IC_t + \frac{1-\tau}{\eta}\mathbb{E}_t \sum_{s=1}^{\infty} \frac{M_{t+s}}{M_t} p_{t+s} q_{t+s}. \tag{4.4.17}$$

One can then verify whether the two approaches yield the same result.

We may wonder when assuming a constant WACC is correct, and then using the classic textbook discounted cash flows model (DCF) to obtain V_t. To answer this question, we may start recalling that, by definition, the weighted average cost of capital $\left\{wacc_{t,t+1}\right\}_{t \geq 0}$ is a stochastic process that satisfies the following equation at each time $t \in \mathbb{N}$,

$$V_t = \frac{\mathbb{E}_t\left(x_{t+1} + V_{t+1}\right)}{1 + wacc_{t,t+1}}, \tag{4.4.18}$$

that is,

$$V_t = \sum_{s=1}^{\infty} \frac{\mathbb{E}_t\left(x_{t+s}\right)}{\prod_{j=1}^{s}\left[1 + \mathbb{E}_{t+s-1}\left(wacc_{t+j-1,t+j}\right)\right]}. \tag{4.4.19}$$

To obtain the classic DCF valuation model, we must show that for each future date $t+j$, $wacc_{t+j-1,t+j} = wacc_{t,t+1} = wacc > 0$. This turns out to be possible if $g_t = \frac{\mathbb{E}_t(Y_{t+1})}{Y_t} = g$, that is, if the expected industry growth rate is constant and below a certain threshold. To prove this claim, recall Eq. (4.3.4) from the previous section,

$$wacc_{t,t+1} = \frac{(1-\tau)\,\Pi}{Q_t} + \left(1 - \frac{1}{Q_t}\right)\mathbb{E}_t\left(\rho_{t+1}\right). \tag{4.4.20}$$

If

$$g_t = g \in (-1, \bar{g}] \implies \mathbb{E}_t\left(\rho_{t+1}\right) = \rho \wedge \mathbb{E}_t\left(Q_{t+1}\right) = Q > 1, \tag{4.4.21}$$

we can conclude that the classic DCF model is consistent with the equilibrium value of the firm, that is,

$$V_t = \sum_{s=1}^{\infty} \frac{\mathbb{E}_t\left(x_{t+s}\right)}{(1 + wacc)^s}. \tag{4.4.22}$$

For a generic time t, we can expand the expression for NPVMR as follows,

$$\Theta_t = \frac{1-\tau}{\eta}\sum_{s=1}^{\infty}\frac{M_{t+s}}{M_t}p_{t+s}q_{t+s} = \frac{1-\tau}{\eta}\mathbb{E}_t\sum_{s=1}^{\infty}\frac{e^{\sum_{j=1}^{s}\mu_{t+j}-\frac{\sigma_\mu^2}{2}}}{(1+r)^s}\left(\frac{A_{t+s}K_{t+s}}{Y_{t+s}}\right)^{-\eta}A_{t+s}K_{t+s} =$$

$$= \frac{1-\tau}{\eta}A^{1-\eta}C_1^{-\eta}\mathbb{E}_t\sum_{s=1}^{\infty}\frac{e^{\sum_{j=1}^{s}\mu_{t+j}-\frac{\sigma_\mu^2}{2}}}{(1+r)^s}e^{\frac{1}{\eta}\left(\varepsilon_{t+1}-\frac{1}{2}\sigma_\varepsilon^2\right)}K_{t+s} =$$

$$\frac{1-\tau}{\eta}(AC_1)^{1-\eta}Y_t\mathbb{E}_t\sum_{s=1}^{\infty}\frac{e^{\sum_{j=1}^{s}\mu_{t+j}-\frac{\sigma_\mu^2}{2}}}{(1+r)^s}e^{\frac{1}{\eta}\left(\varepsilon_{t+s}-\frac{1}{2}\sigma_\varepsilon^2\right)}(1+g)^s,$$

eventually obtaining,

$$\Theta_t = \frac{1-\tau}{\eta}(AC_1)^{1-\eta}Y_t\mathbb{E}_t\sum_{s=1}^{\infty}\left(\frac{1+g}{1+\omega}\right)^s. \tag{4.4.23}$$

where $\left(\frac{1}{1+\omega}\right)^s = \mathbb{E}_t\left[\frac{e^{\sum_{j=1}^{s}\mu_{t+j}-\frac{\sigma_\mu^2}{2}}}{(1+r)^s}e^{\frac{1}{\eta}\left(\varepsilon_{t+s}-\frac{1}{2}\sigma_\varepsilon^2\right)}\right]$ follows from the strong stationarity and serial independence of $\{\varepsilon_t, \mu_t\}_{t\geq 0}$. Thus, provided that $g < \bar{g} = \omega$, the RHS of Eq. (4.4.21) is bounded and the following results hold,

$$Q_t = Q = 1 + \frac{\frac{1-\tau}{\eta}A^{1-\eta}C_1^{-\eta}C_5}{1+\kappa}\frac{1}{\omega-g} \geq 1, \tag{4.4.24}$$

$$\frac{F_{t+1}}{V_t} = \frac{(1-\alpha)(1-\delta)}{1+c}\frac{\mathbb{I}(\tau c \geq \varphi)}{Q} \geq 0, \tag{4.4.25}$$

$$wacc_{t,t+1} = wacc = \frac{\Pi(1-\tau)}{Q} + \left(1-\frac{1}{Q}\right)g. \tag{4.4.26}$$

As a result, the DCF model in Eq. (4.4.22) is valid. However, as g_t is constant, it is immediate to check that Eq. (4.4.20) is a more specific version of the basic model presented in Sect. 2.4.4, that is,

$$V_t = \frac{\mathbb{E}_{t+1}(x_{t+1})}{wacc-g} = \frac{OM\left[(1-\tau)-\frac{g}{\Pi}\right]}{wacc-g}. \tag{4.4.27}$$

Despite its apparent simplicity, Eq. (4.4.27) makes clear the channel through which growth creates value for shareholders. Holding g constant, the larger the spread $\Pi - wacc$, the larger the value creation through the growth is. This spread is often used as multiple of the value of invested capital (IC_{t+1}), and the resulting metric is the Residual Income or Economic Value Added (Stewart 1991) used to assess the value creation of growth strategies. In this regard, the value of the firm can be obtained as,

$$V_t = IC_{t+1} + \frac{\mathbb{E}_t\left(RI_{t+1}\right)}{wacc - g} \tag{4.4.28}$$

where $RI_{t+1} = [\Pi\,(1-\tau) - wacc]\,IC_{t+1}$. We thereby provide an heuristic link between NPVMR and EVA^{TM}.

4.5 Related Literature

The "Q" theory of investment is originally due do Kaldor (1966), Tobin and Brainard (1976) and Hayashi (1982), later extended by Abel (1981, 1983) and Abel and Eberly (1996, 1997). Fama and French (1993) show that Tobin's Q and the firm's size add explanatory power to the cross sectional returns. In this regard, investment-based asset pricing, or "supply-side", models provide an empirically consistent equilibrium explanation of Fama and French (1993). Most of these models adopt a partial equilibrium approach, as we did in this and in the previous chapter. An example is Berk et al. (1999). However, there are examples of general equilibrium models as well, such as Gomes et al. (2003) or Zhang (2005), which analyzes the effects of irreversibility costs in a general equilibrium model with countercyclical equity risk premia (i.e. investors discounts cash flows more aggressively in bad times).

The model presented in this chapter is inspired by the discussion of Tobin's Q and imperfect competition in Balvers et al. (2017). Schiantarelli and Georgoutsos (1990), Abel and Eberly (2011), and Crouzet and Eberly (2020) are other examples of models consistent with our approach. Nevertheless, our model distinguishes from others in the literature because of the presence of a *lag* between the purchase of intermediate goods and the collection of revenues resulting from the production process. This mechanism, which comes from Cooley and Quadrini (2006) and Quadrini (2011), allows to introduce the working capital consistently with the *operating cycle* concept in corporate finance. From an accrual perspective, the model includes quasi-fixed costs, in that the use of inventories purchased in the previous period is a cost item of the current period's *Profit and Loss account*. In this regard, Carlson et al. (2004) is an example of monopolistic competition model with quasi-fixed production costs. However, in our model the timing is different, as the cost of intermediate inputs must be paid in advance. For this reason, contrary to Carlson et al. (2004), there is no *operating leverage* effect in terms of free cash flows to the firm, which is the only relevant asset pricing metric.

Our model can be also extended by including intangible assets, following the $Q+$ framework of Crouzet and Eberly (2020). In this regard, one may question the ultimate source of market power in our model. For instance, a brand could be viewed itself as an intangible asset. This is actually an old problem in accounting, and the answer depends on whether the expenses to preserve the brand's strengthens should be considered as a capital expenditure or production costs.

References

Abel, A. B. (1981). A dynamic model of investment and capacity utilization. *The Quarterly Journal of Economics, 96*(3), 379.

Abel, A. B. (1983). Optimal investment under uncertainty. *The American Economic Review, 73*(1), 228–233.

Abel, A. B., & Eberly, J. C. (1996). Optimal investment with costly reversibility. *The Review of Economic Studies, 63*(4), 581–593.

Abel, A. B., & Eberly, J. C. (1997). An exact solution for the investment and value of a firm facing uncertainty, adjustment costs, and irreversibility. *Journal of Economic Dynamics and Control, 21*(4–5), 831–852.

Abel, A. B., & Eberly, J. C. (2011). How q and cash flow affect investment without frictions: An analytic explanation. *The Review of Economic Studies, 78*(4), 1179–1200.

Bai, H., Li, E. X. N., Xue, C., & Zhang, L. (2019). Does costly reversibility matter for U.S. public firms? *SSRN Electronic Journal.*

Balvers, R. J., Gu, L., & Huang, D. (2017). Profitability, value, and stock returns in production-based asset pricing without frictions. *Journal of Money, Credit and Banking, 49*(7), 1621–1651.

Berk, J. B., Green, R. C., & Naik, V. (1999). Optimal investment, growth options, and security returns. *The Journal of Finance, 54*(5), 1553–1607.

Carlson, M., Fisher, A., & Gianmarino, R. (2004). Corporate investment and asset price dynamics: Implications for the cross-section of returns. *The Journal of Finance, 59*(6), 2577–2603.

Christensen, P. O., & Feltham, G. A. (2009). Equity valuation. *Foundations and Trends in Accounting, 4*(1), 1–112.

Coase, R. H. (1972). Durability and monopoly. *The Journal of Law and Economics, 15*(1), 143–149.

Cooley, T. F., & Quadrini, V. (2006). Monetary policy and the financial decisions of firms. *Economic Theory, 27*(1), 243–270.

Cochrane, J. H. (2009). *Asset pricing*. Princeton University Press.

Cooper, R., & Ejarque, J. (2003). Financial frictions and investment: Requiem in Q. *Review of Economic Dynamics, 6*(4), 710–728.

Crouzet, N., & Eberly, J. (2020). Rents and intangible capital: a q+ framework. *Working Paper.*

Edwards, E. O., & Bell, P. W. (1995). *The theory and measurement of business income*. Garland Pub.

Fama, E. F., & French, K. R. (1993). Common risk factors in the returns on stocks and bonds. *Journal of Financial Economics, 33*(1), 3–56.

Feltham, G. A., & Ohlson, J. A. (1995). Valuation and clean surplus accounting for operating and financial activities. *Contemporary Accounting Research, 11*(2), 689–731.

Gomes, J. F., Yaron, A., & Zhang, L. (2003). Asset prices and business cycles with costly external finance. *Review of Economic Dynamics, 6*(4), 767–788.

Gul, F., Sonnenschein, H., & Wilson, R. (1986). Foundations of dynamic monopoly and the coase conjecture. *Journal of Economic Theory, 39*(1), 155–190.

Hall, R. E. (2004). Measuring factor adjustment costs. *The Quarterly Journal of Economics, 119*(3), 899–927.

Hayashi, F. (1982). Tobin's marginal q and average q: A neoclassical interpretation. *Econometrica, 50*(1), 213.

Hou, K., Mo, H., Xue, C., and Zhang, L. (2020). An augmented q-factor model with expected growth. *Review of Finance, 25*(1), 1–14.

Kaldor, N. (1966). Marginal productivity and the macro-economic theories of distribution: Comment on Samuelson and Modigliani. *The Review of Economic Studies, 33*(4), 309.

Lindenberg, E. B., & Ross, S. A. (1981). Tobin's q ratio and industrial organization. *The Journal of Business, 54*(1), 1.

Miao, J. (2020). *Economic dynamics in discrete time*. MIT Press.

Novy-Marx, R. (2013). The other side of value: The gross profitability premium. *Journal of Financial Economics, 108*(1), 1–28.

Ohlson, J. A. (1995). Earnings, book values, and dividends in equity valuation. *Contemporary Accounting Research, 11*(2), 661–687.

Peasnell, K. V. (1982). Some formal connections between economic values and yields and accounting numbers. *Journal of Business Finance and Accounting, 9*(3), 361–381.

Quadrini, V. (2011). Financial frictions in macroeconomic fluctuations. *Economic Quarterly, 97*(3), 209–254.

Schiantarelli, F., & Georgoutsos, D. (1990). Monopolistic competition and the q theory of investment. *European Economic Review, 34*(5), 1061–1078.

Stewart, G. B. (1991). *The quest for value*. Harper Business.

Tirole, J. (1988). *The theory of industrial organization*. MIT Press.

Tobin, J., & Brainard, W. C. (1976). Asset markets and the cost of capital. *Cowles Foundation Discussion Papers*.

Zhang, L. (2005). The value premium. *The Journal of Finance, 60*(1), 67–103.

Chapter 5
Continuous Time Models, Unsecured Debt and Commitment

This chapter is dedicated to continuous time methods in corporate finance, focusing on capital structure models in which the firm is assumed to be financed by equity and unsecured debt. The major difference with the discrete time setting is that investment and financing decisions take place at each $t \in \mathbb{R}$, with free cash flows and payments on outstanding securities accruing continuously. Admittedly, while continuous time models are based on this purely theoretical abstraction, they are notwithstanding useful to characterize the occurrence of default episodes. We use the standard Ito's processes to model the sources of randomness affecting free cash flows dynamics. Ito's processes can be extended to include *jumps*, that is, a set of countable discontinuities occurring at deterministic or random Poisson times. In order to keep the discussion self-contained, jumps are excluded from both the exogenous processes driving the firm's free cash flows, as well as discrete or lump sum payments to the firm claimholders, with the only possible exceptions of (i) the date at which the firm is established, say $t = 0$, and (ii) the date in which a default episode takes place.

The rest of the chapter is organized as follows. In Sect. 5.1 we derive a general valuation formula for the firm in continuous time setting. In doing this we consider a very simple capital structure, composed by equity and pari-passu unsecured bonds.

In Sect. 5.2 we deal with the Hamilton–Jacobi–Belmann (HJB) approach, which consists in translating asset pricing problems in partial differential equations. As the name suggests, there is an intrinsic connection with dynamic programming in continuous time, which we will largely exploit to derive shareholders' optimal decisions. Specifically, we explore the way in which investors' risk-aversion, which is factored in the stochastic discount factor (SDF), should be handled.

The tools we develop are then used to inspect corporate finance models in which the firm commits at a certain point in time to a static debt's policy. The workhorse of this approach is the Leland (1994) model, which is thoroughly presented in Sect. 5.3. The Leland model assumes that shareholders commit to not issue additional debt after a first and last tranche of bonds is issued. Despite the time inconsistency of

U. Sagliaschi, R. Savona, *Dynamical Corporate Finance*, Contributions to Finance and Accounting, https://doi.org/10.1007/978-3-030-77853-8_5

this assumption, as we shall see in Sect. 6.1, the importance of this model is at least twofold. Firstly, the model played a key role in the last 25 years of research in corporate finance. Secondly, its algebraic derivation suggests a general methodology to tackle more complicated problems. In particular, part of the model's results remains valid in the more general circumstances of Chap. 6, where we restore the firm's flexibility to adjust its net financial position.

The original version of the Leland model is based on the assumption of an exogenous process for the value of the firm. Since then, it has been customary to replace this assumption with that of an exogenous unlevered free cash flows process. As we did in the previous chapter, we extend the analysis to the inclusion of endogenous investment decisions, through which shareholders affect the dynamics of unlevered free cash flows. We do this in Sect. 5.4, where we scrutinize the problems of debt overhang and risk shifting. We will use very schematic models that help to understand the economics behind both phenomena.

5.1 General Setting and Valuation

5.1.1 *The Setting*

For a generic stochastic process y in continuous time (CT), we write $y(t)$, as opposed to y_t in the discrete time (DT) case. In this way we avoid confusion when using the compact notation $f_x = \frac{\partial f}{\partial x}$ for partial derivatives.

To handle the complexity of CT models, we assume that at each trading date t, the holders of a generic security i have equal claims over the differential $dH_i(t) = H_i(t + dt) - H(t) = n_i(t)\, dY_i(t)$, where $H(t)$ is the cumulative cash flows paid by the class of securities i from the conventional date $t = 0$, and given the number of outstanding securities of the same class at time t, $n_i(t)$. In CT model, $n_i(t)$ is the number of securities at the "end" of date t. Contrary to the DT case, we can no longer make use of the more handy notation $n_i(t + 1)$, as the number of oustanding securities could change during the next dt interval.

To get a sense of the CT approach, consider the case in which $H(t)$ follows a *smooth* process, in the sense that $dY_i(t) = y_i(t)\, dt$, where $y_i(t)$ is an Ito diffusion process. It is evident that securities trade in each period at a price which includes the cash flows accruing smoothly between two converging dates, say t and $t + dt$. This is in contrast with DT models, and it is exactly this difference that may preclude a direct interpretation of a CT model as the limit of an assimilable DT model. For this reason, models that differ only from their CT or DT formulation should not be literally considered one as the limiting case of the other, although in several cases it might be a good qualitative approximation. Another consequence, which is valid as long as $dY(t) = y(t)\, dt$ holds for all securities, is that there is no difference between *ex* and *cum* cash flows prices. In fact, at each instant there is always a cash flow that is potentially paid out *over* the next dt interval. As a result, contrary to the DT case, there is no difference between shareholders value and equity market value (see Sect. 2.1). However, allowing for occasional lump-sum equity payments (e.g. discrete dividends or share buybacks), the difference between cum-dividend and ex-dividend equity market value is reinstated.

The idea underlying the approach is inspired by the *integral representation* of the firm's budget constraint. Let assume that between two instants t and $t+\Delta,\ \Delta>0$, the firm is solvent. Let $x(s)$ be the unlevered cash flows that would be available to the firm at date $s+1$ if $x(j)=x(s)$ for all $j\in[s,s+1]$. Adopting the same interpretation for what concerns the tax benefits of capital structure $\pi(s)$ decisions and primary markets transaction costs $\Theta(s)$, the total change in liquidity $L(t)$ between t and $t+\Delta$ is equal to,

$$L(t+\Delta)-L(t)=\underbrace{\int_0^{\Delta} L(t+s)\,r(t+s)\,ds}_{\text{Interest income}}+\underbrace{\int_0^{\Delta}[x(t+s)+\pi(t+s)-\Theta(t+s)]\,ds}_{\text{Free Cash Flows}}-\underbrace{\sum_{i\in\mathcal{S}_t}\int_0^{\Delta} n_i(t)\,dY_i(t)-p_i(t)\,dn_i(t)}_{\text{Payments to security holders plus proceeds from capital structure adjustments}}, \tag{5.1.1}$$

where $p_i(t)$ is the price of a security $i\in\mathcal{S}_t$ at time t and $n_i(t)$ is related amount oustanding. Two observations are important. First, $p_i(t)$ comprehensive of the cash flows $dY_i(t)$ is received immediately after t. Second, $n_i(t)$ is comprehensive only of discrete adjustments taking place at the same date. In other words, $n_i(t)$ does not include the effect of its smooth change over the next dt interval.

The following working hypotheses will be maintained in the rest of the chapter. First, the firm is financed with equity and unsecured debt instruments with equal seniority (*pari passu*). We shall refer to these securities as bonds without loss of generality. Namely, each bond is an exponential maturing perpetuity of unit face value, with coupon rate $c\geq 0$ and contractual retirement rate $\xi\geq 0$ such that $c\cdot\xi>0$. This means that in each period $(t,t+dt]$, the holder of a bond is entitled to receive a fraction ξ of the residual principal at time t, and a coupon payment equal to c times the same amount. This is a very common assumption in the literature to introduce the effects of debt maturity, while preserving the independence on time of the price functions. Second, issuing equity and bonds is costless for the firm. As in Chaps. 3–4, without loss of generality we will assume that any injection of outside equity will occur through negative dividends (see Eq. (3.1.7) in Sect. 3.2.1).

Third, unlevered free cash flows follow an Ito's diffusion process, as well as dividends and the process underlying the issuance of new bonds. As a result, $dY_i(t)=y_i(t)\,dt,\ \forall t\in(0,t_d)$ for the cash flows paid by both stocks and bonds, and there are no discrete adjustments in the number of outstanding securities, with the exception of $t\in\{0,t_d\}$. As a consequence, there is no need to make distinction between ex and cum-dividend market value of equity for all $t\in(0,t_d)$. Finally, the stochastic discount factor process $M(t)$ is supposed to follow an Ito diffusion process.

5.1.2 The Value of the Firm and Its Securities

Having clarified the interpretation we make of the CT models, and specified the main hypotheses we refer to in our analysis, we can now proceed to derive a general formula for the value of the firm. As long as $x(t)$ is supposed to be exogenously given, we assume that the underlying investment policy is individually rational (cf. Sect. 2.1.1),

$$\mathbb{E}_t \int_0^{\infty} \frac{M(t+s)}{M(t)} x(t+s)\, ds \geq 0. \tag{5.1.2}$$

The value of the unlevered firm (V^u) is defined as the maximum value of the LHS of Eq. (5.1.2) (cf. Sect. 1.4). Since we have already analyzed time the different bankruptcy resolution mechanisms in Chap. 1, we will simply assume that in case of default the total recovery value is a fraction $1-\theta(t_d)$ of the firm's unlevered value, plus any amount of liquidity $L(t_d)$ left as available. Notice that the value of future tax benefits is lost in the bankruptcy process.

Let $F(t)$ be the amount of debt oustanding at time t. Contrary to the DT case, we do not allow for discrete debt adjustments. Rather, debt is always adjusted "smoothly", that is, according to the following dynamics,

$$dF(t) = [G(t) - \xi F(t)]\, dt. \tag{5.1.3}$$

In this regard, $G(t)$ is a stochastic process which denotes the firm's debt's policy. Hence, during any generic time interval $[t, t+\Delta]$ in which the firm is solvent, the budget constraint in Eq. (5.1.1) is equivalent to,

$$\begin{aligned} L(t+\Delta) - L(t) = & \int_t^{t+\Delta} [x(s) + \pi(s) + L(s)r(s)]\, ds \\ + \int_t^{t+\Delta} & p(s)G(s)\, ds - \int_t^{t+\Delta} dD(s) - \int_t^{t+\Delta} (c+\xi) F(s)\, ds, \end{aligned} \tag{5.1.4}$$

where $D(s)$ are cumulative dividends paid to shareholders between $t=0$ and $t=s$.

In each period, the holder of a dollar of debt is entitled to receive $(c+\xi)\, dt$ during the next infinitesimal interval (dt). As a result, the price per dollar of debt's notional (p) must be equal to,

$$p(t) = \mathbb{E}_t \int_t^{t_d} \frac{M(s)}{M(t)} e^{-\xi(s-t)} (c+\xi)\, ds + \mathbb{E}_t \left[\frac{M(t_d)}{M(t)} \frac{R^B(t_d)}{F(t_d)} \right], \tag{5.1.5}$$

where $R^B(t_d)$ is debt holders' recovery value. Accordingly, the total market value of the outstanding bonds $\left(V^B\right)$ is obtained as $p(t)F(t)$. It is important to stress the difference relative to DT setting. Being absent discrete adjustments, there is no need to make distinction between the amount of debt outstanding at the beginning or at the end of time $t \in (0, t_d)$. As a result, there is no need to make distinction between cum and ex-dividend market value of the firm. Namely, the value of the firm is defined as $V(t) = V^E(t) + V^B(t) - L(t)$, where $V^E(t)$ is the market value of equity,

$$V^E(t) = \mathbb{E}_t \int_t^{t_d} \frac{M(s)}{M(t)} D(s)\, ds + \mathbb{E}_t \left[\frac{M(t_d)}{M(t)} R^E(t_d) \right]. \tag{5.1.6}$$

Since Eq. (5.1.4) holds for any arbitrary small value of Δ, we can apply Leibniz's rule to derive both its side with respect to Δ. As a result, we find that the following differential equation must be verified $\forall t \in (0, t_d)$,

$$D(t) = x(t) + \pi(t) + p(t) G(t) - \frac{dL(t)}{dt} - (c + \xi) F(t). \tag{5.1.7}$$

The previous relation is the *differential form* of the firm's budget constraint. Putting together, Eq. (5.1.6–5.1.7) allow us to obtain the value of the firm as,

$$\begin{aligned} V(t) = V^E(t) + p(t) F(t) - L(t) = \\ \mathbb{E}_t \int_t^{t_d} \frac{M(s)}{M(t)} [x(s) + \pi(s)]\, ds + \\ \underbrace{p(t) F(t) + \mathbb{E}_t \int_t^{t_d} \frac{M(s)}{M(t)} \{p(s) G(s) - (c + \xi) F(s)\}\, ds +}_{\Xi(t)} \\ \mathbb{E}_t \left\{ \frac{M(t_d)}{M(t)} \left[R^E(t_d) - L(t_d) \right] \right\}. \end{aligned} \tag{5.1.8}$$

The next, purely algebraic, step consists in simplifying the expression defining $\Xi(t)$ in Eq. (5.1.8). Solving Eq. (5.1.3) for $j \in [t, s < t_t]$ we get,

$$F(s) = e^{-\xi(s-t)} F(t) + \int_t^s G(j) e^{-\xi(j-t)} dj, \tag{5.1.9}$$

and, by induction,

$$\begin{aligned} \Xi(t) = \mathbb{E}_t \left\{ \frac{M(t_d)}{M(t)} p(t_d) \left[e^{-\xi(t_d-t)} F(t) + \int_t^{t_d} G(s) e^{-\xi(s-t)} dt_d \right] \right\} = \\ \mathbb{E}_t \left[\frac{M(t_d)}{M(t)} p(t_d) F(t_d) \right]. \end{aligned} \tag{5.1.10}$$

At default, the value of debt $p(t_d) F(t_d)$ is equal to the recovery value of debtholders, $R^B(t_d)$. Consequently, Eq. (5.1.8) simplifies to,

$$V(t) = \mathbb{E}_t \int_t^{t_d} \frac{M(s)}{M(t)} [x(s) + \pi(s)] ds + \mathbb{E}_t \left\{ \frac{M(t_d)}{M(t)} \left[R^E(t_d) + R^B(t_d) - L(t_d) \right] \right\}. \tag{5.1.11}$$

For a firm that makes no use of debt, the previous equation is equivalent to $V(t) = \mathbb{E}_t \int_0^\infty \frac{M(s)}{M(t)} x(s) ds$. As anticipated, we let $V^u(t)$ be the unlevered firm value, that is, the value of the firm that adopts the investment policy generating the process $x(t) = x^*(t)$ with the highest NPV among all the alternatives available to the firm and its shareholders. By assumption, the expression $R^E(t_d) + R^B(t_d) - L(t_d)$ is equal to $[1 - \theta(t_d)] V^u(t_d)$, and, in analogy with Chap. 1, we can define $BC(t) := \mathbb{E}_t \left[\frac{M(t_d)}{M(t)} \theta(t_d) V^u(t_d) \right]$ and $DTS(t) := \mathbb{E}_t \int_0^{t_d} \frac{M(s)}{M(t)} \pi(s) ds$. Thus, the expression for the value of the firm can be written as,

$$V(t) = V^u(t) + DTS(t) - AC(t) - BC(t), \tag{5.1.12}$$

where $AC(t)$ is the value of the agency costs related to pursuing an investment policy different from the one maximizing the NPV of unlevered free cash flows, that is,

$$AC_t = \mathbb{E}_t \int_0^{t_d} \frac{M(s)}{M(t)} \left[x^*(s) - x(s) \right] ds. \tag{5.1.13}$$

As in the DT case (cf. Sects. 2.2.3 and 2.4), the value of the firm is equal to the NPV of the total free cash flows generated through production, investment and financing decisions, and it can be represented by considering the algebraic sum of few "standard" components. In the remainder of the analysis we will assume that, being transaction costs absent, the firm will never make use of liquidity reserves. The argument is the same as in the previous chapters. Since holding liquidity is costly to the firm, due to the taxation of interest income, it is never convenient for shareholders to set $L(t) > 0$, being transaction costs and limits to outside equity injections both absent.

5.2 The Hamilton–Jacobi–Bellman Approach

The Hamilton–Jacobi–Bellman approach (HJB) is a very convenient tool that allows to translate asset pricing problems, which are formulated as stochastic integrals, in systems of partial derivative equations (PDE). Suppose that the value of equity and the price of debt are only function of the firm's fundamentals, that is, $x(t)$ and $F(t)$. A sufficient condition for this to be true is that of a Markov Perfect Equilibrium (MPE), which will be discussed in Chap. 6.

The SDF is a drift-diffusion process with drift coefficient equal to $-r(t)\,M(t)$.[1] To get a first intuition of the HJB approach, let us consider the case in which investors are risk-neutral and the risk-free rate is constant, that is, $\frac{M(t)}{M(0)} = e^{-rt}$, $r > 0$. If we let t_n be a random future date, the value of equity and the price of debt can be represented according to their integral form as, respectively,

$$V^E(t) = \mathbb{E}_t \int_0^{t_n} e^{-r(s-t)} D(s)\,ds + \mathbb{E}_t\left[e^{-rt_n} V^E_{t_n}\right], \tag{5.2.1}$$

and,

$$p(t) = \mathbb{E}_t \int_0^{t_n} e^{-(r+\xi)(s-t)} (c+\xi)\,ds + \mathbb{E}_t\left[e^{-rt_n} p_{t_n}\right]. \tag{5.2.2}$$

Notice that the previous relation holds also for $t_n = t_d$, as it is enough to apply the *boundary conditions* $V^E_{t_d} = R^E_{t_d}$ and $p^B_{t_d} = \frac{R^B_{t_d}}{F_{t_d}}$ which both stem from the absence of arbitrage opportunities in equilibrium. If wet let t_n approach to t, we obtain the following differential equations,

$$V^E(t)\left[1 - e^{-rdt}\right] = D(t)\,dt + \mathbb{E}_t\left[dV^E(t)\right], \tag{5.2.3}$$

$$p(t)\left[1 - e^{-(r+\xi)dt}\right] = (c+\xi)\,dt + \mathbb{E}_t\left[dp(t)\right]. \tag{5.2.4}$$

Suppose that $G = G(x, F)$ is a twice continuously differentiable function, so that we can apply Ito's lemma in order to obtain closed form expressions for $\mathbb{E}_t\left[dV^E(t)\right]$ and $\mathbb{E}_t\left[dp(t)\right]$ respectively, thereby obtaining the following PDE for the value of equity and the price of debt, respectively,

$$\begin{aligned} rV^E(x,F) &= x + \pi + pG - (c+\xi)F + \mu(x,F)\,V^E_x(x,F) \\ &\quad + \frac{1}{2}\sigma(x,F)^2\,V^E_{xx}(x,F) + (G - \xi F)\,V^E_x(x,F), \end{aligned} \tag{5.2.5}$$

$$rp = c + \xi(1-p) + \mu(x,F)\,p_x(x,F) + \frac{1}{2}\sigma(x,F)^2\,p_{xx}(x,F) + (G - \xi F)\,p_x(x,F). \tag{5.2.6}$$

With risk-neutral investors, the expected return of any security must be equal to the risk-free rate. Eq. (5.2.5) is just a formal restatement of this basic result. If we multiply both sides of Eq. (5.2.3) by $\frac{dt}{V^E(x,F)}$, we notice that

[1]See Chapter 1 in Cochrane (2009)'.

RHS of the resulting expression is the sum of the current dividend yield $\left(\frac{x+dts+pG-(c+\xi)F}{V^E(x,F)}dt\right)$ plus the expected capital gain $\left(\frac{\mathbb{E}_t\left[dV^E(t)\right]}{V^E(t)}\right)$, which is equal to $\left[\mu V_x^E + \frac{1}{2}\sigma^2 V_{xx}^E + (G - \xi F)\, V_x^E\right] dt$ from the application of Ito's lemma. An identical interpretation holds for Eq. (5.2.6). The term $[c + \xi\,(1-p)]\,dt$ is the instantaneous payoff of a dollar of debt, while $\left[\mu p_x + \frac{1}{2}\sigma^2 p_{xx} + (G - \xi F)\, p_x\right] dt$ is the expected price appreciation (depreciation, if negative).

Equations (5.2.5–5.2.6) are examples of Hamilton–Jacobi–Bellman equations (HJB). In general, HJB equations provide the expected-returns formulation of equilibrium asset pricing problems. In fact, if we follow the same procedure for a generic SDF process,

$$dM(t) = -rM(t)\,dt + \upsilon(M(t))\,dW^{(M)}(t), \tag{5.2.7}$$

we obtain the following system of differential equations,

$$\begin{cases} M(t)\,V^E(t) = M_t D(t)\,dt + \mathbb{E}_t\left[M(t+dt)\,V^E(t+dt)\right] & \text{Equity Value,} \\ M(t)\,p(t) = M(t)(c+\xi)\,dt + \mathbb{E}_t\left[M(t+dt)\,p(t+dt)\right] & \text{Price of debt per} \\ & \text{unit of face value.} \end{cases} \tag{5.2.8}$$

The assumption of a constant risk-free rate is not crucial for the validity of what comes next, but it helps in this case to simplify the solution. Besides, in order to obtain closed-form results, which is the actual reason why we discuss CT models, it is usually necessary to make such an assumption. Recalling that, $\mathbb{E}_t\left[dM(t)\right] = -rM(t)\,dt$, we obtain,

$$rdt - \mathbb{E}_t\left[\frac{dM(t)}{M(t)}\frac{dV^E(t)}{V^E(t)}\right] = \frac{D(t)}{V^E(t)}dt + \mathbb{E}_t\left[\frac{dV^E(t+dt)}{V^E(t)}\right] \tag{5.2.9}$$

and,

$$[r+\xi]\,dt - \mathbb{E}_t\left[\frac{dM(t)}{M(t)}\frac{dp(t)}{p(t)}\right] = (c+\xi)\,dt + \mathbb{E}_t\left[\frac{dp(t+dt)}{p(t)}\right] \tag{5.2.10}$$

for the value equity and the price of debt, respectively.

Let ρ be the correlation between $dW^{(M)}(t)$ and $dW(t)$, which is supposed to be constant, to simplify the discussion. The application of Ito's lemma leads to the following relation for the expected value of cross-products in the RHS of

Eq. (5.2.10),

$$\mathbb{E}_t\left[\frac{dM(t)}{M(t)}\frac{dV^E(t)}{V^E(t)}\right] = \rho\sigma(x(t), F(t))\, V_x^E \upsilon(M(t))\, dt, \tag{5.2.11}$$

Consequently, the following PDE characterizes the value of equity as a function of the fundamentals (x, F),

$$\left[r - \sigma(x, F)\, V_x^E \upsilon(M)\,\rho\right] V^E = x + \pi + pG - (c + \xi)\, F + \mathcal{A}^{\mathbb{P}} \circ V^E \tag{5.2.12}$$

where $r - \sigma(x, F)\,\upsilon(M)\,\rho(x, F)$ is the equilibrium expected return for the firm's stocks, while $\mathcal{A}$ is the characteristic operator under the objective probability measure ($\mathbb{P}$), that is, $(\mathcal{A} \circ f)\, dt := \mathbb{E}_t[df(t)]$. Likewise, the price per unit of debt is the solution of,

$$[r - \sigma(x, F)\, p_x \upsilon(M)\,\rho]\, p(x, F) = c + \xi(1 - p(x, F)) + \mathcal{A}^{\mathbb{P}} \circ p(x, F), \tag{5.2.13}$$

where $r - \sigma(x, F)\, p_x \upsilon(M)\,\rho$ is the equilibrium expected return for a dollar of the firm's debt. See also Brennan and Schwartz (1984) for additional insights on the structure of equilibrium expected returns in continuous time corporate finance models.

5.2.1 *Risk-Neutral Valuation*

The risk-neutral probability measure ($\mathbb{Q}$) is obtained by setting the Radon–Nikodym derivative with respect to $\mathbb{P}$ equal to the normalized SDF, that is,

$$\frac{d\mathbb{Q}_t}{d\mathbb{P}_t} = \frac{M(t + dt)}{\mathbb{E}_t[M(t + dt)]} = e^{r(t)dt}\frac{M(t + dt)}{M(t)}. \tag{5.2.14}$$

Under the newly defined probability measure $\mathbb{Q}$, which is *equivalent* to $\mathbb{P}$,[2] Eq. (5.2.8) becomes,

$$\begin{cases} V^E(t) = D(t)\, dt + e^{-r(t)dt}\mathbb{E}_t^{\mathbb{Q}}\left[V^E(t + dt)\right] & \text{Equity Value,} \\ p(t) = (c + \xi)\, dt + e^{-[r(t)+\xi]dt}\mathbb{E}_t^{\mathbb{Q}}[p(t + dt)] & \text{Price of debt per unit of face value.} \end{cases} \tag{5.2.15}$$

[2]Here, the word *equivalent* should be intended as in probability theory. $\mathbb{Q}$ is equivalent to $\mathbb{P}$ iff $\mathbb{P}(A) = 0 \iff \mathbb{Q}(A) = 0$ for every measurable event A.

Solving forward both equations, we obtain,

$$V(x_t, F_t) = \mathbb{E}_t^{\mathbb{Q}} \int_0^{t_d} e^{-\int_0^s r(j)dj} x(s)\, ds + \mathbb{E}_t^{\mathbb{Q}} \int_0^{t_d} e^{-\int_0^s r(j)dj} \pi(s)\, ds \\ + \mathbb{E}_t^{\mathbb{Q}} \left[e^{-rt_d} (1-\theta_d) V_{t_d}^u \right], \tag{5.2.16}$$

$$V^E(x_t, F_t) = \mathbb{E}_t^{\mathbb{Q}} \int_0^{t_d} e^{-\int_0^s r(j)dj} D(s)\, ds + \mathbb{E}_t^{\mathbb{Q}} \left[e^{-rt_d} R^E(t_d) \right], \tag{5.2.17}$$

and,

$$p(x_t) = \mathbb{E}_t^{\mathbb{Q}} \int_0^{t_n} e^{-(r+\xi)s} (c+\xi)\, ds + \mathbb{E}_t^{\mathbb{Q}} \left[e^{-rt_n} F \right]. \tag{5.2.18}$$

This result is commonly known as Feyman–Kac lemma. Starting from Eq. (5.2.17) for the value of equity, the application of Ito's lemma to $\mathbb{E}_t^{\mathbb{Q}}\left[V^E(t+dt)\right]$ allows us to write,

$$r(s) V^E(s) = x(s) + \pi(s) + p(s) G(s) - (c+\xi) F(s) + \mathcal{A}^{\mathbb{Q}} \circ V^E, \tag{5.2.19}$$

where $\mathcal{A}^{\mathbb{Q}}$ is the characteristic operator under the newly defined probability measure $\mathbb{Q}$. Next, we multiply both sides times $e^{-r(s-t)}ds$, obtaining,

$$-\left[r(s) e^{-r(s)(s-t)} V^E(s) + e^{-r(s-t)} \mathcal{A}^{\mathbb{Q}} \circ V^E \right] ds \\ = e^{-r(s-t)} \left[x(s) + \pi(s) + p(s) G(s) - (c+\xi) F(s) \right] ds. \tag{5.2.20}$$

The LHS of the previous equation is equal to $-\mathbb{E}_t^{\mathbb{Q}}\left[d\left(V^E(s)\, e^{-r(s)(s-t)}\right)\right]$. Integrating both sides of Eq. (5.2.21) between t and the stochastic default time t_d, after imposing the boundary condition $V_{t_d}^E = R_{t_d}^E$, we eventually conclude that,

$$V^E(x_t) = \mathbb{E}_t^{\mathbb{Q}} \int_0^{t_d} e^{-\int_0^s r(j)dj} \left[x(s) + \pi(s) + p(s) G(s) - (c+\xi) F(s) \right] ds \\ + \mathbb{E}_t^{\mathbb{Q}} \left[e^{-rt_d} R_{t_d}^E \right]. \tag{5.2.21}$$

An identical argument can be then used to prove Eq. (5.2.18).

The proof of Eq. (5.2.16) deserves some additional considerations. Because the amount of debt is changing over time, characteristic operator for the value of the firm must take into account the effects of the presence of $G(t)$. Starting from the definition of characteristic operator, $\mathcal{A}^{\mathbb{Q}} \circ V_t := \mathbb{E}_t^{\mathbb{Q}}\left[dV^E + d(pF)\right]$, we get,

$$\begin{aligned} \mathcal{A}^{\mathbb{Q}} \circ V = \mathbb{E}_t^{\mathbb{Q}}\left[dV^E + Fdp + pdF\right] = \\ \mathcal{A}^{\mathbb{Q}} \circ V^E + F\mathcal{A}^{\mathbb{Q}} \circ p + p(G - \xi F). \end{aligned} \tag{5.2.22}$$

Thus, if we multiply both sides of Eq. (5.2.18) times $F(t)$, and add each side of the resulting equation to the respective sides of Eq. (5.2.19), we obtain the following PDE for the value of the firm,

$$r(s)V(s) = x(s) + \pi(s) + \mathcal{A}^{\mathbb{Q}} \circ V. \tag{5.2.23}$$

Finally, by repeating the same steps used to show the validity of Eq. (5.2.17), we obtain Eq. (5.2.16) from the application of the boundary condition,

$$V(t_d) = V^E(t_d) + V^B(t_d) = R^E(t_d) + R^B(t_d) = [1 - \theta(t_d)]V^u(t_d). \tag{5.2.24}$$

Notice that, for a firm financed by equity only, the value of the firm is again the NPV of unlevered free cash flows. In CT models it is often convenient to work under a risk-neutral probability measure. Once the probability measure is switched from $\mathbb{P}$ to $\mathbb{Q}$, we can proceed as if all decision makers in the model were risk-neutral. Admittedly, all of this may sound a bit abstract at first. The next sections are intended to clarify the advantage of this theoretical framework.

5.3 Commitment, Optimal Default and the Static Trade-off Theory of Capital Structure

This section focuses on a milestone of modern corporate finance, the Leland model of optimal static capital structure (Leland 1994). The model is based on the assumption that shareholders are for some reason able to commit to a static capital structure policy. This hypothesis is not necessary verified, neither in theory nor in practice, but it remains an important starting point for more advanced and (perhaps) more accurate analysis.

In particular, the Leland model assumes that, after an initial amount of debt is issued at $t = 0$, shareholders neither issue nor buyback additional debt in future, that is, $G(t) = 0$. Moreover, the Leland model is based on the following working hypotheses (HPs):

(1) a constant risk-free rate, $r(t) = r > 0$;
(2) the firm operates with the same investment policy of the unlevered firm, and unlevered free cash flows evolves according to $dx(t) = \mu x(t) dt + \sigma x(t) dW^{\mathbb{Q}}(t)$ under the risk neutral probability measure;[3]
(3) $\theta_{t_d} = \theta$ is constant and equal to $\theta \geq 0$;
(4) $\pi(t) = \tau c F(t)$;[4]
(5) shareholders have no bargaining power in case of default, and the absolute priority rule holds.

Some comments are needed to be more clear in the discussion. First, HP2 implies that $V^u(t) = \frac{x(t)}{r-\mu}$, where μ is the drift of $x(t)$ under the risk-neutral probability measure $\mathbb{Q}$. To see this, it is sufficient to solve Eq. (5.3.1) forward,

$$V^u(t) = \mathbb{E}_t \int_0^{\infty} \frac{M(t+s)}{M(t)} x(s) ds, \tag{5.3.1}$$

and apply he change of probability measure from $\mathbb{P}$ to $\mathbb{Q}$, that is, $\mathbb{E}_t \int_0^{\infty} \frac{M(t+s)}{M(t)} x(s) ds = \mathbb{E}_t^{\mathbb{Q}} \int_0^{\infty} e^{-rs} x(s) ds$. Second, a result of HP5, we have,

$$R^E(t_d) = \max\left\{0, (1-\theta) V^u(t_d) - \frac{c+\xi}{r+\xi} F\right\}, \tag{5.3.2}$$

where $R^B(t_d) = \min\left\{(1-\theta) V^u(t_d); \frac{c+\xi}{r+\xi}\right\}$ is bond holders' recovery value.

The roadmap of this section is the following. First, we assume that shareholders commits to default at a given threshold x_b for x_t. In other words, once this threshold is hit for the first time, the firm enters irreversibly in the bankruptcy procedure that we discussed in Sect. 5.1.1. Secondly, we take the amount of debt outstanding at each instant t as given, thereby obtaining an optimal default threshold consistent with the shareholders goal to maximize the equity market value, which for each date $t > 0$ coincides with shareholders value, by the lack of discrete cash flows. Finally, at time $t = 0$ we analyze the optimal static capital structure of the firm, assuming that at $t = 0_-$ shareholders are able to issue a discrete amount of debt $F \geq 0$.

[3]Notice that we have dropped the asterisk (*) for ease of notation.

[4]Notice that, with this hypothesis, in case operating earnings are insufficient to cover coupon payments, the firm obtains a net positive cash transfer from the government.

5.3.1 Option to Default and Expected Default Time

The first step is to solve the differential equation for V^E as a parametric function of the default threshold x_b,

$$\begin{aligned} rV^E(x, F|x_b) &= x + \tau cF - (c+\xi)F + \mu x V_x^E(x, F) \\ &+ \frac{1}{2}\sigma^2 x^2 V_{xx}^E(x, F) - \xi F V_F(x, F). \end{aligned} \tag{5.3.3}$$

Notice that we have suppressed the time dependency, as we have transformed the dynamic asset pricing problem in a PDE with x and F as only state variables. Now, we shall use the letter y to denote the scaled unlevered free cash flows, that is,

$$y(t) := \frac{x(t)}{F(t)}. \tag{5.3.4}$$

We guess, and verify later, that the general solution of Eq. (5.3.3) is homogenous of degree one in (x, F), that is,

$$V^E(x, F|x_b) = FV^E(y, 1|y_b) = Fv^E\left(y|y_b := \frac{x_b}{F}\right), \tag{5.3.5}$$

obtaining the following ordinary differential equation (ODE) for the scaled equity value $v^E(y)$,

$$\begin{aligned} rv^E(y|y_b) &= y + \tau c - (c+\xi) + \mu y v_y^E(y) + \frac{1}{2}\sigma^2 y^2 v_{yy}^E(y|y_b) \\ &- \xi\left(v^E(y|y_b) - yv_y^E(y|y_b)\right). \end{aligned} \tag{5.3.6}$$

The advantage of this approach is hat solving an ODE is usually simpler than a PDE. In other words, once we find a solution for Eq. (5.3.6) we can multiply by F and verify that it is indeed a solution for Eq. (5.3.3).

We start from the boundary conditions of the problem, and then turn to analyze the *general solution* of Eq. (5.3.6). If $\frac{y}{y_b} \to \infty$, the firm never default and, consequently,

$$v^E(y|y_b) \to \frac{y}{r-\mu} + \int_0^\infty e^{-(r+\xi)s}\left[c(1-\tau)+\xi\right]ds = \frac{y}{r-\mu} + \frac{c(1-\tau)+\xi}{r+\xi}. \tag{5.3.7}$$

Likewise, if $\frac{y}{y_b} = 1$, $v^E\left(y = y_b | y_b\right) = \max\left\{0, (1-\theta)\frac{y_b}{r-\mu} - \frac{c+\xi}{r+\xi}\right\}$. The *general solution* of Eq. (5.3.6) has the following structure,

$$f(y) = \frac{y}{r-\mu} - \frac{c(1-\tau)+\xi}{r+\xi} + Ay^{-\gamma} + By^{\beta}, \;\; A, B \in \mathbb{R}. \tag{5.3.8}$$

To prove this assertion, it is sufficient to establish the existence of γ, β such that Eq. (5.3.6) is verified for every $A, B \in \mathbb{R}$ once we replace $v^E(y)$ with $f(y)$. The derivative of f with respect to y is provided by,

$$f_y(y) = \frac{1}{r-\mu} - \gamma Ay^{-\gamma-1} + \beta By^{\beta-1}. \tag{5.3.9}$$

Observing that $v^E - yv^E_y = \frac{c(1-\tau)+\xi}{r+\xi}$, and substituting Eq. (5.3.8–5.3.9) in Eq. (5.3.6) we obtain the following polynomial,

$$\begin{aligned}(r+\xi)\left(Ay^{-\gamma} + By^{\beta}\right) = &-(\hat{\mu}+\xi)\left(\gamma Ay^{-\gamma} - \beta By^{\beta}\right)\\ &+\frac{1}{2}\sigma^2\left[(\gamma+1)\gamma Ay^{-\gamma} + (\beta-1)\beta By^{\beta}\right]\end{aligned} \tag{5.3.10}$$

as $f_{yy}(y) = (\gamma+1)\gamma Ay^{-\gamma-2} + (\beta-1)\beta By^{\beta-2}$. Since the constants A, B are arbitrary by definition,[5] it must be the case that the tuple (γ, β) solves the following system of equations,

$$\begin{cases}\frac{1}{2}\sigma^2\gamma^2 - \gamma\left(\mu - \frac{1}{2}\sigma^2\right) - (r+\xi) = 0\\ \frac{1}{2}\sigma^2\beta^2 + \beta\left(\mu - \frac{1}{2}\sigma^2\right) - (r+\xi) = 0\end{cases}, \tag{5.3.11}$$

Let $z_{1,2}$ be the solution of the quadratic equation $\frac{1}{2}\sigma^2 z^2 + z\left(\mu + \frac{1}{2}\sigma^2\right) - (r+\xi) = 0$, that is,

$$\begin{cases}z_1 = \dfrac{-\left(\mu+\xi-\frac{1}{2}\sigma^2\right) - \sqrt{\left(\mu+\xi-\frac{1}{2}\sigma^2\right)^2 + 2\sigma^2(r+\xi)}}{\sigma^2} < 0\\ z_2 = \dfrac{-\left(\mu+\xi-\frac{1}{2}\sigma^2\right) + \sqrt{\left(\mu+\xi-\frac{1}{2}\sigma^2\right)^2 + 2\sigma^2(r+\xi)}}{\sigma^2} > 0\end{cases} \tag{5.3.12}$$

It is then immediate to conclude that, for $\gamma = |z_1|$ and $\beta = z_2$, Eq. (5.3.8) is a general solution of Eq. (5.3.6).

---

[5]Recall that we are looking at the structure of the general solution of a second order ODE. The constants A, B must be allowed to be chosen arbitrary consistently with the number of boundary conditions (two) characterizing a specific solution.

Thus, in order to obtain $v^E(y)$ we are left with the task of determining which specific values for A and B in Eq. (5.3.8) are consistent with the boundary conditions for $\frac{y}{y_b} \to \infty$ and $\frac{y}{y_b} = 1$. Starting from the latter, we immediately conclude that B must be equal to zero and $Ay^{-\gamma} \to 0$, otherwise Eq. (5.3.7) would be violated. Since default entails the loss of future tax shield, and debtholders have absolute priority in the bankruptcy process, it is never convenient for shareholders to fill for bankruptcy protection when their recovery value is positive. As a consequence, we have to consider only the case in which $v^E(y = y_b|y_b) = 0$. Consequently, the value of A consistent with the rational behavior of shareholders' is the solution of the following equation,

$$0 = \frac{y_b}{r-\mu} - \frac{c(1-\tau)+\xi}{r+\xi} + Ay_b^{-\gamma} \tag{5.3.13}$$

that is,

$$A = \left(\frac{c(1-\tau)+\xi}{r+\xi} - \frac{y_b(1-\tau)}{r-\hat{\mu}}\right) y_b^{\gamma}. \tag{5.3.14}$$

Setting $B = 0$, and substituting the RHS of the previous equation in $\frac{y(1-\tau)}{r-\mu} + \frac{c(1-\tau)+\xi}{r+\xi} + Ay^{-\gamma}$, we eventually obtain,

$$v^E(y|y_b) = \frac{y}{r-\mu} - \frac{c(1-\tau)+\xi}{r+\xi} + \left(\frac{c(1-\tau)+\xi}{r+\xi}F - \frac{y_b(1-\tau)}{r-\mu}\right)\left(\frac{y}{y_b}\right)^{-\gamma}. \tag{5.3.15}$$

Multiplying both sides of Eq. (5.3.15) by F we obtain the candidate solution to the original PDE for $V^E(x, F|x_b)$,

$$Fv^E(y) = \frac{x}{r-\mu} - \frac{c(1-\tau)+\xi}{r+\xi}F + \left(\frac{c(1-\tau)+\xi}{r+\xi}F - \frac{x_b(1-\tau)}{r-\mu}\right)\left(\frac{x}{x_b}\right)^{-\gamma}. \tag{5.3.16}$$

Taking first and second order partial derivatives it is immediate to verify that the previous equation is a solution of Eq. (5.3.3), thus confirming our initial guess. Therefore, for every choice of x_b such that $V^E(x, F|x_b) = 0$,

$$V^E(x, F|x_b) = \frac{x}{r-\mu} - \frac{c(1-\tau)+\xi}{r+\xi}F + \left(\frac{c(1-\tau)+\xi}{r+\xi}F - \frac{x_b(1-\tau)}{r-\mu}\right)\left(\frac{x}{x_b}\right)^{-\gamma}. \tag{5.3.17}$$

The expression $\frac{x}{r-\mu} - \frac{c(1-\tau)+\xi}{r+\xi}$ is the value of equity if shareholders never took advantage of their option to default ($x_b \to \infty$). Consequently, the term

$\left(\frac{c(1-\tau)+\xi}{r+\xi}F - \frac{x_b}{r-\mu}\right)\left(\frac{x}{x_b}\right)^{-\gamma}$ is the value of shareholders' option to default, which comes as a consequence of their limited liability. Furthermore, we can show that,

$$\mathbb{E}_t^{\mathbb{Q}}\left[e^{-rd}\right] = \mathbb{E}_t^{\mathbb{Q}}\left[e^{-rd(y)}\right] = \left(\frac{y}{y_b}\right)^{-\gamma} = \left(\frac{x}{x_b}\right)^{-\gamma}, \tag{5.3.18}$$

where $d := t_d - t$ is the *time to default,* while $t_d := \inf_{s\geq 0}\{y(t+s) = y_b\}$ is the (stochastic) default date. To see this, we may start from the integral representation of $V^E(x, F)$,

$$\begin{aligned} V^E(x(t), F(t)) = F(t)\Bigg\{&\mathbb{E}_t^{\mathbb{Q}}\int_0^{t_d} e^{-r(s-t)} y(s)(1-\tau)\, ds \\ &-\mathbb{E}_t^{\mathbb{Q}}\int_0^{t_d} e^{-(r+\delta)(s-t)}\left[(1-\tau)c+\xi\right] ds\Bigg\}, \end{aligned} \tag{5.3.19}$$

and observe that it can be formulated as,

$$\begin{aligned} V^E(x(t), F(t)) = F\Bigg\{&\frac{x(t)}{r-\hat{\mu}} - \mathbb{E}_t^{\mathbb{Q}}\left[e^{-r(t_d-t)}\mathbb{E}_{t_d}^{\mathbb{Q}}\int_{t_d}^{+\infty} e^{-r(s-t_d)} y(s)(1-\tau)\, ds\right] - \Bigg\} \\ &\frac{c(1-\tau)+\xi}{r+\xi} + \mathbb{E}_t^{\mathbb{Q}}\left\{e^{-r(t_d-t)}\mathbb{E}_{t_d}^{\mathbb{Q}}\int_0^{t_d} e^{-(r+\delta)(s-t_d)}\left[(1-\tau)c+\xi\right]\right\} ds, \end{aligned}$$

that is,

$$\begin{aligned} V^E(x(t), F(t)) = F\Bigg\{&\frac{y(t)}{r-\mu} - \mathbb{E}_t^{\mathbb{Q}}\left[e^{-rd}\right]\frac{y_b}{r-\mu} - \frac{c(1-\tau)+\xi}{r+\xi} \\ &+\mathbb{E}_t^{\mathbb{Q}}\left(e^{-rd}\right)\frac{c(1-\tau)+\xi}{r+\xi}\Bigg\}. \end{aligned} \tag{5.3.20}$$

Rearranging Eq. (5.3.17) as $V^E(x, F) = F\left[\frac{y}{r-\mu} - \left(\frac{y}{y_b}\right)^{-\gamma}\frac{y_b}{r-\mu} - \frac{c(1-\tau)+\xi}{r+\xi}y \right.$ $\left. + \frac{c(1-\tau)+\xi}{r+\xi}\left(\frac{y}{y_b}\right)^{-\gamma}\right]$, it is immediate to conclude that Eq. (5.3.18) must be always valid. Furthermore, we can exploit this result to obtain $p(x, F)$. Recall that, in equilibrium, the market price of a dollar of debt's face value is given by the following equation,

$$p(x(t), F(t)) = \mathbb{E}_t^{\mathbb{Q}}\int_0^{t_d} e^{-(r+\xi)(s-t)}(c+\xi)\, ds + \mathbb{E}_t^{\mathbb{Q}}\left[e^{-(r+\xi)d}\frac{R_{t_d}^B}{F}\right]. \tag{5.3.21}$$

Since shareholders obtain nothing at y_b, it follows that $\frac{R^B_{t_d}}{F} = (1-\theta)\frac{1}{r-\mu}y_b$. At the same time, we have just shown that $\mathbb{E}^{\mathbb{Q}}_t \int_0^{t_d} e^{-(r+\xi)s}(c+\xi)\,ds = \frac{c+\xi}{r+\xi}\left[1-\mathbb{E}^{\mathbb{Q}}_t\left(e^{-rd}\right)\right]$ and $\mathbb{E}^{\mathbb{Q}}_t\left[e^{-rd}\right] = \left(\frac{y}{y_b}\right)^{-\gamma}$. Therefore, given x_b, the equilibrium price of debt is equal to,

$$p(x,F) = p(y) = \frac{c+\xi}{r+\xi}\left[1-\left(\frac{y}{y_b}\right)^{-\gamma}\right] + (1-\theta)\frac{y_b}{r-\mu}\left(\frac{y}{y_b}\right)^{-\gamma} \tag{5.3.22}$$

which is the NPV of the coupon and principal payments until default, $\mathbb{E}^{\mathbb{Q}}_t \int_0^{t_d} e^{-(r+\xi)(s-t)}(c+\xi)$, plus the expected recovery value per unit of outstanding debt, $(1-\theta)\frac{y_b}{r-\mu}\left(\frac{y}{y_b}\right)^{-\gamma}$.

5.3.2 *The Optimal Default Boundary*

Shareholders choose x_b as a function of (x, F) in order to maximize the value of their claims, that is,

$$\begin{aligned} rV^E(x,F) = \max_{x_b}\Big\{ & x + \tau cF - (c+\xi)F + \hat{\mu}xV^E_x(x,F) \\ & + \frac{1}{2}\sigma^2 x^2 V^E_{xx}(x,F) - \xi F V_F(x,F)\Big\}. \end{aligned} \tag{5.3.23}$$

Since we have a closed form expression for $V^E(x, F|x_b)$,[6] we can obtain the optimal default threshold through the solution of the equivalent static problem,

$$\max_{x_b}\left\{V^E(x,F|x_b)\right\} = F\max_{y_b}\left\{v^E(y|y_b)\right\}, \tag{5.3.24}$$

that is,

$$\max_{y_b}\left\{\frac{y}{r-\mu} - \frac{c(1-\tau)+\xi}{r+\xi} + \left(\frac{c(1-\tau)+\xi}{r+\xi}F - \frac{y_b(1-\tau)}{r-\mu}\right)\left(\frac{y}{y_b}\right)^{-\gamma}\right\}. \tag{5.3.25}$$

[6]When a closed-form expression for $V^E(x, F|x_b)$ is not available we can use the value matching and smooth pasting conditions (see Dixit 1993).

As $v^E(y|y_b)$ is strictly concave in y_b, $v^E_{y_b}(y|y_b) = 0$ is sufficient to characterize the optimal default threshold,

$$\gamma\frac{c(1-\tau)+\xi}{r+\xi}(y_b)^{\gamma-1} - (1+\gamma)(y_b)^{\gamma}\frac{1}{r-\mu} = 0 \tag{5.3.26}$$

that is,

$$x_b^* = \frac{\gamma}{1+\gamma}\frac{c(1-\tau)+\xi}{r+\xi}(r-\mu)F. \tag{5.3.27}$$

For notational simplicity, we avoid the use of asterisks when the value of equity is no longer intended as a function of a generic default threshold. Putting together, the previous results provide the following equation for the value of the firm,

$$\begin{gathered} V(x,F) = \left[v^E\left(y|y_b = \frac{x_b}{F}\right) + p\left(y|y_b = \frac{x_b}{F}\right)\right]F = \\ V^u(x) + \frac{\tau c F}{r+\xi}\left(\frac{x}{x_b}\right)^{-\gamma} - \theta\frac{x_b}{r-\mu}\left(\frac{x}{x_b}\right)^{-\gamma}, \end{gathered} \tag{5.3.28}$$

where $V^u(Y) = \frac{x}{r-\mu}$ is the unlevered firm value, $x_b = \frac{\gamma}{1+\gamma}\frac{c(1-\tau)+\xi}{r+\xi}(r-\mu)F$, while $\frac{\tau c F}{r+\xi}\left(\frac{x}{x_b}\right)^{-\gamma}$ and $\theta\frac{x}{r-\mu}\left(\frac{x}{x_b}\right)^{-\gamma}$ are respectively the value of debt tax shield and expected bankruptcy costs. Notice that shareholders' equilibrium behavior prevents the maximization of the total firm value. Indeed, the RHS of Eq. (5.3.28) could be always improved by setting the default threshold a bit higher. In other words, the value of the firm is maximized if shareholders never exercise their option to default. However, contrary to Chaps. 3 and 4, shareholders may find the alternative of default attractive. As a result, the equivalence between the maximization of shareholders value and total firm's value breaks up in the Leland model. It is also worth observing that the optimal default threshold is independent on the severity of bankruptcy costs. This is an immediate consequence of the fact that shareholders recover nothing at default, and, consequently, bankruptcy costs are entirely absorbed by bond holders.

5.3.3 *Optimal Static Capital Structure*

At time $t = 0$ the firm inherits a given amount of debt F_0, which is optimally set beforehand by shareholders subject to their commitment to $G(t) = 0$. Thus, the cum-dividend market value at time $t = 0$ differs from the ex-dividend value by the proceeds related to the issuance of F_0. Consequently, at $t = 0$, shareholders solve the following optimization problem,

$$\hat{V}(x_0) = \max_{F_0} \{pF_0 + V(x_0, F_0) - pF_0\} = \max_{F_0} V(x_0, F_0). \tag{5.3.29}$$

where $x_0 := x(0)$. Thus, the optimal initial debt level F^* is the one that maximizes the total value of the firm,

$$F^* = \operatorname{argmax}_{F_0 \geq 0} \left\{ V^u(x_0) + \frac{\tau c F_0}{r+\xi} \left[1 - \left(\frac{x}{x_b(F_0)} \right)^{-\gamma} \right] - \theta \frac{x_b(F_0)}{r-\mu} \left(\frac{x}{x_b(F_0)} \right)^{-\gamma} \right\}, \tag{5.3.30}$$

subject to the optimal choice of the bankruptcy threshold, that is, $x_b(F_0) = \frac{\gamma}{1+\gamma} \frac{c(1-\tau)+\xi}{r+\xi} (r-\mu) F_0$. Due to the concavity of the objective function in F_0, the following first order condition is necessary and sufficient to obtain the optimal static capital structure of the firm,

$$V_F(x, F) = \frac{\tau c}{r+\xi} + \frac{\tau c}{r+\xi} \left(\frac{x_b}{x} \right)^{\gamma} + \frac{\tau c F}{r+\xi} \frac{\gamma}{x_b} \left(\frac{x_b}{x} \right)^{\gamma} \frac{dx_b}{dF} - (\gamma+1) \frac{\theta}{r-\hat{\mu}} \left(\frac{x_b}{x} \right)^{\gamma} \frac{dx_b}{dF} = 0. \tag{5.3.31}$$

Since $\frac{dx_b}{dF} = \frac{\gamma}{1+\gamma} \frac{c(1-\tau)+\xi}{r+\xi} (r-\mu) = \frac{x_b}{F}$, the previous equation simplifies to,

$$\tau c \left(\frac{x_b}{x} \right)^{-\gamma} + (1+\gamma) \tau c - \theta \gamma c (1-\tau) + \xi = 0 \tag{5.3.32}$$

that is,

$$F^* = \frac{x}{(r-\mu)} \frac{1+\gamma}{\gamma} \frac{r+\xi}{c(1-\tau)+\xi} \left[(1+\gamma) - \frac{\theta\gamma(1-\tau)+\xi}{\tau} \right]^{-\frac{1}{\gamma}} \tag{5.3.33}$$

With Markov perfect strategies, the static model of optimal capital structure is time-inconsistent (cf. Chap. 6). In other words, absent specific frictions that prevents shareholders to adjust debt in the future, $G(t) \neq_{a.s.} 0$. Postponing the more technical discussion in the next chapter, for the moment we only claim that if debtholders believe that the firm will not issue additional debt in future, then shareholders may have the incentive to deviate from their commitment to $G(t) = 0$.

5.3.4 *Credit Spreads in the Leland Model*

The Leland model is largely used to derive equilibrium credit spreads. The credit spread (ς) is defined as the difference between the *internal rate of return* of a dollar invested in corporate bonds and the risk-free rate, where the former is obtained by assuming that the firm will never renege on its debts. Applying the general definition to the case of the Leland model, we have the following equation for ς,

$$\varsigma(y) = \frac{c + \xi(1 - p(y))}{p(y)} - r. \tag{5.3.34}$$

Credit spreads are inversely related to scaled y, as $p_y > 0$ from Eq. (5.3.22). In this regard, y^{-1} can be interpreted as a *leverage ratio*, $l(Y, F) := \frac{F}{Y} = y^{-1}$, or, being the coupon rate constant, as a proxy of the *interest coverage* $\left(\frac{cF}{Y} = cy^{-1}\right)$. Higher interest coverage or low leverage ratios reduce credit spreads, and the other way around. From a qualitative perspective, the model seems to work well, as it is natural to expect that firms with lower indebtedness ratios have also a lower default risk. However, the model is quantitatively fragile. Indeed, quantitative predictions lead to credit spreads which are low compared to those observed on the market. This is perhaps one of the major shortcomings of the Leland model, which is likely to have its roots in the hypothesis of shareholders commitment to $G(t) = 0$ (cf. Chap. 6). Rather than going through additional algebra, we provide a concrete example.

A major producer of soft drinks has a capital structure composed by ordinary shares and about 80 different senior unsecured bonds. None of them is protected by covenants, so we can calibrate the Leland model as follows. First, since we have a large number of *issues*, we can calibrate ξ to the inverse of the weighted average life of the debt capital structure, which is equal to 10.5 years.[7] Likewise, we set c equal to 2.7%, which is the average coupon rate. Second, the company has almost no cash on its balance sheet, and both the Debt-to-NOPaT and Debt-to-unlevered free cash flows ratio are close to 4.2×. This suggests to calibrate y to 23.8%. All debt is issued in US Dollars and the real risk-free rate for the same maturity is roughly 1%. Finally, we need to calibrate also the risk-neutral drift and volatility of $x(t)$. To this purpose, it is reasonable to assume that, being the soft drinks industry quite competitive, μ and σ should be similar across industry peers. Hence, we can look for an unlevered peer and obtain μ, σ from $V^E = \frac{x}{\mu - \sigma}$ and observing that σ is also the volatility of stock returns. Considering the last 5 years of market data, we can calibrate μ to -3.5% and σ to 20.4%. As a result we obtain $\gamma = 4.90$, $\frac{x_b}{F} = 0.034$.

Consider now the worst case scenario in which the recovery value is null, that is, $\theta = 1$. It is evident that, as $\frac{\partial p}{\partial \theta} < 0$, the credit spread is increasing in θ. Even with such an extreme assumption, the credit spread predicted by the Leland model is approximately zero. However, the company that we have analyzed is paying an average credit spread slightly above 40 bps. A sensitivity analysis of the calibration assumption reveals that the result obtained is quite robust, unless we consider the case of a distressed issuer. To sum up, for a safe company, the Leland model suggests that default can be considered as negligible and credit spread should be close to zero. This is perfectly logical in the model, as debt is never going to increase further. The

[7] See Leland (1998) or DeMarzo and He (2021).

problem is that firms issue additional debt over time, and shareholders may try to take advantage of incumbent debt holders in so doing. This will be actually the topic of the next chapter, and we will show that, by considering the same data of this example, we obtain an equilibrium credit spread close to the one observed in the market.

5.4 Endogenous Investment and Agency Costs of Capital Structure

In this section we introduce endogenous investment decisions. The key idea is to study the impact of agency costs of debt within the perimeter of commitment to a static debt policy, in particular one in which shareholders commit to $G(t) = 0$ forever. We will show that agency costs will add on top of bankruptcy costs in trading-off the tax benefits of debt financing. Section 5.4.1 deals with debt overhang while Sect. 5.4.2 with risk-shifting. Both models are intentionally very simple, with the action space of shareholders being quite limited. Yet, they provide an extremely clear explanation of both phenomena which remains valid even for more sophisticated models.

5.4.1 Debt Overhang

Let $K(t)$ be the firm's capital stock, which is composed by homogeneous goods that do not depreciate over time. In case of default, the total recovery value is a fraction $\theta \in [0, 1]$ of the unlevered firm value, and the absolute priority rule is applied. The firm's production function is $Y(t) = Z(t) K(t)$, where $Y(t)$ measures the firm's EbIT (operating earnings),[8] while $Z(t)$ is an exogenous GBM process that characterizes the before-tax return on invested capital,

$$dZ(t) = \mu^* Z(t)\, dt + \sigma Z(t)\, dW^{\mathbb{Q}}(t)\,. \tag{5.4.1}$$

Investment in each period is restricted with the action space $I(t) \in \{0, -kK(t)\}$, and,

$$dK(t) = I(t)\,, \tag{5.4.2}$$

In other words, shareholders can either keep the capital stock as constant or reduce it by selling a fraction $k > 0$ per unit of time. A unit of capital generates a stream of

[8] We hope that the different use of the letter Y in this section will not create confusion to the reader.

after-tax cash flows with NPV equal to $\frac{Z(t)(1-\tau)}{r-\mu^*} = \nu Z(t)$, where $\nu := \frac{1-\tau}{r-\mu^*}$, and the resale price of a unit of capital is supposed to be proportional to $\upsilon Z(t)$ through the constant $\psi < 1$. Consequently, unlevered free cash flows are equal to operating earnings plus the proceeds from divestitures, that is,

$$x(t) = Y(t)(1-\tau) - \psi \nu Z(t) I(t). \tag{5.4.3}$$

If we let $\vartheta(t) := -\frac{I(t)}{K(t)} \in \{0, k\}$, we can reformulate Eq. (5.4.3) in the following way,

$$x(t) = Y(t)(1-\tau) + \psi \nu Y(t) \vartheta(t), \tag{5.4.4}$$

and, as an application of Ito's lemma, the dynamics of operating earnings is the following,

$$\begin{aligned} dY(t) &= d[Z(t) K(t)] = -Z(t) K(t) \vartheta dt + K(t) dZ(t) = \\ &= \left[\mu^* - \vartheta(t)\right] Y(t) dt + \sigma Y(t) dW^{\mathbb{Q}}(t). \end{aligned} \tag{5.4.5}$$

Thus, the effect of assets disposal is equivalent to choose a lower drift for the firm's operating earnings. As a result, we can characterize investment decisions by considering the choice of a drift rate $\mu(t) \in \left\{\mu', \mu^*\right\}$, where $\mu' := \mu^* - k$, and writing Eq. (5.4.5) equivalently as,

$$dY(t) = \mu(t) Y(t) dt + \sigma Y(t) dW^{\mathbb{Q}}(t). \tag{5.4.6}$$

The unlevered firm never sell assets, that is, $\mu(t) = \mu^*$. To see this, it is sufficient to formulate the HJB equation for the shareholders of the unlevered firm,

$$rV^u(Y) = \max_{\mu \in \{\mu', \mu^*\}} \left\{ Y(1-\tau) + \psi \nu \left(\mu^* - \mu\right) Y + \mu Y V_Y^u(Y) + \frac{1}{2}\sigma^2 Y^2 V_{YY}^u(Y) \right\} \tag{5.4.7}$$

where $\vartheta \psi \nu Y = \psi \nu (\mu^* - \mu)$ are the proceeds from assets sales. If we derive the RHS of the previous equation with respect to μ, we obtain,

$$\frac{\partial \left(Y(1-\tau) + \psi \nu (\mu^* - \mu) Y + \mu Y V_Y^u(Y) + \frac{1}{2}\sigma^2 Y^2 V_{YY}^u(Y) \right)}{\partial \mu} = \left[V_Y^u(Y) - \psi \nu\right] Y. \tag{5.4.8}$$

Consider the strategy $\mu(t) = \mu^*$. Then, it is immediate to verify that the value of the unlevered firm would be equal to $\nu Y = \frac{1-\tau}{r-\mu^*}$. By Eq. (5.4.8), deviating to $\mu = \mu' < \mu^*$ results in an immediate loss equal to $k \nu Y$ per unit of time. Hence,

$\mu(t) = \mu^*$ is optimal for the unlevered firm's shareholders and,

$$V^u(K, Z) = \frac{1-\tau}{r-\mu^*} K = \nu K. \tag{5.4.9}$$

The economic interpretation of this result is straightforward. Since $\psi < 1$, the resale price of capital is always below its marginal value. As a result, the proceeds obtained from assets sales are not sufficient to offset the negative capital gain deriving form the expected reduction of future dividends.

Let assume now that the firm has an amount of debt equal to $F(t)$, and shareholders are for some reason able to commit to $G(t) = 0$. The shareholders' optimization problem becomes,

$$\begin{aligned} rV^E(Y, F) = \max_{\mu\in\{\mu',\mu^*\},Y_b} &\Big\{Y(1-\tau) + \tau c F - (c+\xi)F + \psi\nu\left(\mu^* - \mu\right)Y \\ &-\xi F V_F^E(y, F) + \mu Y V_Y^E(Y, F) + \frac{1}{2}\sigma^2 Y^2 V_{YY}^E(Y, F)\Big\}, \end{aligned} \tag{5.4.10}$$

where Y_b denotes the choice of the bankruptcy threshold. We guess, and verify later, that $V^E(Y, F) = FV^E\left(y = \frac{Y}{F}, 1\right) = Fv^E(y)$, so that Eq. (5.4.10) can be reformulated as a two-steps problem,

$$\begin{cases} (r+\xi)\,v^E(y|y_b) = \max_{\mu\in\{\mu',\mu^*\}}\Big\{y(1-\tau) + \tau c - (c+\xi) + \psi\nu(\mu^* - \mu)\,y \\ \qquad\qquad +\mu y v^E(y) + \frac{1}{2}\sigma^2 y^2 v_{yy}^E(y|y_b)\Big\} \\ v^E(y) = F\max_{y_b} v^E(y|y_b) \end{cases}. \tag{5.4.11}$$

Applying the same logic adopted in the unlevered case, the solution of the previous problem can be obtained from the following set of first order conditions,

$$\begin{cases} v_y^E(y) \geq \psi\nu & \mu = \mu^* \\ v_y^E(y) < \psi\nu & \mu = \mu'. \end{cases} \tag{5.4.12}$$

Basically, if the levered marginal value of capital stock is below the resale price of capital, shareholders prefer to get rid of assets and increase the current dividends flow. Namely, as the firm's profitability decreases, shareholders have the incentive to sell part of their assets at the expense of debt holders, who will obtain a lower recovery value in bankruptcy. Since $v^E(y)$ is strictly increasing in y, Eq. (5.4.12) is equivalent to determine a threshold $y_k^* > y_b$ below which shareholders prefer

μ' to μ^*, that is,

$$\mu = \mu^{**} = \begin{cases} \mu^* & y > y_k^* \\ \mu' & y \leq y_k^*. \end{cases} \tag{5.4.13}$$

In order to show that $v^E(y)$ is strictly increasing in y, it is sufficient to consider the integral form of $V^E(Y, F)$, that is,

$$V^E(Y, F) = \max_{\mu, Y_b}\left\{\mathbb{E}_t^{\mathbb{Q}}\int_0^{t_d} e^{-rs}\left[Y(1-\tau) - (c+\xi)F(s,\alpha) + \psi\nu\left(\mu^* - \mu^{**}(s)\right)Y\right]ds\right\}, \tag{5.4.14}$$

and apply the envelope theorem to Y and F.

Hence, we can formulate shareholder's problem as,

$$(r+\xi)v^E(y) = \max_{y_b, y_k \geq y_b}\left\{\frac{1}{2}y(1-\tau) + \tau c - (c+\xi) + \mathbb{I}(y \leq y_k)\psi\nu k y \right.$$
$$\left. + \mu(y)yv^E(y) + \frac{1}{2}\sigma^2 y^2 v_{yy}^E(y)\right\} \tag{5.4.15}$$

Since debtholders cannot prevent assets sales, shareholders have the incentive to capture as much as possible of debt holders recovery value. Consequently, $y_k \geq y_b$ always and we can break the optimization problem in Eq. (5.4.15) again in three components,

$$\begin{cases} rv^E\left(y|y_{k,}, y_b\right) = y(1-\tau) + \tau c - (c+\xi) + \mathbb{I}(y \leq y_k)\psi\nu k y \\ \qquad +\mu^* y v^E(y) + \frac{1}{2}\sigma^2 y^2 v_{yy}^E(y) & y > y_k \\ rv^E\left(y|y_{k,}, y_b\right) = y(1-\tau) + \tau c - (c+\xi) + \psi\nu k y \\ \qquad +\mu' y v^E(y) + \frac{1}{2}\sigma^2 y^2 v_{yy}^E(y) & y \in [y_b, y_k] \\ v^E(y) = \max_{y_b, y_k} v^E(y|y_b, y_k) \end{cases} \tag{5.4.16}$$

The solution of the two ODEs can be obtained adapting the strategy of the Leland model. Starting from the case $y \in [y_b, y_k]$, we have,

$$v^E(y|y_b \leq y \leq y_k) = \frac{(1-\tau) + \psi\nu k}{r+k-\mu^*}y - \frac{c(1-\tau)+\xi}{r+\xi}$$
$$+\left[\frac{c(1-\tau)+\xi}{r+\xi} - \frac{(1-\tau)+\psi\nu k}{r+k-\mu^*}y_b\right]\left(\frac{y}{y_b}\right)^{-\gamma_{NI}}, \tag{5.4.17}$$

where $\gamma_{NI} := \frac{\left(\mu^* - k + \xi - \frac{1}{2}\sigma^2\right) + \sqrt{\left(\mu^* - k + \xi - \frac{1}{2}\sigma^2\right)^2 + 2\sigma^2 (r+\xi)}}{\sigma^2}$. Likewise, in the region $y \in (y_k, +\infty)$, the firm is always solvent but has the option to divest as soon as y hits the threshold y_k. Hence,

$$\begin{aligned} v^E(y | y > y_k) &= \frac{(1-\tau)}{r - \mu^*} y - \frac{c(1-\tau) + \xi}{r + \xi} \left[1 - \left(\frac{y}{y_k} \right)^{-\gamma_I} \right] \\ &+ \left[v^E(y = y_k | y_b \le y \le y_k) - \frac{(1-\tau)}{r - \mu^*} y_k \right] \left(\frac{y}{y_k} \right)^{-\gamma_I}, \end{aligned} \tag{5.4.18}$$

where $\gamma_I := \frac{\left(\mu^* + \xi - \frac{1}{2}\sigma^2\right) + \sqrt{\left(\mu^* + \xi - \frac{1}{2}\sigma^2\right)^2 + 2\sigma^2 (r+\xi)}}{\sigma^2}$.

Hence, shareohlders' optimization problem eventually becomes,

$$v^E(y) = \max_{y_b, y_k} \left\{ [1 - \mathbb{I}(y \le y_k)] \, v^E(y | y > y_k) + \mathbb{I}(y \le y_k) \, v^E(y | y_b \le y \le y_k) \right\}. \tag{5.4.19}$$

Since the objective function is concave in (y_b, y_k), the optimal solution thresholds $\left(y_b^*, y_k^*\right)$ are obtained by setting $\frac{\partial w(y, y_k, y_b)}{\partial y_b} = \frac{\partial w(y, y_k, y_b)}{\partial y_k} = 0$, where $w(y, y_k, y_b) := [1 - \mathbb{I}(y \le y_k)] \, v^E(y | y > y_k) + \mathbb{I}(y \le y_k) \, v^E(y | y_b \le y \le y_k)$. Once obtained $\left(y_b^*, y_k^*\right)$, it is immediate to show that there exists an optimal static capital structure based on a trade-off between DTS and $AC + BC$. Notably, agency costs stem from the presence of assets sales for $y \le y_k^*$, that are in turn consistent with shareholders value maximization, but prevent at the same time the maximization of total claim holders value.

5.4.2 Risk-Shifting

Debt overhang is one of the possible investment distortions related to the presence of debt in the firm's capital structure. Another distortion is risk-shifting, we analyze using a setting to the one we adopted in the previous section. The only differences are the following. First, the capital stock is fixed, and, without loss of generality, we set $K(t) = 1$. Second, the drift of $Z(t)$ is equal to zero under the objective probability measure ($\mathbb{P}$), and debt is never retired, that is, $\xi = 0$. Third, shareholders have now the possibility to choose the "business risk" of the firm, by changing the diffusion coefficient of $Z(t)$. Namely, shareholders can choose $\sigma \in \{\sigma_L, \sigma_H\}$, $0 < \sigma_L < \sigma_H$, as a function of (Z, F). Consequently, under the objective probability measure, operating earnings evolve according to,

$$dY(t) = \sigma(Y(t))\,dW_t^{\mathbb{P}}. \tag{5.4.20}$$

It is important to notice that the stochastic model *must* be formulated in this case with respect to the objective probability measure ($\mathbb{P}$). In fact, changes in σ affect the "shape" of $\mathbb{Q}$. For the same reason, it is important to specify the evolution of the stochastic discount factor, which is set equal to,

$$dM(t) = -rM(t)\,dt + \eta M(t)\left[\rho\,dW^{\mathbb{P}}(t) + (1-\rho)\,dw^{\mathbb{P}}(t)\right], \tag{5.4.21}$$

where $w^{\mathbb{P}}(t)$ is a Wiener process orthogonal to $W^{\mathbb{P}}(t)$, and $\rho \in [-1, 0]$ is the correlation coefficient between $dw^{\mathbb{P}}(t)$ and $dW^{\mathbb{P}}(t)$.[9]

As in Sect. 5.4.1, our analysis starts from the unlevered case, in which shareholders solve,

$$rV^u(Y) = \max_{\sigma}\left\{Y(1-\tau) + \mathcal{A}(\sigma)\circ V^u + \mathbb{E}_t\left[\frac{dM(M)}{M}\frac{dV^u(Y)}{V^u(Y)}\right]V^u(Y)\right\}. \tag{5.4.22}$$

Applying Ito's product rule, we can easily show the validity of the following expression,

$$\mathbb{E}_t\left[\frac{dM}{M}\frac{dV^u}{V^u}\right] = \frac{V_y^u(y)}{V^u(y)}\rho\sigma(y)\,y\eta. \tag{5.4.23}$$

Thus, the HJB equation for the unlevered firm value is,

$$rV^u(Y) = \max_{\sigma\in\{\sigma_L,\sigma_H\}}\left\{Y(1-\tau) - \sigma|\rho|\eta V_y^u(Y) + \frac{1}{2}\sigma^2(Y)\,Y^2 V_{YY}^u(Y)\right\}. \tag{5.4.24}$$

We claim that $\sigma = \sigma_H$ is never optimal for the unlevered firm's shareholders. To prove this, we guess that $V^u(Y)$ is proportional to Y. As a result, the objective function of shareholders' maximization problem is equal to $Y(1-\tau) - \sigma|\rho|\eta V_y^u(Y)$, which is strictly decreasing in σ, and it is optimal for the unlevered firm's shareholders to set $\sigma = \sigma_L$ for every possible value of $Y \in \mathbb{R}^+$. This implies,

[9] With complete markets, the stochastic discount factor is proportional to the ratio between the marginal utility of future consumption to that of current consumption (cf. Sect. 1.3.2). Assuming a negative correlation coefficient is equivalent to say that earnings are positively correlated with the aggregate economic activity.

in turn, the following equation for the unlevered firm value,

$$V^{u}(Y) = \frac{Y(1-\tau)}{r + |\rho|\eta\sigma_L}. \tag{5.4.25}$$

Observing that the LHS of the Eq. (5.4.25) is proportional to Y, as originally guessed, concludes the proof of our assertion. Hence, the optimal investment policy for the unlevered firm is equivalent to minimizing its business risk. The economic intuition is straightforward. Since changing the level of risk does not affect the available growth opportunities, the lower the volatility of earnings, the lower the cost of capital. Indeed, it is immediate to show that $(r + |\rho|\eta\sigma_L)\,dt$ is the instantaneous expected return for the unlevered firm's stocks. Another way to read such a result is that a lower business risk, reflects positively on the risk-neutral growth rate, which is equal to $-\frac{1}{2}\sigma_L|\rho|\eta$.

We now consider the case in which the firm has an amount of debt equal to F, which is constant over time as $G(t) = \xi = 0$ by assumption. As in Sect. 5.4.1 we guess, and later verify, that $V(Y, F) = Fv^{E}\left(y = \frac{Y}{F}\right)$. Hence, the levered firm's shareholders solve the following optimization problem,

$$rv^{E}(y) = \max_{\sigma\in\{\sigma_L,\sigma_H\},y_b}\left\{y(1-\tau) - (1-\tau)c - \sigma|\rho|\eta y v^{E}_{y}(y) + \frac{1}{2}\sigma^{2}(y)\,y^{2}v^{E}_{yy}(y)\right\}. \tag{5.4.26}$$

We claim that $\sigma = \sigma_L$ is no longer an optimal policy. To see this, recall that such a policy is optimal if the value function is homogenous degree one in y. However, since shareholders have now the option to default, given $\sigma(Y) = \sigma_L$, the scaled equity value would be equal to,

$$\max_{y_b}\left\{\frac{1-\tau}{r+\frac{1}{2}\sigma_L|\rho|\eta}y - \frac{1-\tau}{r}c + \left[\frac{1-\tau}{r}c - \frac{1-\tau}{r+\frac{1}{2}\sigma_L|\rho|\eta}y_b\right]\left(\frac{y}{y_b}\right)^{-\gamma_L}\right\} \tag{5.4.27}$$

which is strictly convex in y, as we can use the same logic of Sect. 5.3.1 to show that $\gamma_L = \frac{-\frac{1}{2}\sigma_L^2+\sqrt{\frac{1}{2}\sigma_L^4+2\sigma_L^2 r}}{\sigma_L^2} > 0$. Hence, the policy $\sigma(Y) = \sigma_L$ is necessary inconsistent with shareholders equilibrium behavior.

Since $v(y)$ is strictly increasing in y (cf. Sect. 5.4.1), following the same steps as in the previous section, we can show that shareholders' optimal risk strategy consists in switching from σ_L to σ_H as soon as y hits a boundary y_s^*,

$$\begin{cases} \sigma = \sigma_L & y > y_s^* \\ \sigma = \sigma_H & y_b^* < y \leq y_s^*. \end{cases} \tag{5.4.28}$$

and solve for $\left(y_b^*, y_s^*\right)$. The economic message from this result, which is generally known as "risk-shifting", is quite simple. As the ratio between profitability and debt (y) worsens, holding $\sigma = \sigma_L$ it becomes less and less likely for shareholders to obtain a positive dividends stream. Consequently, shareholders may benefit from an increase in cash flows volatility, because of the positive skewness resulting from their limited liability in case of default. As a result, there are agency costs in the model, which depend in this case on higher level of business risk compared to the unlevered case when the firm is already in financial distress or close to.

5.5 Related Literature

Additional references to the use of CT methods in corporate finance can be found in Dixit (1993), Dixit and Pindyck (1994), Duffie (2010), Dumas and Luciano (2017), Stokey (2009) and Back (2017).

Merton (1973) is the first example of continuous time corporate finance model. Contrary to the Leland (1994) model, in the Merton model default can take place only at a pre-determined date, which coincides with the maturity of a single zero coupon bond issued by the firm. Besides, the default threshold is exogenously given, and corresponds to the level of x at which the value of the firm is equal to the face value of debt, as neither taxes nor bankruptcy costs were included in the analysis. Longstaff and Schwartz (1995) extended the Merton model including the presence of tax benefits of debt financing as well as bankruptcy costs and the possibility of *floating rate* debt. Nevertheless, they assumed default to occur as soon as the NPV of $x(t)$ hit financial distress or close to $F(t)$, as in the case of a positive net worth covenant. The contribution of Leland (1994) is that a similar threshold is inconsistent with shareholders' optimizing behavior, as we argued in Sect. 5.3.1.

The original Leland model features the presence of a single perpetual bond and exogenous investment decisions. Leland and Toft (1996) provides an extension to the case of finite maturity debt, while Leland (1998) incorporates agency costs of debt, focusing on the problem of risk-shifting. Hennessy (2004) considers the relation between Tobin's Q and debt overhang, within an investment model closely related to the one presented in Sect. 3.2, while Hackbarth and Mauer (2011) introduces the effect of multiple class of bonds. Instead, He (2011) analyzes the optimal contracting problem between shareholders and managers in the Leland model, and study the effects to equilibrium leverage decisions. This is an example of one analysis that does not assume, contrary to our case, the presence of governance mechanisms protecting shareholders interests.The Leland model can also be adapted to limits to outside equity injections, equity flotation costs, and the study of optimal cash hoardings. The interested reader may refer to chapters 2 and 3 in Moreno-Bromberg and Rochet (2018).

Leland (1994) based models are also known as static trade-off models or theories of the firm's capital structure. For the empirical testing of trade-off models the reader may refer to Titman and Wessels (1988), Shyam-Sunder and Myers (1999), Fama and French (2002) and Strebulaev (2007).

References

Back, K. E. (2017). *Asset pricing and portfolio choice theory* (2nd ed.). Oxford University Press.

Brennan, M. J., & Schwartz, E. S. (1984). Optimal financial policy and firm valuation. *The Journal of Finance, 39*(3), 593–607.

Cochrane, J. H. (2009). *Asset pricing*. Princeton University Press.

DeMarzo, P. M., & He, Z. (2021). Leverage dynamics without commitment. *The Journal of Finance, 73*(3), 1195–1250.

Dixit, A. K. (1993). *The art of smooth pasting*. Harwood Academic Publishers.

Dixit, A. K., & Pindyck, R. S. (1994). *Investment under uncertainty*. Princeton University Press.

Duffie, D. (2010). *Dynamic Asset Pricing Theory*. Princeton University Press.

Dumas, B., & Luciano, E. (2017). *The economics of continuous-time finance*. The MIT Press.

Fama, E. F., & French, K. R. (2002). Testing trade-off and pecking order predictions about dividends and debt. *Review of Financial Studies, 15*(1), 1–33.

Hackbarth, D., & Mauer, D. C. (2011). Optimal priority structure, capital structure, and investment. *Review of Financial Studies, 25*(3), 747–796.

He, Z. (2011). A model of dynamic compensation and capital structure. *Journal of Financial Economics, 100*(2), 351–366.

Hennessy, C. A. (2004). Tobin's q, debt overhang, and investment. *The Journal of Finance, 59*(4), 1717–1742.

Leland, H. E. (1994). Corporate debt value, bond covenants, and optimal capital structure. *The Journal of Finance, 49*(4), 1213–1252.

Leland, H. E. (1998). Agency costs, risk management, and capital structure. *The Journal of Finance, 53*(4), 1213–1243.

Leland, H. E., & Toft, K. B. (1996). Optimal capital structure, endogenous bankruptcy, and the term structure of credit spreads. *The Journal of Finance, 51*(3), 987–1019.

Longstaff, F. A., & Schwartz, E. S. (1995). A simple approach to valuing risky fixed and floating rate debt. *The Journal of Finance, 50*(3), 789–819.

Merton, R. C. (1973). Theory of rational option pricing. *The Bell Journal of Economics and Management Science, 4*(1), 141.

Moreno-Bromberg, S., & Rochet, J. C. (2018). *Continuous-time models in corporate finance*. Princeton University Press.

Shyam-Sunder, L., & Myers, S. C. (1999). Testing static tradeoff against pecking order models of capital structure. *Journal of Financial Economics, 51*(2), 219–244.

Stokey, N. L. (2009). *Economics of inaction: Stochastic control models with fixed costs*. Princeton University Press.

Strebulaev, I. A. (2007). Do tests of capital structure theory mean what they say? *The Journal of Finance, 62*(4), 1747–1787.

Titman, S., & Wessels, R. (1988). The determinants of capital structure choice. *The Journal of Finance, 43*(1), 1–19.

Chapter 6
Dynamic Capital Structure without Commitment

The static trade-off theory of capital structure is based on the unsatisfactory premise that firms do not adjust debt over time. While alternative forms of commitment could be considered, of which the target interest coverage ratio is an example, there is a clear problem of time-consistency that must be taken into account. To clarify this point, consider again the case of the Leland model, in which shareholders commit to never issue additional debt in the future. Absent legal constraints preventing shareholders to adjust debt in the future, will they maintain their commitment? As we shall see in Sect. 6.2, shareholders may have the incentive to issue additional debt as soon as they could. In general, commitment to policies that are not dynamically consistent cannot be supported in equilibrium; either bond holders would fail to incorporate shareholders incentives in their expectations, or shareholders would not take advantage of profitable opportunities. One stark implication is that commitment may be valuable for shareholders, as their future debt flexibility could result in equilibria in which they obtain a lower payoff. Albeit counterintuitive, this is an old time problem in game theory which is related to subgame perfection. As the set of achievable payoffs for each player depends on the behavior of other players, restricting ex-ante part of their (future) action space could lead to more efficient equilibria.

The problem of (lack of) commitment is not always evident, although it is pervasive in many real-life situations. To make an example, consider the case of an husband (H) and his wife (W) who are spending their last day of vacation on a very windy island. Both love windsurfing, but H prefers to read comics and sleep in the evening, while W is very active and enjoy dancing, although she does so only if H comes with her. Unfortunately, due to his limited skills with gusty winds, H has broken his board and there is no place for rent another one. The breeze is perfect and H proposes W to lend him her board, in exchange of going with her dancing in the evening. Will W accept H's bid? Sadly, W anticipates that after sailing H will have the option to say he will be tired and not feeling in the mood of going on a dance-floor. As a result, H will stay on the beach watching his wife enjoying

U. Sagliaschi, R. Savona, *Dynamical Corporate Finance*, Contributions to Finance and Accounting, https://doi.org/10.1007/978-3-030-77853-8_6

the stiff breeze, and W will spend her last vacation evening watching his husband reading comics. Notice that a similar outcome is in fact an equilibrium of the game, as both players are dynamically best responding one to the strategy of the other. However, if H could restrict his evening's actions space, both his wife and himself could improve their payoffs.

Going back to the case of shareholders and debt holders, suppose the former announce they will not issue additional debt in the future. Suppose that, if debt holders believe this announcement, shareholders would then find it optimal to issue more debt in the future. As this cannot be an equilibrium, debt holders will be willing to buy bonds only at a credit spread that protects them from the potential capital losses related to future issuances of debt. Consequently, as they are paying a larger credit spreads because of their financing flexibility, shareholders will not refrain from issuing additional debt in the future whenever it results convenient for them. Based on our previous considerations, it is reasonable to advance the hypothesis that incorporating leverage dynamics without commitment (DeMarzo & He 2020) could be a promising direction to explain the credit risk puzzle (cf. Jones et al. 1984; Chen et al. 2008). Indeed, as we discussed in Sect. 5.3.4, Leland-type models predict low credit spreads compared to those observed on corporate bonds markets. Although, this may be related to the shape of the reference yield curve, the presence of tax asymmetries or embedded optionalities in debt contracts, even more sophisticated "commitment-based" models fail to predict sufficiently large spreads (Huang & Huang 2012).

The windsurfing example suggests an important insight that will be useful here and in the following chapter. Consider H and W will go once again on vacation together. W could say to H that, if he failed to keep his promise to bring her out in the evening, she won't trust him again. Provided that H does not dislike dancing so much, he will prefer to go windsurfing and then stick to his commitment, even if tired and still tempted to read comics. This is also an equilibrium of the game, but completely different from the one described before. Indeed, the strategies played by H and W are not Markov perfect, as their equilibrium behaviors depend on an outcome (H staying in bed, W never trusting her husband again) that will be not observed in equilibrium. In general, we should expect players, unless we assume they know very well each other and can establish long-run relationships, to coordinate on much simpler conjectures and strategies. For this reason, in this chapter we shall focus on Markov Perfect Equilibria, in which shareholders and debt holders strategies depend only on *payoff-relevant* variables, which correspond to the firm's fundamentals. Later, in Sect. 7.4, we will show how the Markov Perfect Equilibrium (MPE) obtained in this chapter could be used to support other equilibria in which commitment is dynamically consistent.

The remainder of this chapter is based on DeMarzo and He (2020) (DH henceforth). For tractability, we work with the usual hypothesis of exponentially maturing *pari-passu* bonds, with equal coupon and retirement rate. As we focus on Markov Perfect Equilbria, all the results obtained must be considered necessary valid only within this class of equilibria. In other words, leverage policies that are not dynamically consistent with Markov perfect strategies may be instead supported by grim trigger strategies, consistent with *Folk theorems* in game theory. In Sect. 6.1, we discuss some preliminaries of the analysis, in particular the extreme agency conflict that manifests between shareholders and bond holders at the bankruptcy threshold. In Sect. 6.2 we present a discrete time version of DH, which clarifies the time-inconsistency problem in the Leland model and provides a first overview of the *leverage ratchet effect* (Admati et al. 2017). In Sect. 6.3 we present the original CT version of the DH model, starting from the case in which the recovery value for the firm is null. One evident consequence of the model is the presence of the leverage ratchet effect. In the unique Markov Perfect Equilibrium of the dynamic game between shareholders and debt holders, the former cannot credibly commit to retire debt in the future, and they keep issuing additional debt until the tax shield on interest expenses is fully exhausted. As it will be clear when discussing Sect. 6.1, the extension to positive recovery values is not immediate, as a consequence of an extreme form of agency conflict that arises at the bankruptcy threshold. In Sect. 6.3.5 we present a potential way to resolve this conflict. Up to Sect. 6.3, the unlevered free cash flows for the firm is considered as exogenously given. In Sect. 6.4 we introduce endogenous investment decisions, revisiting the stylized models of debt overhang and risk-shifting presented in Sects. 5.4.1 and 5.4.2, respectively. Finally, in Sect. 6.4.3 we show the effect of no-commitment on the weighted average cost of capital to the firm.

A word of caution. The theoretical results that emerge from the DH model can be seen as a bit of extreme. We should not worry too much about that though. As we argued in Chap. 5, it is in our opinion that CT models should be mostly adopted to obtain useful economic intuitions, rather than for precise quantitative calibrations. Of course, this is possible in several cases, but it is generally easier to do so with DT models.

6.1 Commitment, Time Consistency and Debt Capacity

We assume the same setting as in Chap. 5, except that shareholders can now adjust the amount of debt over time (cf. Sect. 5.1–5.2). In equilibrium, debt holders take as given the firm's debt issuance policy. Since higher future debt levels will make the existing bonds riskier, then the debt price eventually depends on shareholders' financing policy. Thus, shareholders must take into account the relationship between their financing decisions and $p(t)$. This is essentially a dynamic game, in which shareholders correctly predict the effect of leverage decisions to the proceeds (outlays, if negative) from current debt issuances (buybacks, if negative), i.e. $p(t)\,\Delta F(t)$. In this chapter we will restrict the analysis to the case of Markov Perfect Equilibria (MPE), in which the optimizing decisions of all agents in the model are function of the firm's fundamentals.[1] Although MPE are only a subset of the possible equilibria of a dynamic game, they have the heuristic property of being "simple", in the sense that equilibrium actions are based only on payoff-relevant variables.

The simplest version of the model features an exogenous unlevered free cash flows stream $x(t)$, a debt tax shield equal to $\pi(x, F)$ in each period and no recovery value in case of default, i.e. $\theta = 1$. With Markov Perfect strategies (MP), the value of equity and the price of debt can be represented as $V^E(t) = V^E(x(t), F(t))$ and $p(t) = p(x(t), F(t))$, respectively. Recall that, with Walrasian secondary financial markets, investors take as given the bond prices, while firms take as given the way in which market-clearing prices are determined (cf. Sect. 1.3.3).

As anticipated, shareholders must take into account the effect of their debt's policy $F(t)$ into the function $p(x(t), F(t))$. This is a very important aspect of the model, which has been absent in Chap. 3 and 4 as considered the debt as risk-free and its price always equal to one. In fact, with unsecured debt and no borrowing constraints, shareholders' may be enticed by the alternative of default, and, as a result, we should expect an inverse relation between $p(t)$ and $F(t)$, i.e. $p_F < 0$. Intuitively, higher debt levels increases the optimal default threshold (cf. Sect. 5.3.2) and accelerate bond holders' *loss given default*. As the recovery of value is null, debt holders will loose earlier, in expectations, the NPV of their residual coupon and principal payments.

In the basic version of the model, the role of the zero recovery value is twofold. First, debt's seniority becomes irrelevant, as, in case of default, each bond holder obtain nothing regardless her specific priority in the firm's capital structure (cf. Sect. 7.3.2). Second, with positive recovery values, the firm's capacity to borrow against its cash flows could be seriously compromised, as we show below.

Consider the case in which, at a future date t, shareholders issue an amount Δ of debt and right after, i.e. at $t + dt$, they decide to put the firm in default. Suppose that, contrary to the case in which $\theta = 0$, $R^B > 0$ is the total recovery value of debt holders. Then, despite the firm was going to be bankrupt in the blink of an eye, the issuance price of the extra-amount of debt $\Delta > 0$ would be strictly positive and equal to $\frac{R^B}{F+\Delta}$. Absent specific constraints on the payment of dividends for highly levered firms, shareholders could pay themselves an *extraordinary dividend* equal to $\frac{R^B}{F+\Delta}$ right before default, thereby expropriating the incumbent bond holders of a fraction $\frac{\Delta}{F+\Delta}$ of their recovery value. The larger Δ, the larger the value created for shareholders at the expense of incumbent bond holders is. As a result, in the limit for $\Delta \to \infty$, shareholders expropriate incumbent bond holders of their recovery value, obtaining the best outcome for themselves. By anticipating this behavior, investors will be not willing to lend their money unless the presence of some protection mechanism at the default threshold. In other words, cash flows are no

[1]For a formal definition of Markov Perfection and Markov Perfect Equilirium see Chapter 13 in Fudenberg and Tirole (1991).

longer pledgeable, that is, the firm cannot borrow against its cash flows. This in an extreme form of agency problem between shareholders and bond holders, which could be mitigated by the presence of specific contractual provisions, such as debt covenants (Gamba & Mao 2020).

6.2 A Discrete Time Model

6.2.1 The Leverage Ratchet Effect

The DH model is formulated in CT. However, it is convenient to start with a DT model, which shows that not issuing debt in the future is dynamically inconsistent with the maximization of shareholders value. The result of this analysis highlights the economic determinants of the so-called leverage ratchet effect (Admati et al. 2017).

The unlevered free cash flows process $\{x_t\}_{t\geq 0}$ is exogenously given. As shareholders can freely inject additional equity in the firm without transaction costs, we can assume without loss of generality that $L_t = 0$ for all dates $t \in \mathbb{N}$. Bonds rank *pari passu* in the firm's capital structure, and they are all senior to ordinary shares. Each bond is issued with infinite maturity and a face value of one dollar. The principal is exponentially amortized at the rate $\xi \geq 0$, and the coupon rate is equal to $c \geq 0$. We will come back at the end of this section to the case of finite maturities, and, specifically, bonds issued with maturity equal to one period (i.e. the principal of a bond issued in t due at $t+1$). At each date, the tax benefits of debt are equal to $\pi(x_t, F_t)$, where the function $\pi(\cdot, \cdot)$ satisfies the following hypothesis, $\pi(x, F), \pi_x(x, F), \pi_F(x, F) \geq 0$, while sign $[\pi_{xF}(x, F)]$ may depend on (x, F).[2] As anticipated, we focus on MPE, in which the value of equity and the price of debt depend on (x, F). Markets are complete and the firm is managed in the best interests of shareholders. Equivalently, shareholders maximize their cum-dividend equity value, that is,

$$\hat{V}^E(x_t, F_t) = \max\left\{\max_{F_{t+1}}\{x_t + \pi(x_t, F_t) + p(x_t, F_{t+1})[F_{t+1} - F_t(1-\xi)]\right.,$$
$$\left. -(\xi + c)F_t + \mathbb{E}_t\left[M_{t,t+1}\hat{V}^E(x_{t+1}, F_{t+1})\right]\right\}, 0\Big\} \tag{6.2.1}$$

where 0 corresponds to the payoff obtained in case default. Notice that $p(x_t, F_{t+1})$ is the price per dollar of debt's face value. It is also the price at which new bonds are issued, since each one comes with an initial face value equal to one dollar.

[2] In this way, we can include the presence of a maximum cap to the tax deductibility of interest expenses.

Accordingly, $[F_{t+1} - F_t(1-\xi)]$ is the change in the face value of debt, as well as the number of new bonds issued, which contribute to a new vintage in the firm's debt capital structure (DCS).

The SDF $\{M_t\}_{t\geq 0}$ is determined according to Eq. (6.2.2) below,

$$M_{t+1} = M(z_t, z_{t+1}), \tag{6.2.2}$$

where $M(\cdot,\cdot) : \mathbb{R} \times \mathbb{R} \to \mathbb{R}^+$ is a positive real valued function, while $\mathbf{z}_t$ is a vector valued stochastic process that satisfies the Markov property. Consequently, the problem in Eq. (6.2.1) can be formulated as,

$$\begin{cases} \hat{V}^E(x,F) = \max\left\{\max_F\left\{W\left(x,F,F'\right)\right\},0\right\} \\ W\left(x,F,F'\right) = x + \pi(x,F) + p\left(x,F'\right)\left[F' - F(1-\xi)\right] - (\xi + c)F \\ \qquad\qquad + \mathbb{E}_t\left[M\left(\mathbf{z},\mathbf{z}'\right)\hat{V}^E\left(x',F'\right)\right] \end{cases} . \tag{6.2.3}$$

In the continuation region $\mathcal{C} = \left\{x, F : \hat{V}^E(x,F) > 0\right\}$ we guess that $\hat{V}^E$ is differentiable, and obtain the necessary optimality conditions through the usual approach we followed in Chaps. 3 and 4,

$$\begin{cases} \frac{\partial W}{\partial F} = p(x,F) + p_F(x,F) + \mathbb{E}_t\left[M\left(\mathbf{z},\mathbf{z}'\right)\tilde{V}_F^E\left(x',F'\right)\right] = 0 & \text{FOC} \\ \frac{\partial}{\partial F}\hat{V}^E(x,F) = \left[\pi_F(x,F) - (1-\xi)\,p\left(x,F'\right) - (c+\xi)\right]\chi(x,F,\mathbf{z}) & \text{Envelope Condition,} \end{cases} \tag{6.2.4}$$

where $\chi(x,F)$ is equal to one if $(x,F) \in \mathcal{C}$, or zero. Since in case of default, debt holders recover nothing, in any MPE the price of debt satisfies the following equation,

$$p(x,F) = \mathbb{E}_t\left\{M\left(\mathbf{z},\mathbf{z}'\right)\left[(\xi + c) + p\left(x',F'\right)(1-\xi)\right]\chi\left(x',F'\right)\right\}, \tag{6.2.5}$$

where $p\left(x',F'\right)(1-\xi)$ is the market value of the remaining portion of debt conditional on $\left(x',F'\right) \in \mathcal{C}$.

If we let $\Delta_t := F_{t+1} - F_t(1-\xi)$ the amount of debt issued (bought back, if negative) in each period, we obtain the following Euler equation characterizing the unique MPE of the dynamic game between share and debt holders,

$$p_F(x_t, F_t + \Delta_t)\,\Delta_t = -\mathbb{E}_t\left\{\frac{M_{t+1}}{M_t}\pi_F(x_{t+1}, F_t + \Delta_t)\,\chi(x_{t+1}, F_t + \Delta_t)\right\}. \tag{6.2.6}$$

Since the stochastic discount factor is necessarily a strictly positive stochastic process (cf. Sect. 1.3), and $\pi_F \geq 0$, the sign of Δ_t eventually depends on that of $p_F(x_t, F_t + \Delta_t)$. A larger value of debt today increases the chance that tomorrow's cash flows will be insufficient to cover interests payments. As shareholders may not consider as convenient additional equity injection, it is reasonable to conjecture that, in equilibrium, the probability of default increases with the amount of debt outstanding and $p_F < 0$. As a result, as long as the expected marginal tax shield is positive, the firm has the incentive to issue additional debt in each period. As a result, shareholders commitment to issue no additional debt in the future is not credible in any MPE. Furthermore, the amount of debt will decrease only if $\Delta_t < \xi F_t$. Thus, in any MPE, the presence of tax deductibility of interests payments will induce firms to accumulate debt over time until the tax benefits of debt are not fully exhausted. This outcome is known as leverage ratchet effect (Admati et al. 2017). Shareholders never buyback debt in equilibrium, as this would entail a positive wealth transfer to bond holders,[3] and they keep issuing additional bonds until the marginal tax shield becomes null.

Notice that, as shareholders have the option to set $\Delta_t = 0$, the equilibrium value of equity cannot be lower than that in the case of $\Delta_t = 0$ commitment. However, the same is not necessary true for the value of the firm as a whole. To see this, notice that the price of debt must be lower compared with the case of $\Delta_t = 0$ commitment, as the probability of default is higher for each future period. Therefore, holding F_t constant, the total effect on the cum-dividend market value of the firm is, in principle, uncertain.

In the next section, we will show that, in a CT model in which shareholders adjust debt smoothly over time, all gains from trade are dissipated and the total value of the firm is strictly lower compared to the case of commitment. This result is reminiscent of the Coase conjecture for the monopolist producer of durable goods, operating with a linear technology. In our case, the firm is the monopolist of its own debt (F_{t+1}), and faces a strictly decreasing inverse demand curve $p_t = p(x_t, F_{t+1})$ from the secondary market. Anticipating future debt issuances, investors demand for a higher credit spread today. At that point, it becomes convenient for shareholders to issue additional debt, otherwise they would be paying for some unexploited financial flexibility. Debt holders' original conjecture is therefore verified, and the unique MPE of the game is dynamically inefficient. Namely, the more frequent the firm will be able to issue additional debt, the larger will be the credit spread. The price of debt will be lower and shareholders will dissipate part of their gains from trade.

Finally, an important remark is necessary for the case of finite maturity. In general, with finite maturities, each vintage of debt must be analyzed in separation. In other words, a first order condition for the optimal adjustment of each vintage's must be obtained. In this regard, suppose that the firm issues only one-period bonds. In this case, it is immediate to verify that Eq. (6.2.6) becomes,

$$p_F(x_t, F_{t+1}) F_{t+1} = -\mathbb{E}_t \left\{ \frac{M_{t+1}}{M_t} \pi_F(x_{t+1}, F_{t+1}) \chi(x_{t+1}, F_{t+1}) \right\}. \quad (6.2.7)$$

[3]Debt becomes safer and shareholders' option to default is worth less.

As a result, the optimal leverage policy is static. In other words, with maturity equal to the trading frequency of the firm, the problem of no-commitment is actually irrelevant, as current debt holders are not impacted by future debt issuances. This is a fundamental difference with the continuous time model, in which maturity does not alleviate the no-commitment issue. In other words, the typical feature of DT models whereby the company can only issue debt at a countable set of dates can be viewed as a form of commitment compared to CT models in which shareholders can adjust debt at every $t \in \mathbb{R}$.

6.2.2 The Coase Conjecture

Let us pause for a moment on the issue of dynamic capital structure models and consider the case of the monopolist producer of a durable good that does not depreciate over time. Assume that goods are produced with a linear technology, i.e. the marginal cost of production is constant (c), and there are no fixed costs. Each consumer is infinitesimal, in that she buys a quantity dF of goods. The demand schedule for the good corresponds to the highest reservation price of the pool of consumers that are willing to buy a certain quantity F. Each consumer has also a different degree of impatience, in the sense that she prefers to buy the good today rather than tomorrow.

Suppose the firm can commit to trade only at a certain date t. Then, profits maximization requires $p_t = \left[1 + p_F \frac{F}{p}\right]^{-1} c$, as we showed in Sect. 4.2.1. However, commitment is not credible. As $p_t > c$, the firm will be tempted to trade with those consumers that found p_t above their reservation price at date t. The reason is simple. As $p_t > c$, at date $t + \Delta$ the firm can set a price $p_t - \delta_{t+\Delta} > c$ and make additional profits by capturing the residual demand for its products. However, by anticipating this outcome, the more patient consumers will be no longer willing to buy the firm's good at $t = 0$, as they prefer to wait until $t + \Delta t$ benefit from the discount $\delta_{t+\Delta}$. In other words, at date t only those consumers with an impatience rate high enough to consider the future discount insufficient will be willing to accept the original price p_t.

Now, suppose that a third round of trade can occur at $t + 2\Delta$, and then a fourth at $t + 3\Delta$ and so on. The larger the number of trading rounds, the more consumers will be able to postpone their trade, if the price at each round is above the marginal cost of production and the firm has in fact the incentive to keep trading. Gul et al. (1986) shows that, as $\Delta t \to 0$ and the number of trading round diverges, the monopolist completely dissipates its market power. As a result, the same outcome of perfect competition is obtained, in which the firm makes zero profits. See also Stokey (1981) and Chapter 1 in Tirole (1988).

6.3 The Continuous Time Case

In this section we present the original version of the DH model, considering the case of an exogenous Ito diffusion process for the firm's unlevered free cash flows $x(t)$. DH provides also the extension to the case of Poisson jumps. Nevertheless, in presence of jumps it may be more convenient to adopt a DT approach directly, especially for quantitative applications. As we are going to see, the CT model entails quite extreme implications. We should view these results on a par with the MM propositions in Sect. 2.2. In other words, the models should be used to obtain useful economic intuitions and for qualitative reasoning, rather than to predict quantitatively the impact of the leverage ratchet effect on equilibrium assets prices.

6.3.1 *An Irrelevance Result*

We begin our analysis by considering a given exogenously process for $x(t)$,

$$dX(t) = \mu(X(t))\,dt + \sigma(X(t))\,dW_t^{\mathbb{Q}}, \tag{6.3.1}$$

where $\mu(\cdot)$ and $\sigma(\cdot)$ are twice continuously differentiable functions of $x(t)$. In principle, debt could be issued with a mix of a continuous process $G(t)$ and discrete issuances at a countable set of dates.[4] However, we fill focus on smooth issuance equilibria, in which debt optimally evolves as,

$$dF(t) = [G(t) - \xi F(t)]\,dt \tag{6.3.2}$$

for some adapted process $G(t)$. Notice that, in equilibrium, shareholders must find optimal to adjust debt smoothly, which means that, along the equilibrium path, it must be never profitable for them to discretely adjust debt. All other features of the model are the same as those of the DT case, namely, a zero recovery value in case of default, and a capital structure composed by ordinary shares and *pari passu* unsecured bonds with infinite maturity, contractual retirement rate $\xi \geq 0$ and coupon rate c. In term of timing convention, $F(t)$ is the amount of debt outstanding before the net adjustment $G(t) - \xi F(t)\,dt$ taking place "smoothly" during the infinitesimal interval $(t, t + dt]$. Since all cash flows are continuous, there is no need to make distinction between cum and ex-dividend value of securities (cf. Sect. 5.1).

[4]Clearly, the firm cannot issue a discrete amount of debt at each point in time, otherwise debt will be infinite.

As anticipated, we consider only equilibria that are Markov perfect. Assuming a Markovian process for the SDF $M(t)$, and a constant risk-free rate $r > 0$, we can formulate shareholders problem under the risk-neutral probability measure $\mathbb{Q}$ as,

$$rV^E(x, F) = \max_{G, x_b} \left\{ x + \pi(x, F) - (c + \xi) F + p(x, F) G + (G - \xi F) V_F^E + \mu(x) V_x^E(x, F) + \frac{\sigma(x)^2}{2} V_{xx}^E(x; F) \right\}, \tag{6.3.3}$$

where x_b is the choice of the default boundary as a function of (x, F). The problem is linear in the choice of G, which is unrestricted, i.e. $G \in \mathbb{R}$. Notice that, in order to ensure the existence of a smooth issuance equilibrium, the optimal issuance rate must be bounded ($|G| < \infty$). Consequently, in any smooth issuance equilibrium, shareholders must be indifferent to any choice of G, that is, for each possible value of (x, F) in the continuation region $\mathcal{C} := \{(x, F) \in \mathbb{R}^+ \times \mathbb{R}^+ : x > x_b(F)\}$, the following first order condition (FOC) must hold,

$$\frac{\partial}{\partial G}\left[pG + (G - \xi F) V_F^E\right] = p(x, F) + V_F^E(x, F) = 0. \tag{6.3.4}$$

This is actually a restatement of the fundamental theorem of linear programming.

Let $V^{E_0}(x, F)$ the value of equity if shareholders were able to commit $G(t) = 0$, or "in case of commitment" for short. Substituting the optimality (indifference) condition $p(x, F) = -V^E(x, F)$ in the PDE for the value of equity, we obtain the same problem that shareholders face in the case of commitment to $G(t) = 0$, that is,

$$rV^E(x, F) = \max_{x_b} \left\{ x + \pi(x, F) - (c + \xi) F - \xi F V_F^E + \mu(x) V_x^E(x, F) + \frac{\sigma(x)^2}{2} V_{xx}^E(x, F) \right\} \tag{6.3.5}$$

As a result, the optimal default threshold is the same that in the case of commitment, $V^{E_0}(x, F)$ and so does the value of equity, that is, $V^E(x, F) = V^{E_0}(x, F)$, provided that we can show the global optimality of the smooth issuance policy. This amounts to show that Eq. (6.3.4) rules out the incentive for discrete debt issuances, and as we show in Sect. 6.3.2, it is eventually equivalent to verify that $p_F < 0$ in equilibrium. For the moment, we focus on the intuition behind the irrelevance result that we have just obtained.

In equilibrium, shareholders do not gain anything from adjusting debt, and they are indifferent to any smooth issuance path. Thus, the future leverage policy is irrelevant for what concerns shareholders value. In fact, we showed that the value of equity is thus the same as if the firm committed not to issue additional debt in the future. In other words, all gains from trades are dissipated regardless the dynamics of $G(t)$. Algebraically, the argument is exactly the same as in Sect. 4.1 for the static problem of profits maximization in the case of perfect competition and a linear production technology.[5] From an economic perspective, this observation suggests an analogy with the Coase (1972) conjecture for the monopolist producer of a durable goods. Indeed, the concept is essentially the same, as the firm is monopolist of its own debt, and can trade continuously. As the price of debt must be decreasing in F in equilibrium (see Sect. 6.3.2), with Markov perfect strategies (see Sect. 7.4) shareholders are tempted to issue additional debt to take profit from the dilution of existing bond holders if they mistakenly conjectured $G(t) = 0$. A similar situation is not an equilibrium for the game, and therefore debt holders anticipate future debt issuances and demand a larger compensation (i.e. a larger credit spread) in exchange of future dilutions (i.e. capital losses). In the limit of continuous time trading, shareholders dissipates their "rents" and the price of debt is equal to the marginal cost, which is marginal reduction in the value of their future claims $\left(-V_F^E\right)$.

In short, all gains from trade are dissipated and shareholders get nothing out of their continuous adjustment in $F(t)$. This is an *irrelevance* result that should be read on a par with the MM irrelevance propositions. In reality, firms cannot adjust debt continuously and, as we move on a DT setting, we observe a strict preference for positive debt issuance rates, which means that issuing additional debt in the future is strictly enticing for shareholders, contrary to what instead is observed in the CT model presented in this section.

6.3.2 *Global Optimality and the Leverage Ratchet Effect*

We remain to show that, along the equilibrium path, which is characterized by the first order condition (FOC),

$$p(x, F) = -V_F^E(x, F), \tag{6.3.6}$$

shareholders are always worse off by considering a discrete debt adjustment, since they are indifferent to any smooth issuance process $G(t)$ when Eq. (6.3.6) is valid. In this regard, we conjecture, and verify later, that $p_F(X, F) < 0$. We can then

[5]The only equilibrium was the one in which the firm made zero profits.

compute explicitly the gain (loss, if negative), in terms of shareholders value creation (dissipation, if negative), from a discrete debt adjustment $\Delta \neq 0$ as,

$$\begin{aligned} & V^E(x, F+\Delta) + p(x, F+\Delta)\Delta - V^E(x,F) = \\ & \int_0^\Delta V^E(x, F+\delta)\,d\delta + p(x, F+\Delta)\Delta < \\ & \int_0^\Delta \left[\underbrace{V^E(x, F+\delta) + p(x, F+\delta)}_{=0,\text{ by FOC (4.3.6)}} \right] d\delta = 0 \end{aligned} \tag{6.3.7}$$

The equation allows us to conclude that, along any optimal smooth issuance path, shareholders are never better off by adjusting debt discretely. Hence, provided that $p_F < 0$, we have shown the global optimality of the smooth issuance path resulting in any MPE. In addition to that, Eq. (4.3.7) establishes that $V^E(x, F)$ is convex and $V_F^E < 0$.

The model admits a unique smooth-issuance MPE, in which the firm never actively reduced debt, that is, $G(t) \geq 0$. To prove this claim, it is sufficient to show that there exists one and only one stochastic process $G(t) \geq 0$ that is consistent with Eq. (6.3.6) and the HJB equations characterizing the equilibrium value of equity and price of debt. Given Eq. (6.3.6), $p(x, F)$ and $V^E(x, F)$ must satisfy respectively the following PDE (cf. Sect. 5.2),

$$(r+\xi)\,p = c+\xi+[G(x,F)-\xi F]\,p_F(x,F)+\mu(x)\,p_x(x,F)+\frac{\sigma(x)^2}{2}p_{xx}(x,F), \tag{6.3.8}$$

and

$$rV^E(x,F) = x+\pi(x,F)-(c+\xi)F-\xi F V_F^E+\mu(x)\,V_x^E(x,F)+\frac{\sigma(x)^2}{2}V_{xx}^E(x,F). \tag{6.3.9}$$

Thus, Eq. (6.3.6) and Eq. (6.3.8–6.3.9) consist of a system of 3 PDE that jointly determine $V^E(x, F)$, $p(x, F)$ and $G(x, F)$, subject to the boundary conditions (cf. Sect. 5.3),

$$\begin{cases} V^E(x_b, F) = 0 & R^E = 0 \\ p(x_b, F) = 0 & R^B = 0 \\ \lim_{x\to\infty} V^E(x,F) = \frac{1}{M(t)}\mathbb{E}_t \int_t^\infty M(s)\,x(s)\,ds - \frac{c(1-\tau)+\xi}{r+\xi}F & \text{Perpetual debt service} \\ \lim_{x\to\infty} p(x,F) = \frac{c(1-\tau)+\xi}{r+\xi} & \text{Vanishing default risk,} \end{cases} \tag{6.3.10}$$

where x_b is the optimal default threshold, which is the same as in case in the case of shareholders' commitment to $G(t) = 0$. Differentiating both sides of Eq. (6.3.9) with respect to F, we obtain,

$$-(r+\xi)\,p = \pi_F(x,F) - (c+\xi) - \xi F p_F + \mu(x)\,p_x(x,F) + \frac{\sigma(x)^2}{2} p_{xx}(x,F), \tag{6.3.11}$$

where we made use of Eq. (6.3.6) to substitute the partial derivatives of V^E with that of p. Adding each side of Eq. (6.3.11) to the respective sides of Eq. (6.3.8) we eventually obtain,

$$G(x,F) = -\frac{\pi_F(x,F)}{p_F(x,F)}. \tag{6.3.12}$$

Recall that, in order to ensure the global optimality of Eq. (6.3.6), we must show that $p_F < 0$. If we can show this, from Eq. (6.3.12) we have a unique smooth issuance MPE with leverage ratchet effect, that is, $G(t) > 0$. Actually, DH shows that the smooth issuance MPE is the only MPE of the game. The proof of this result is rather technical and relies on the convexity of the equity value function (see DeMarzo & He 2020).

6.3.3 *The Value of the Firm*

Suppose that $p_F < 0$, so that we can prove the existence of a unique smooth issuance MPE in which shareholders have no gain from the continuous adjustment of debt outstanding. It is easy to see that the value of the firm, $V(x,F) = V^E(x,F) + p(x,F)\,F$, is always lower than in the case of commitment. Indeed, while the value of equity is the same, the price of debt will be lower due to the presence of the term $-\pi_F(x,F)$ in Eq. (6.3.11), which corresponds to the additional compensation that bond holders require anticipating future debt issuances. Thus,

$$V(x,F) = V^E(x,F) + p(x,F)\,F < V^{E_0}(x,F) + p^0(x,F), \tag{6.3.13}$$

where $V^0(x,F)$, and $p^0(x,F)$ are the value of the firm and the price of debt, respectively, if shareholders were able to commit to $G(t) = 0$.

Moreover, by applying Eq. (5.1.13), the value of the firm can be obtained as,

$$V(t) = V(x(t), F(t)) = \underbrace{\frac{1}{M(t)}\mathbb{E}_t \int_t^{\infty} M(s)\, x(s)\, ds}_{NPV^{(x)}(x)} + \underbrace{\frac{1}{M(t)}\mathbb{E}_t \int_t^{t_d} \pi(x(s), F(s))\, ds}_{DTS(x,F)} - \underbrace{\mathbb{E}_t\left[\frac{1}{M(t)} \int_{t_d}^{\infty} M(s)\, x(s)\, ds\right]}_{BC(x,F)}, \tag{6.3.14}$$

where $t_d = \inf\left\{s > t : x(s) = x_b^*(F)\right\}$. Writing the value of the equity as,

$$V^E(x, F) = NPV^{(x)}(x) + DTS(x, F) - BC(x, F) - p(x, F)\, F, \tag{6.3.15}$$

we get the following alternative representation of Eq. (6.3.6),

$$DTS_F(x, F) - BC_F(x, F) = -p_F(x, F)\, F. \tag{6.3.16}$$

Recall that the optimal default threshold is the same as in the case of commitment, that is, the same as in the Leland model. From Sect. 5.3.2 we know that x_b is an increasing function of F. Thus, holding constant x, we can partially integrate Eq. (6.3.16) with respect to the face value of debt outstanding over the closed interval $[0, F]$,

$$\int_0^F \left[DTS_F(x, f) - BC_F(x, f)\right] df = \int_0^F p_f(x, f)\, f df. \tag{6.3.17}$$

For $F = 0$, the value of the firm is equal to the value of its equity. Since the value of the equity is the same as in the case of commitment to $G(t) = 0$, it follows that,

$$V(x, F = 0) = V^E(x, F = 0) = V^{E_0}(x, F = 0) = NPV^{(x)}(x), \tag{6.3.18}$$

where $NPV^{(x)}(x)$ is the net present value of the exogenous unlevered free cash flows process. Therefore, in equilibrium we have $DTS(x, F = 0) = BC(x, F = 0)$, and, consequently,

$$DTS(x, F) - BC(x, F) = \int_0^F p_f(x, f)\, f df < 0. \tag{6.3.19}$$

As the price of debt must be decreasing in F in any smooth issuance MPE, the value of expected bankruptcy costs (BC) more than offsets the NPV of the tax benefits of debt (DTS). In other words, the dynamic game between shareholders and debt holders results in such an aggressive leverage policy that results in the full dissipation of the debt tax shield at the firm level. Notice that, if a firm is initially unlevered (i.e. $F(0) = 0$), commitment to $G(t) = 0$ is credible as shareholders have no gain from a smooth issuance debt program. Hence, for firms that have no oustanding debt, there is always an additional MPE is which the firm remains an all-equity firm forever. This is a potential explanation for the zero leverage puzzle (Strebulaev & Yang 2013), that is, the existence of firms that do not make use of debt despite the potential tax benefits.

6.3.4 Leverage Dynamics

Another remarkable property of the model is the path dependency of *leverage ratios*, in the sense that the amount of debt oustanding is a function of past operating earnings. To prove this, we consider a specific case for the dynamics of $x(t)$, that will be useful in the next discussions (cf. Sect. 6.4).

The corporate tax rate applied to the firm's EbIT (Y) is equal to $\tau > 0$, and the total taxes paid in each period is the sum of taxes on operating earnings (τY), plus a linear tax shield applied to coupon payments, $\pi(x, F) = \tau c F$. The firm's production function is $Y(t) = Z(t)$, where $Z(t)$ is an exogenous GBM,

$$dZ(t) = \mu Z(t)\, dt + \sigma Z(t)\, dW^{\mathbb{Q}}(t), \tag{6.3.20}$$

which measures the profitability of the firm's capital stock. The latter is assumed to be fixed and equal to one. Consequently, depreciation expenses are equal to investment expenditure, and $x(t) = Y(t)(1-\tau)$.

We conjecture, and verify later, that $p_F < 0$. With this conjecture, we can obtain the value of equity and the price of debt by using the Leland model presented in Sect. 3.3, as the value of equity is the same as in the case of commitment. Indeed, we have $Y_b = \frac{\gamma}{1+\gamma}\frac{c(1-\tau)+\xi}{r+\xi}\frac{r-\mu}{1-\tau}F$, and letting $y(t) =: \frac{Y(t)}{F(t)}$, we get,

$$V^E(Y, F) = F v^E(y) = \frac{1-\tau}{r-\mu}Y - \frac{(1-\tau)c+\xi}{r+\xi}F + \left[\frac{(1-\tau)c+\xi}{r+\xi} - \frac{1-\tau}{r-\mu}Y_b^*\right]\left(\frac{y}{y_b}\right)^{-\gamma}, \tag{6.3.21}$$

where $\gamma = \frac{\left(\mu+\xi-\frac{1}{2}\sigma^2\right)+\sqrt{\left(\mu+\xi-\frac{1}{2}\sigma^2\right)^2+2\sigma^2(r+\xi)}}{\sigma^2}$ and $y_b = \frac{\gamma}{1+\gamma}\frac{c(1-\tau)+\xi}{r+\xi}\frac{r-\mu}{1-\tau}$. The price of debt is obtained from Eq. (6.3.6), and it is equal to,

$$p(Y, F) = p(y) = \underbrace{\frac{c+\xi}{r+\xi}\left[1-\left(\frac{y}{y_b}\right)^{-\gamma}\right]}_{p^0(Y,F):\text{price of debt if } G(t)=0} - \underbrace{\frac{\tau c}{r+\xi}\left[1-\left(\frac{y}{y_b}\right)^{-\gamma}\right]}_{DTS^0(Y,F):\text{NPV tax shield on interests if } G(t)=0}. \tag{6.3.22}$$

From Eq. (6.3.22) we can then conclude that $p_F < 0$, thereby confirming the conjecture (we have found a Markov Perfect Equilibrium of the game).

Notice that, contrary to the case of commitment, even firms with a low leverage ratio, $l(t) := \frac{F(t)}{Y(t)} = \frac{1}{y(t)}$, are paying significant credit spreads. The model thus provides an equilibrium explanation for the credit risk puzzle observed in the market. Putting together, Eq. (6.3.21–6.3.22) allows to obtain the value of the firm,

$$V(Y, F) = \frac{1-\tau}{r-\mu} Y - \frac{1-\tau}{r-\mu} Y \left(\frac{Y}{Y_b^*} \right)^{-\gamma}, \tag{6.3.23}$$

With GBM cash flows, the value of the firm is equal to NPV of the unlevered free cash flows, $\frac{1-\tau}{r-\mu} Y$, minus the expected bankruptcy costs in the case of commitment to $G(t) = 0$. The equilibrium rate of debt's issuance is obtained using Eq. (6.3.12),

$$G(Y, F) = -\frac{\tau c}{p_F(Y, F)} = \frac{\tau c}{\frac{c(1-\tau)+\xi}{r+\xi} \frac{\partial}{\partial F} \left(\frac{Y_b^*}{Y} \right)^{\gamma}} = \frac{\tau c}{\gamma \frac{c(1-\tau)+\xi}{r+\xi}} F \left(\frac{y}{y_b^*} \right)^{\gamma} = F g(y), \tag{6.3.24}$$

with $g(y) := \frac{\tau c}{\gamma \frac{c(1-\tau)+\xi}{r+\xi}} \left(\frac{y}{y_b} \right)^{-\gamma}$.

We define *target leverage* the positive real number $\hat{l} < \frac{1}{y_b}$ that solves the following equation,

$$\xi = g\left(\frac{1}{\hat{l}} \right), \tag{6.3.25}$$

that is,

$$\hat{l} = \left[\frac{\tau c}{\xi \gamma \frac{c(1-\tau)+\xi}{r+\xi}} \right]^{\frac{1}{\gamma}} \left(\frac{1}{y_b} \right). \tag{6.3.26}$$

The interpretation of $\hat{l}$ is straightforward. If $l(t) = \hat{l}$, the amount of new debt issued during the next infinitesimal time interval, $G(t)\,dt$, is equal to the amount retired, $\xi F(t)\,dt$. Holding Y constant, the firm leverage ratio will thus remain unchanged. Likewise, we should expect $l(t)$ to fall when $y(t)$ is above $\hat{l}^{-1}$ and the other way around. To prove this, we can show that $F(t)$ is a function of past operating earnings, as claimed at the beginning of this section. We first obtain the instantaneous equilibrium rate of change in debt's face value,

$$\begin{aligned} \frac{dF(t)}{F(t)} &= \frac{\tau c}{\gamma \frac{c(1-\tau)+\xi}{r+\xi}} \left(\frac{y(t)}{y_b^*} \right)^{\gamma} - \xi = \\ \xi \left[\hat{l} y(t) \right]^{\gamma} - \xi &= \frac{1}{\gamma} \frac{\gamma \xi \left[\hat{l} Y(t) \right]^{\gamma} - \gamma \xi F(t)^{\gamma}}{F(t)^{\gamma}}. \end{aligned} \tag{6.3.27}$$

Then, we can formulate the differential,

$$F(t+dt)^{\gamma} - F(t)^{\gamma} = \gamma\xi\left[\hat{l}Y(t)\right]^{\gamma} dt - \gamma\xi F(t)^{\gamma}, \tag{6.3.28}$$

from which we eventually obtain,

$$F(t) = \left[F(0)\, e^{-\gamma\xi t} + \hat{l}^{\gamma}\int_0^t e^{-\gamma\xi(t-s)} Y(s)^{\gamma}\, ds\right]^{\frac{1}{\gamma}}. \tag{6.3.29}$$

Thus, at each point in time the amount of debt outstanding is a sort of weighted moving average of past operating earnings. From Eq. (6.3.29) we can establish the convergence in mean γ of $l(t)$ to $\hat{l}$ for the non-degenerate case $\hat{l} < \frac{1}{y_b}$,

$$\lim_{t\to\infty}\mathbb{E}_t\left\{\left[\frac{F(t)}{Y(t)}\right]^{\gamma}\right\} = \hat{l}^{\gamma}\lim_{t\to\infty}\mathbb{E}_t\left\{\int_0^t e^{-\gamma\xi(t-s)}\left[\frac{Y(s)}{Y(t)}\right]^{\gamma} ds\right\} = \hat{l}^{\gamma}, \tag{6.3.30}$$

which is equivalent to say that $l(t)$ tends to fall when $y(t)$ is above $\hat{l}$ and the other way around. Put differently, although firms never actively reduce debt, when the leverage ratio is very high, $G(t) < \xi F(t)$ and leverage slowly revert to target ratio $\hat{l}$. Hence, we have an equilibrium foundation of the *partial leverage adjustment* models, which are used in many empirical studies (cf. Jalilvand & Harris 1984; Leary & Roberts 2005; Fama and French 2002).

6.3.5 Positive Recovery Values

So far we have assumed that the value of the firm jumps down to zero when default occurs. Here, we follow DH and discuss a potential mechanism to introduce positive recovery values while resolving the extreme agency conflict we discussed in Sect. 6.1.

With *pari passu* bonds and positive recovery values, in Sect. 6.1 we argued that shareholders find optimal to issue a large (unbounded) amount of debt right before $x(t)$ hits the optimal default threshold x_b. In this way they can expropriate incumbent bond holders of their recovery value. In a more realistic setting, debt holders, by anticipating this possibility, will try to take preemptive legal actions to avoid this unpleasant outcome. Shareholders, by anticipating bond holders behavior, will try to sell some of the firm's assets or take other actions in order to obtain a positive payoff even in case of default. This conflict is detrimental for both parties, and could be solved through a restructuring procedure in which the liquidation of the firm is avoided, and both stockholders and debt holders obtain a positive recovery value. A precise micro-foundation of this process should require an extensive discussion. Following DH, we adopt a quasi-reduced form approach, we present using the same example as the one discussed in the previous section.

At Y_b shareholders can choose between different restructuring regimes $j \in J$, where J is an exogenous set of all the *take-it-or-leave* it offers that debt holders are willing to accept.[6] Each restructuring regime j consists in a debt-for-equity swap, in which the company continues to exist as an all-equity firm for the time being. Namely, all assets, including intangibles and growth options, even if not modelled explicitly, are put in a newly constituted company (NewCo). However, if we let t_d the restructuring date, only a fraction $\beta_j \in (0, 1)$ of the NPV of $x\,(t_d + s)$ is recovered, as a consequence of direct restructuring costs and other potential inefficiencies. Let Y_b the (optimal) restructuring threshold. Given the (optimal) choice of Y_b, shareholders will propose to debt holders the restructuring regime maximizing their recovery value,

$$\max_{j \in J} \alpha_j \left(1 - \beta_j\right) \nu Y_b, \tag{6.3.31}$$

where $\nu := \frac{1-\tau}{r-\mu}$ is the Enterprise Value-to-EbIT multiple in absence of debt while α_j is the recovery rate of shareholders for a given restructuring regime j. Since the set of regimes is independent from Y_b, the previous problem is to choose j to maximize $\alpha_j \left(1 - \beta_j\right)$.

The extension of the model is straightforward. Shareholders' problem is unchanged,

$$\begin{aligned} rV^E(x, F) = \max_{Y_b, G} \Big\{ & x + \tau c F - (c + \xi) F + p(Y, F) G + [G - \xi F] V_F^E \\ & + \mu x V_x^E(x, F) + \frac{\sigma^2 x^2}{2} V_{xx}^E(x, F) \Big\} \end{aligned} \tag{6.3.32}$$

except for the boundary condition at the restructuring threshold Y_b. The first order condition characterizing the smooth issuance equilibrium is again $p(Y, F) = -V_F^E(Y, F)$, and, consequently, the value of equity is the same as if the firm committed to $G(t) = 0$, provided that $p_F < 0$ in equilibrium. Nevertheless, shareholders obtain a higher equity valuation relative to the one computed in Sect. 6.3.4, thanks to the positive recovery value obtained in the restructuring process. The HJB equation for rational debt pricing is the same as before,

$$(r + \xi) p(Y, F) = c(1 - \tau - \tau c) + \xi - \xi F p_F(Y, F) + \mu Y p_Y(Y, F) + \frac{\sigma^2 x^2}{2} p_{FF}(Y, F) \tag{6.3.33}$$

[6]In order to reach an agreement with debt holders, shareholders' offer must be incentive compatible. In other words, restructuring should be at least profitable as the alternative of default for bond holders.

and, consequently, the equilibrium rate of debt's issuance is again equal to,

$$G(Y, F) = -\frac{\tau c}{p_F(Y, F)}. \tag{6.3.34}$$

Using the solution technique developed for the Leland model in Chap. 5, the value of equity and the price for debt are equal to,

$$\begin{aligned} V^E(Y, F) = V^{E_0}(Y, F) = & \underbrace{\frac{1-\tau}{r-\mu} Y - \frac{(1-\tau)c+\xi}{r+\xi} F}_{\text{NPV of dividends if the firm never defaults}} + \\ & \underbrace{\left[\frac{(1-\tau)c+\xi}{r+\xi} - \frac{1-\tau}{r-\mu} Y_b \left(1-\alpha_j\right)\left(1-\beta_j\right)\right]\left(\frac{Y}{Y_b}\right)^{-\gamma}}_{\text{Value of the restructuring option}} \end{aligned} \tag{6.3.35}$$

and,

$$\begin{aligned} p(Y, F) = & \underbrace{\frac{c+\xi}{r+\xi}\left[1-\left(\frac{Y}{Y_b^*}\right)^{-\gamma}\right]}_{p^0(Y,F)\text{:price of debt if } G=0} - \underbrace{\frac{\tau c}{r+\xi}\left[1-\left(\frac{Y}{Y_b^*}\right)^{-\gamma}\right]}_{DTS^0(Y,F)\text{:NPV tax shield on interests if } G=0} \\ & + \underbrace{\frac{1-\tau}{r-\mu} Y_b^* \left(1-\alpha_{j^*}\right)\beta_{j^*}\left(\frac{Y}{Y_b^*}\right)^{-\gamma}}_{\text{Expected Recovery Value}} \end{aligned} \tag{6.3.36}$$

from which we eventually verify that $p_F < 0$. Consequently, all the conclusions in Sect. 6.3.4 regarding the evolution of leverage remain valid. Furthermore, the total value of the firm continues to be lower than in the case of commitment, and strictly lower than the NPV of the firm's unlevered free cash flows,

$$\begin{aligned} V(Y, F) = V^E(Y, F) + p(Y, F) F = \\ \frac{1-\tau}{r-\mu} Y - \frac{1-\tau}{r-\mu}\left(1-\alpha_j\right) Y \left(\frac{Y}{Y_b}\right)^{-\gamma}. \end{aligned} \tag{6.3.37}$$

To summarize, when shareholders have the opportunity to adjust their leverage continuously, the following results hold for what concerns the unique MPE of the model:

(1) shareholders are indifferent to any future debt issuance policy;
(2) the value of equity is the same as if the firm committed to $G(t) = 0$;
(3) as long as $\pi_F > 0$, the firm issues additional debt;
(4) the price of debt is lower compared to the case of commitment to $G(t) = 0$;

(5) credit spreads may be large also for firms having low leverage ratio;
(6) the total value of the firm is strictly lower than in the case of commitment to $G(t) = 0$;
(7) leverage is a function of past earnings and, absent default, we should observe a reversion towards a "target" ratio.

6.4 Endogenous Investment and The Cost of Capital

In this section we extend the CT model to include endogenous investment decisions. In Sect. 6.4.1 we focus on debt overhang, while Sect. 6.4.2 inspects the case of risk-shifting. In other words, we repeat the analysis of Sect. 5.4.1–5.4.2 in absence of the firm's commitment to $G(t) = 0$. Most of the required algebraic steps were already covered, so we can now focus on the issue of no-commitment. Finally, in Sect. 6.4.3 we illustrate the effects of no-commitment on the firm cost of capital.

6.4.1 Debt Overhang

The framework is the same as in Sect. 5.4.1, except that shareholders can now adjust debt according to Eq. (6.3.2). The firm's operating earnings (EbIT) are equal to $Y(t) = Z(t)K(t)$, where $Z(t)$ is an exogenous GBM process,

$$dZ(t) = \mu^* Z(t)\,dt + \sigma Z(t)\,dW^{\mathbb{Q}}(t). \tag{6.4.1}$$

The capital stocks does not depreciate over time, $dK(t) = I(t)$, and investments are either null or negative, i.e. $I(t) \in \{0, -kK(t)\}$, $k > 0$. The resale price of the capital stock is equal to $\psi\nu Z(t)$, with $\nu = \frac{1-\tau}{r-\mu^*}$ and $\psi < 1$. The application of Ito's lemma allows to reformulate the problem in terms of risk-neutral drift $\mu(t) \in \left\{\mu' = \mu^* - k, \mu^*\right\}$, as

$$dY_t = \mu(t) Y(t)\,dt + \sigma Y(t)\,dW^{\mathbb{Q}}(t). \tag{6.4.2}$$

On the one hand, the unlevered firm never choose to reduce its capital stock, and $V^u(Y) = \nu Y$. On the other, subject to shareholders commitment to $G(t) = 0$,

$$\begin{aligned} rV^E(Y, F) = & \max_{\mu\in\{\mu',\mu^*\},Y_b} \Big\{Y(1-\tau) + \tau cF - (c+\xi)F + \psi\nu\left(\mu^* - \mu\right)Y \\ & -\xi F V_F^E(y, F) + \mu Y V_Y^E(Y, F) + \frac{1}{2}\sigma^2 Y^2 V_{YY}^E(Y, F)\Big\}, \end{aligned} \tag{6.4.3}$$

there exists an optimal boundary $Y_k > Y_b$ such that for $Y \in (Y_b, Y_k]$ shareholders prefer $\mu' = \mu^* - k$ to μ^*. The growth rate μ^* is instead optimal for $Y \in (Y_k, +\infty)$.

We now introduce the possibility that shareholders adjust debt smoothly over time. Considering again a smooth issuance MPE, we can formulate the shareholders problem as,

$$rV^E(Y,F) = \max_{\mu\in\{\mu',\mu^*\},G,Y_b} \{Y(1-\tau) + \tau cF - (c+\xi)F + p(Y,F)G + \psi\nu(\mu^*-\mu)Y$$

$$+[G - \xi F]V_F^E(y,F) + \mu Y V_Y^E(Y,F) + \frac{1}{2}\sigma^2Y^2V_{YY}^E(Y,F)\Big\}, \tag{6.4.4}$$

which implies the same first order condition $p(Y,F) = -V^E(Y,F)$ for G. As a result, shareholders are indifferent to the choice of G. Substituting Eq. (6.3.6) in Eq. (6.4.4), we obtain the same problem as in the case of commitment,

$$rV^E(Y,F) = \max_{\mu\in\{\mu',\mu^*\},Y_b} \{Y(1-\tau) + \tau cF - (c+\xi)F + \psi\nu(\mu^*-\mu)Y$$

$$-\xi F V_F^E(y,F) + \mu Y V_Y^E(Y,F) + \frac{1}{2}\sigma^2Y^2V_{YY}^E(Y,F)\Big\}, \tag{6.4.5}$$

and consequently the optimal threshold for Y_k at which shareholders cut investments is the same as in the case of commitment. Proceeding as in Sect. 6.3.1–6.3.2, we can then check the global optimality of a smooth issuance policy, given the conjecture $p_F < 0$, and then verify that the equilibrium price of debt is effectively decreasing in F. Thus, regardless the presence of the leverage ratchet effect, we obtain the same investment policy and equity market value as in the case of commitment. In other words, the Leland model remains a convenient tool to solve models without commitment.

6.4.2 *Risk Shifting*

Extending the risk-shifting model presented in Sect. 5.4.2 is also straightforward. We briefly recall the salient features of the model. The capital stock is fixed, and equal to one without loss of generality. Rather than choosing the investment rate, shareholders engage in *assets substitution*; operating earnings evolves according to,

$$dY(t) = \sigma(Y(t))\,dW_t^{\mathbb{P}}, \tag{6.4.6}$$

where $\sigma(Y) \in \{\sigma_L, \sigma_H\}$, $0 < \sigma_L < \sigma_H$ denotes the level of business risk decided by the firm's stockholders. The restructuring process in case of default is the same as in the previous section. The asset pricing equation for the value of equity is formulated with respect to the objective probability measure $\mathbb{P}$. The SDF of the model economy evolves as,

$$dM(t) = -rM(t)\,dt + \eta M(t)\left[\rho dW^{\mathbb{P}}(t) + (1-\rho)\,dw^{\mathbb{P}}(t)\right], \tag{6.4.7}$$

where $w^{\mathbb{P}}(t)$ is a Wiener process orthogonal to $W_t^{\mathbb{P}}$, and $\rho < 0$.

As shown in Sect. 5.4.2, the unlevered firm solves the problem,

$$rV^u(Y) = \max_{\sigma\in\{\sigma_L,\sigma_H\}} \left\{Y(1-\tau) - \sigma|\rho|\eta Y V_y^u(Y) + \frac{1}{2}\sigma^2 Y^2 V_{YY}^u(Y)\right\}, \tag{6.4.8}$$

which always results in the choice of the lowest level of volatility, i.e. $\sigma = \sigma_L$, in order to minimize the cost of capital. Therefore, $V^u(Y) = \frac{Y(1-\tau)}{r+|\rho|\eta\sigma_L}$. On the other hand, given the commitment $G(t) = 0$, in the presence of debt, shareholders find optimal to increase risk when the scaled operating earnings $\left(y = \frac{Y}{F}\right)$ fall below a certain threshold $y_s > y_b$,

$$\begin{cases} \sigma = \sigma_L & y > y^s \\ \sigma = \sigma_H & y_b < y \le y_s, \end{cases} \tag{6.4.9}$$

where y_b is the scaled restructuring threshold.

We now extend the model to take into account the effects of continuous leverage adjustments, focusing on smooth-issuance MPE. Since the evolution of debt is locally deterministic, $dF(t) = [G(t) - \xi F(t)]\,dt$, the characteristic operator for the expected change in the levered firm's equity value is equal to,

$$\mathcal{A}\circ V^E(Y,F) = [G - \xi F]\,V_F^E(Y,F) - \sigma|\rho|\eta Y V_Y^E(Y,F) + \frac{1}{2}\sigma^2(Y)\,Y^2 V_{YY}^E(Y,F). \tag{6.4.10}$$

Therefore, in the no-commitment case, shareholders problem can be formulated as,

$$rV^E(Y,F) = \max_{G,\sigma\in\{\sigma_L,\sigma_H\}} \{Y(1-\tau) - (1-\tau)cF + pG - \xi F +$$

$$[G - \xi F]\,V_F^E(Y,F) - \sigma|\rho|\eta Y V_Y^E(Y,F) + \frac{1}{2}\sigma^2(Y)\,Y^2 V_{YY}^E(Y,F)\Big\}. \tag{6.4.11}$$

The equilibrium condition for G is the same of Eq. (6.3.6), that is, $p(Y,F) = -V_F^E(Y,F)$. Thus, proceeding as in Sect. 6.4.1, we eventually conclude that the value of equity is the same as in the case of commitment, provided that the conjecture $p_F < 0$ is verified. Combining the methodologies developed in Sect. 5.4.1–5.4.2, and 6.3.3, it is immediate to obtain the price of debt and show that, in equilibrium, $p_F < 0$. Furthermore, the value of the firm is equal to that in case of commitment, net of the debt tax shield component, namely,

$$V(Y,F) = \underbrace{\frac{Y(1-\tau)}{r+|\rho|\eta\sigma_L}}_{\text{Unlevered firm value}} - \underbrace{\left[\frac{(1-\tau)}{r+|\rho|\eta\sigma_L} - \frac{(1-\tau)}{r+|\rho|\eta\sigma_H}\right] Y_s \left(\frac{Y}{Y_s}\right)^{-\gamma_1}}_{\text{Agency costs in the case of commitment to } G=0} - \underbrace{\frac{(1-\tau)}{r+|\rho|\eta\sigma_H}(1-\alpha_j) Y_b \left(\frac{Y}{Y_k}\right)^{-\gamma_I}\left(\frac{Y_k}{Y_b}\right)^{-\gamma_{NI}}}_{\text{Bankruptcy costs in the case of commitment to } G=0} \tag{6.4.12}$$

where $\gamma_1 = \frac{\left(\mu+\xi-\frac{1}{2}\sigma_L^2\right)+\sqrt{\left(\mu+\xi-\frac{1}{2}\sigma_L^2\right)^2+2\sigma_L^2(r+\xi)}}{\sigma_L^2}$ and $\gamma_2 = \frac{\left(\mu+\xi-\frac{1}{2}\sigma_H^2\right)+\sqrt{\left(\mu+\xi-\frac{1}{2}\sigma_H^2\right)^2+2\sigma_H^2(r+\xi)}}{\sigma_H^2}$ respectively. As in the previous section, we observe the same investment policy as in the case of commitment.

6.4.3 The Weighted Average Cost of Capital

Recall the example of Sect. 5.3.4, in which we showed the inability of the Leland model to predict a credit spread greater than zero for a financially healthy company active in the soft drink industry. If we repeat the analysis with the same data, the application of Eq. (6.3.22) provides a credit spread close to 0.5%, regardless the specific value for the recovery rate θ. The model's prediction is consistent with what we observe for the specific company that we analyzed in this example, which pays an average credit spread, relative to the treasury curve, equal to 0.40%. Thus, it is reasonable to expect that shareholders' lack of commitment ultimately results in a higher cost of capital for the firm. In other words, differently from the case of Chaps. 3 and 4, the presence of debt does not reduce the weighted average cost of capital (WACC). Intuitively, we can prove this result by using the same setting described in the previous section.

Under the objective probability measure $\mathbb{P}$, shareholders solve the following dynamic program,

$$rV^E(Y,F) = \max_{\sigma\in\{\sigma_L,\sigma_H\},G,Y_b}\Big\{Y(1-\tau)-(1-\tau)cF+pG+(G-\xi F)\left[V_F^E(Y,F)-1\right]$$
$$-\sigma|\rho|\eta V_Y^E(Y,F)+\frac{1}{2}\sigma^2(Y)Y^2V_{YY}^E(Y,F)\Big\}. \tag{6.4.13}$$

The optimality condition for G is $p = -V_F^E$, which makes irrelevant the choice of G in equilibrium for shareholders. Given the choice of the optimal default and risk-shifting thresholds, the following PDE can be formulated,

$$k^uV^E = Y(1-\tau)-c(1-\tau)-\xi F-\xi FV_F^E+[\mu+(\sigma_L-\sigma)|\rho|\eta]YV_Y^u+\frac{\sigma^2Y^2}{2}V_{YY}^u, \tag{6.4.14}$$

where $k^u := r+\sigma_L|\rho|\eta$ is the expected return of the unlevered firm. As we showed in the previous section, the value of the firm is strictly lower than the unlevered firm value,

$$V(Y,F) < V^u(Y), \tag{6.4.15}$$

due to the presence of agency and bankruptcy costs. The levered firm's value satisfies the HJB equation,

$$r+\sigma|\rho|\eta V_Y(Y,F) = \frac{1}{V(Y,F)}\Big[Y(1-\tau)-\xi FV_F(Y,F)$$
$$+\mu YV_Y(Y,F)+\frac{1}{2}\sigma^2(Y)Y^2V_{YY}(Y,F)\Big], \tag{6.4.16}$$

which is equivalent to say that the value of the firm is the same that would be obtained if: (i) there was no tax shield on interests expenses, and (ii) shareholders committed to $G(t) = 0$. Notably, the term $rV(Y,F)+\sigma|\rho|\eta V_Y(Y,F)$ is the expected return for the levered firm. Since in CT the WACC of the firm is defined as a stochastic process $wacc(t)$ which solves, in analogy with the DT case (see Sect. 3.1.3),

$$wacc(Y(t),F(t))V(Y(t),F(t))dt = \underbrace{Y(1-\tau)dt}_{\text{Unlevered Free Cash Flows}} + \underbrace{\mathbb{E}_t[dV(Y(t),F(t))]}_{\text{Expected Capital Gain}}. \tag{6.4.17}$$

In the unique MPE of the model, the funding cost advantage of debt is completely dissipated, namely, holding the operating earnings (Y) constant, the levered firms "pays" a higher WACC compared to its unlevered benchmark. To prove this, we start expressing Eq. (6.4.15) as,

$$\frac{Y(1-\tau)}{V^u(Y)} < \frac{Y(1-\tau)}{V(Y,F)}, \tag{6.4.18}$$

obtaining eventually,

$$wacc(Y, F>0) - k^u > \frac{1}{V(Y,F)}\left[\underbrace{-\xi F V_F(Y,F) + \mu Y V_Y(Y,F) + \frac{\sigma^*(Y,F)^2 Y^2}{2} V_{YY}(Y,F)}_{\text{Expected Capital Gain: Levered Firm}}\right]$$
$$-\frac{1}{V^u(Y,F)}\left[\underbrace{\mu Y V_Y^u(Y) + \frac{\sigma_L^2 Y}{2} V_{YY}^u(Y)}_{\text{Expected Capital Gain: Unlevered Firm}}\right], \tag{6.4.19}$$

as $wacc(Y, F=0) = k^u$. In fact, at $F=0$ we have $V = V^u$.

From Eq. (6.4.12) it is easy to check that,

$$\mu Y V_Y(Y,F) + \frac{\sigma^*(Y,F)^2 Y}{2} V_{YY}(Y,F) \geq \mu Y V_Y^u(Y) + \frac{\sigma_L^2 Y}{2} V_{YY}^u(Y). \tag{6.4.20}$$

The economic intuition is that a small increase in operating earnings has a larger impact to the levered firm's value, since it reduces the deadweight cost of future debt service. Furthermore $V_F(Y,F) < 0$, and we can conclude that,

$$wacc(Y, F>0) - k^u > -\frac{\xi F}{V(Y,F)} V_F(Y,F) > 0, \tag{6.4.21}$$

that is,

$$wacc(Y, F>0) > k^u. \tag{6.4.22}$$

This result is actually a restatement of the tax shield's dissipation in the MPE of the game only. As the presence of debt reduces the total firm value below its unlevered benchmark, unlevered free cash flows must be discounted at a higher rate to guarantee consistency with equilibrium prices.

6.5 Related Literature

Earlier models of dynamic capital structure decisions are Fischer et al. (1989), Leland (1998), Goldstein et al. (2001) and Titman and Tsyplakov (2007). These models share the common feature of exogenous frictions, such as debt covenants or transaction costs, that mitigate the no-commitment problem that arises in DeMarzo and He (2020). For instance, in Goldstein et al. (2001), the firm must retire all the existing debt at par value before issuing additional bonds. Dangl and Zechner (2004) is an application of this type of models on structural credit risk analysis. Another example of dynamic capital structure models with exogenous frictions is Abel (2017), where the presence of an exogenous borrowing constraint generates a regime switching between states in which the trade-off theory holds, and states in which the firm is credit constrained. Differently from the models of Chaps. 3 and 4, the borrowing constraint is applied to the issuance of unsecured debt and does not protect debt holder from losses in case of default.

The dynamic capital structure model presented in Chap. 3 is time-consistent, but, as a consequence of the presence of collateral, the price of debt is not sensitive to future leverage decisions, even for the case of longer maturities (cf. Sect. 7.1). DeMarzo (2019) shows that collateral is a *commitment device*, as it restricts the set of leverage policies that shareholders can pursue over time. The literature on dynamic capital structure without commitment is indeed evolving and is stimulating a vivid academic debate. Examples are Benzoni et al. (2019), which incorporates the presence of transaction costs, or Malenko and Tsoy (2020), in which non-Markov Perfect Equilibria are considered (cf. Sect. 7.4). Both papers argue that DH's results are too restrictive, in that small frictions or other types of equilibria can largely mitigate the leverage ratchet effect of the frictionless MPE framework. Gamba and Saretto (2018) considers the application of quantitative discrete time model to analyze the agency component of credit spread, while Xiang (2019) analyzes the time-consistency of financial debt covenants (cf. Sect. 7.2). In this regard, Gamba and Mao (2020) consider a MPE in which shareholders and incumbent debt holders can continuously renegotiate the structure of covenants. Johnson et al. (2018) extend the basic DH model in a general equilibrium framework, and analyze the value of commitment in terms of social welfare.

We have focused on smooth-issuance equilibrium strategies, without discussing the possibility of non-smooth equilibria in which debt is adjusted rarely. DeMarzo and He (2020) shows that non-smooth MPE can be ruled out as a consequence of the convexity of the equity value function. The proof is rather technical and articulated, and the interested reader may refer to Appendix C of their paper. In other words, the unique smooth issuance MPE is also the unique MPE of the continuous time model presented is Sect. 5.3.

The DH model provides an appealing explanation of the credit spread puzzle (Jones et al. 1984; Chen et al. 2008), as the anticipation of future debt issuances increases the cost of debt of high grade borrowers (cf. Gamba & Saretto 2018). The theory presented in this chapter provides also an equilibrium foundation of the *partial adjustment models* often adopted in empirical studies, of which notable examples are Jalilvand and Harris (1984), Leary and Roberts (2005). The model very well explains also the zero leverage puzzle (Strebulaev & Yang 2013). A direct empirical application of the DH model is in Chaderina et al. (2020), in which the authors analyze the effects of no-commitment on the term structure of levered equity risk premia.

References

Abel, A. B. (2017). Optimal debt and profitability in the trade-off theory. *The Journal of Finance, 73*(1), 95–143.

Admati, A. R., DeMarzo, P. M., Hellwig, M. F., & Pfleiderer, P. (2017). The leverage ratchet effect. *The Journal of Finance, 73*(1), 145–198.

Benzoni, L., Garlappi, L., Goldstein, R. S., & Ying, C. (2019). Optimal debt dynamics, issuance costs, and commitment. *SSRN Electronic Journal.*

Chaderina, M., Weiss, P., & Zechner, J. (2020). The maturity premium. *SSRN Electronic Journal.*

Chen, L., Collin-Dufresne, P., & Goldstein, R. S. (2008). On the relation between the credit spread puzzle and the equity premium puzzle. *Review of Financial Studies, 22*(9), 3367–3409.

Coase, R. H. (1972). Durability and monopoly. *The Journal of Law and Economics, 15*(1), 143–149.

Dangl, T., & Zechner, J. (2004). Credit risk and dynamic capital structure choice. *Journal of Financial Intermediation, 13*(2), 183–204.

DeMarzo, P. M. (2019). Presidential address: Collateral and commitment. *The Journal of Finance, 74*(4), 1587–1619.

DeMarzo, P. M., & He, Z. (2020). Leverage dynamics without commitment. *The Journal of Finance, 73*(3), 1195–1250.

Fama, E. F., & French, K. R. (2002). Testing trade-off and pecking order predictions about dividends and debt. *Review of Financial Studies, 15*(1), 1–33.

Fischer, E. O., Heinkel, R., & Zechner, J. (1989). Dynamic capital structure choice: Theory and tests. *The Journal of Finance, 44*(1), 19–40.

Fudenberg, D., & Tirole, J. (1991). *Game theory*. MIT Press.

Gamba, A., & Mao, L. (2020). Debt covenants and the value of commitment. *SSRN Electronic Journal.*

Gamba, A., & Saretto, A. (2018). The agency credit spread. *WBS Finance Group Research Paper, 213.*

Goldstein, R., Ju, N., & Leland, H. (2001). An EBIT-based model of dynamic capital structure. *The Journal of Business, 74*(4), 483–512.

Gul, F., Sonnenschein, H., & Wilson, R. (1986). Foundations of dynamic monopoly and the coase conjecture. *Journal of Economic Theory, 39*(1), 155–190.

Huang, J.-Z., & Huang, M. (2012). How much of the corporate-treasury yield spread is due to credit risk? *Review of Asset Pricing Studies, 2*(2), 153–202.

Jalilvand, A., & Harris, R. S. (1984). Corporate behavior in adjusting to capital structure and dividend targets: An econometric study. *The Journal of Finance, 39*(1), 127–145.

Johnson, T. C., Liu, P., & Yu, Y. (2018). The private and social value of capital structure commitment. *SSRN Electronic Journal.*

Jones, E. P., Mason, S. P., & Rosenfeld, E. (1984). Contingent claims analysis of corporate capital structures: An empirical investigation. *The Journal of Finance, 39*(3), 611–625.

Leary, M. T., & Roberts, M. R. (2005). Do firms rebalance their capital structures? *The Journal of Finance, 60*(6), 2575–2619.

Leland, H. E. (1998). Agency costs, risk management, and capital structure. *The Journal of Finance, 53*(4), 1213–1243.

Malenko, A., & Tsoy, A. (2020). Optimal time-consistent debt policies. *SSRN Electronic Journal.*

Stokey, N. L. (1981). Rational expectations and durable goods pricing. *The Bell Journal of Economics, 12*(1), 112.

Strebulaev, I. A., & Yang, B. (2013). The mystery of zero-leverage firms. *Journal of Financial Economics, 109*(1), 1–23.

Tirole, J. (1988). *The theory of industrial organization.* MIT Press.

Titman, S., & Tsyplakov, S. (2007). A dynamic model of optimal capital structure. *Review of Finance, 11*(3), 401–451.

Xiang, H. (2019). Time inconsistency and financial covenants. *SSRN Electronic Journal.*

Chapter 7
Extensions

In this chapter we extend in several ways the models developed in the previous chapters. Section 7.1 presents a more general version of the model of imperfect competition we discussed in Chap. 4. In particular, we introduce the presence of investment adjustment costs, production costs other than the consumption of inventories as well as the possibility for the firm to issue unsecured debt. The model does not admit a closed-form solution, but we will show that, within the class of Markov Perfect Equilibria, the capital structure of the firm is a combination of the results we obtained in the previous chapters. On the one hand, the firm issues as much as secured debt possible, provided the related tax benefits exceeds transaction costs, whereas a leverage ratchet effect manifests in relation to the gradual issuance of unsecured debt. On the other, the investment Euler equation is affected by investment adjustment costs and probability of default, which add on top of decreasing returns to scale in the firm's capital stock.

In presence of investment adjustment costs or unsecured debt, or both, the model in Sect. 7.1 must be solved numerically. In this regard, unsecured debt is a major complication to implement numerical solution methods. As shareholders decisions may depend on the price of unsecured debt, one should solve for the value of equity given an estimate of the debt price, and then repeat the procedure until the shareholders decisions lead the actual debt price to converge towards the estimated price. For this reason, in Sect. 7.2 we re-examine the case in which the firm is financially constrained, namely it cannot issue unsecured debt. The model is essentially a combination of those presented in Sect. 3.2 and 4.2, and proves to be extremely useful in empirical studies. In particular, in Sect. 7.2.2 we show that the implications for the cross-section of stock returns are essentially the same as in Sect. 4.3.1.

One drawback of the empirical strategy presented in Sect. 7.2.2, is that, when statistically robust, the model cannot help us to conclude whether investment adjustment costs are relevant or not. In general, the validity of the relationship between expected stock returns and fundamentals is not depending on specific

U. Sagliaschi, R. Savona, *Dynamical Corporate Finance*, Contributions to Finance and Accounting, https://doi.org/10.1007/978-3-030-77853-8_7

assumptions about production and capital dynamics. For this reason, in Sect. 7.3 we introduce the Generalized method of Moments (GMM) through which we estimate the model's parameters and test for the validity of the investment Euler equation.

In Sect. 7.3 we also discuss numerical methods, focusing in particular on the borrowing constraints case (cf. Sect. 7.3.1). In this regard, Appendix of this chapter provides a coding example in Python of the numerical solution method presented in Sect. 7.3.1. Instead, in Sect. 7.3.2 we provide a sketch of the algorithm when considering the unsecured debt. A synthetic guide to numerical methods for SDP can be found in Chapter 12 of Miao (2020).

With fully secured debt only, default is always suboptimal for shareholders (cf. Proposition 3.2 in Sect. 3.1). As a result, there is no dynamic game between shareholders and debt holders, in that the price of debt is unaffected by investment and financing decisions. However, in the case of unsecured debt, we consider the Markov Perfect Equilibria only. In Sect. 7.4 we re-examine the DH model (cf. Sect. 6.3), by focusing on a specific class of equilibria in which the DH equilibrium is played as a punishment in case the firm deviates from a constant leverage policy. With GBM cash flows, we show that shareholders never default and the firm maintains a leverage ratio which minimizes the tax burden, as in Tserlukevich (2008).

7.1 A Quantitative Corporate Finance Model

In this section, we present an extension of the model of imperfect competition discussed in Sect. 4.2. The model does not admit a closed form solution, and then we rely on numerical methods to obtain quantitative predictions. An overview on numerical dynamic programming methods is in Sect. 7.3. Compared to Chap. 4, the model includes investment adjustment costs, unsecured debt and production expenses that must be paid in the same period in which the revenues are collected. In Sect. 7.1.1 we describe the model set-up, while optimal production and pricing decision are discussed in Sect. 7.1.2. In Sect. 7.1.3 we derive the first order conditions characterizing optimal investment and financing decisions when the firm is solvent, and discuss some qualitative results which are consistent with Chap. 3–6. Zhang (2005), Livdan et al. (2009), Gomes and Schmid (2010), Li et al. (2009), Li et al. (2016), DeMarzo (2019) and Gomes and Schmid (2021) are the key papers for this section.

7.1.1 Model Set-Up

The firm produces homogeneous goods that are non-storable and non-durable. Therefore, in each period the quantity sold cannot exceed the maximum quantity that can be produced, and it is always suboptimal to produce more goods than those actually sold to consumers. The assumptions on the working capital dynamics are the same discussed in Sect. 4.2. The firm purchases inventories of raw materials that will be used in the following period's production process, and based on the end-of-period capital stock (K_{t+1}). Namely, working capital at the end of each period t is equal to κK_{t+1}, $\kappa \geq 0$. Inventories are always fully exhausted. Either they are fully consumed within the production process, or, in case the firm is operating under its maximum capacity, any residual quantity perishes. To add more realism to the model, we also introduce production expenses in the same period when production takes place. Namely, given the firm's invested capital at a date t, which is equal to $K_t + \kappa K_t$, if we let J_t be the amount of goods sold at the same date, the firm's technology constraint is the following,

$$J_t \leq \underbrace{A_t K_t^{\sigma} L_t^{1-\sigma}}_{\text{Maximum Capacity}}, \quad \sigma \in (0, 1), \tag{7.1.1}$$

where L_t is a composite production input (e.g. labor hours). Contrary to intermediate production goods, which must be purchased in advance, L_t is decided at the same time the production takes place. The cost per unit of L_t is $w_t > 0$, which is exogenously given and paid simultaneously to the collection of date t revenues. The demand schedule for the firm's products is $Y_t P_t^{-\eta}$, where P_t is the price set by the firm in each period for a unit of produced goods. The price of capital goods is set equal to one (*numeraire*), and the evolution of the capital stock (K_t) is governed by,

$$K_{t+1} = K_t (1 - \delta) + I_t, \tag{7.1.2}$$

provided that the firm is solvent at date t. As in Sect. 3.3, investment is subject to (possibly) asymmetric quadratic adjustment costs $\phi(K_t, K_{t+1}) = \frac{\theta_t}{2}\left(\frac{I_t}{K_t}\right)^2 K_t > 0$ where θ_t satisfies,

$$\theta_t = \theta(I_t) = \begin{cases} \theta^+ \geq 0 & I_t \geq 0 \\ \theta^- \geq 0 & I_t < 0. \end{cases} \tag{7.1.3}$$

The firm is financed by equity, fully secured bonds and unsecured bonds. Shareholders can exercise their option to default only after production takes place. As a result, the invested capital available at default is equal to $(1 - \delta) K_t$. An event of default is resolved with the immediate liquidation of the firm, in which secured bond holders are served first. Namely, the holders of secured bonds are paid with the proceeds obtained from the liquidation of the firm's fixed assets, that are equal to $(1 - \alpha) K_t (1 - \delta)$, where $\alpha \in [0, 1]$ is a constant haircut rate. Secured bonds have infinite maturity and a time-varying coupon rate equal to the risk-free rate r_{t+1}. Let S_{t+1} be the amount of secured debt outstanding at the end of time t; we impose the following collateral constraint (CC),

$$S_{t+1} \leq \frac{K_{t+1}(1-\delta)(1-\alpha)}{1+c_{t+1}}, \tag{7.1.4}$$

where $c_{t+1} = r_{t+1}+\varphi$ is the total cost of secured debt, which includes a fixed charge φ per dollar of secured debt outstanding related to monitoring costs. The latter is paid out directly by the firm to one or more financial intermediaries, and does not contribute to the cash-flows obtained by the holders of secured bonds. Eq. (7.1.4) ensures that secured debt holders are always paid back in full. Furthermore, the price of secured debt is always equal to one as in each period secured bond holders obtain the risk-free rate with certainty. In case of default, unsecured bond holders have absolute priority on any proceeds from the liquidation of fixed assets in excess of $S_{t+1}(1+c_{t+1})$. Unsecured bonds are exponentially decaying perpetuities with floating coupon rate equal to r_{t+1} and contractual retirement rate equal to $\xi \geq 0$. Let U_{t+1} be the amount of unsecured debt outstanding at the end of date t. We guess, and verify later, that in each period the firm obtains positive cash flows from production decisions (cf. Sect. 7.1.2). For simplicity, we assume that, in case of default, the resulting operating cash flows are lost (a form of bankruptcy costs). Thus, at the (stochastic) default date t_d, the recovery value for unsecured debt holders is equal to,

$$R^U_{t_d} = \min\left\{K_{t+1}(1-\delta)(1-\alpha) - S_{t+1}(1+c_{t+1}), U_{t_d}\right\}, \tag{7.1.5}$$

and, consequently, the recovery value for shareholders is,

$$R^E_{t_d} = \min\left\{K_{t+1}(1-\delta)(1-\alpha) - S_{t+1}(1+c_{t+1}) - U_{t_d}, 0\right\}. \tag{7.1.6}$$

Implicitly, we have assume that shareholders cannot issue additional debt at t_d. This is an important difference relative to CT models (see Sects. 6.1 and 6.3).

As in the previous chapters, we assume that shareholders can freely inject additional equity in the firm, without any transaction cost. The tax system is linear and the corporate tax rate is equal to $\tau \geq 0$. As a consequence, holding liquidity is always detrimental for shareholders value, because of the interest income taxation. Therefore, we can set liquidity equal to zero in each period without loss of generality, and assume that any equity injection will occur through negative dividends (cf. Chap. 3). Let p_t be the price per dollar of unsecured debt, $\Delta^U_{t+1} := U_{t+1} - (1-\xi)U_t$ and $\Delta^S_{t+1} := S_{t+1} - S_t$. Furthermore, let J_t be the amount of goods sold at time t, and recall that the firm's goods are non storable and non-durable, which implies that $J_t \leq A_t K_t^{\sigma} L_t^{1-\sigma}$. Then, shareholders solve the following maximization problem,

$$\begin{cases} \hat{V}^E(K_t, S_t, U_t) = \max\left\{\max_{J_t, P_t, U_{t+1}, S_{t+1}, K_{t+1}}\{D_t \right. \\ \qquad\qquad \left. +\mathbb{E}_t\left[\frac{M_{t+1}}{M_t}\hat{V}^E(K_{t+1}, S_{t+1}, U_{t+1})\right]\right\}, R_t^E\Big\} \\ s.t. \\ D_t = NI_t + p_t\Delta_{t+1}^U + \Delta_{t+1}^S - (1+\kappa)(K_{t+1} - K_t) - \xi U_t & \text{Dividends} \\ NI_t = [P_t J_t - w_t L_t - c_t S_t - r_t U_t - (\kappa+\delta)K_t - \phi(K_t, K_{t+1})](1-\tau) & \text{Net Income} \\ S_{t+1} \le \frac{(1-\alpha)(1-\delta)K_{t+1}}{1+c_{t+1}} & \text{CC} \\ J_t \le A_t K_t^\sigma L_t^{1-\sigma} & \text{Capacity} \\ J_t \le Y_t P_t^{-\eta} & \text{Demand} \\ R_{t_d}^E = \min\left\{K_{t+1}(1-\delta)(1-\alpha) - S_{t+1}(1+c_{t+1}) - U_{t_d}, 0\right\} & \text{Recovey Value.} \end{cases} \tag{7.1.7}$$

where p_t is the price per dollar of unsecured debt outstanding at the end of time t.

A few comments may help to better understand the underlying logic we follow in formalizing the problem. First, invested capital ($IC_{t+1} = \kappa K_{t+1} + K_{t+1}$) at the end of time t is defined as the sum of fixed assets (K_{t+1}) and working capital (κK_{t+1}) accounting book-values, that is, $IC_{t+1} = \kappa K_{t+1} + K_{t+1}$ (cf. Sect. 4.2). Second, dividends are equal to net income plus proceeds from new debt issuances $\left(p_t\Delta_{t+1}^U + \Delta_{t+1}^S\right)$ and minus change in invested capital ($IC_{t+1} - IC_t$). Third, we are implicitly focusing on Markov Perfect Equilibria (MPE), in which shareholders value and the price of unsecured debt are both function of the payoff of key variables only. Fourth, for reasons of space, we do not explicit here the dependence of $\hat{V}^E$ on the exogenous stochastic processes (e.g. w_t). In this regard, in Sect. 7.1.2 we are going to show how to include all sources of random variation within a single stochastic process (z_t) affecting shareholders investment and financing decisions.

7.1.2 Optimal Production and Pricing Decisions

The choice of J_t and P_t has no effect on $\hat{V}^E(K_{t+1}, S_{t+1}, U_{t+1})$. Therefore, we can proceed as in Sect. 4.2 and solve, first, the auxiliary problem for optimal pricing and production decisions, that is,

$$\begin{aligned} &\max_{P_t, J_t, L_t} \; P_t J_t - w_t L_t \\ &J_t \le A_t K_t^\sigma L_t^{1-\sigma} \\ &J_t \le Y_t P_t^{-\eta}. \end{aligned} \tag{7.1.8}$$

Following the same argument as in Sect. 4.2.1, both constraints must be binding, that is,

$$\begin{cases} Y_t P_t^{-\eta} = A_t K_t^{\sigma} L_t^{1-\sigma} \\ J_t = A_t K_t^{\sigma} L_t^{1-\sigma}. \end{cases} \tag{7.1.9}$$

for a given value of J_t. Hence, the problem in Eq. (7.18) simplifies to,

$$\max_{J_t} \left(\frac{J_t}{Y_t}\right)^{-\frac{1}{\eta}} J_t - w_t \left(\frac{J_t}{A_t K_t^{\sigma}}\right)^{\frac{1}{1-\sigma}} \tag{7.1.10}$$

from which we obtain that the optimal sales level J_t^* must be equal to,

$$J_t^* = Y_t^{\frac{1-\sigma}{\eta\sigma+1-\sigma}} \left(\frac{\eta-1}{\eta}\frac{1-\sigma}{w_t}\right)^{\frac{\eta(1-\sigma)}{\eta\sigma+1-\sigma}} \left(A_t K_t^{\sigma}\right)^{\frac{\eta}{\eta\sigma+1-\sigma}}. \tag{7.1.11}$$

Now, with few algebraic steps, it is immediate to show that, in equilibrium,

$$P_t J_t^* - w_t L_t = z_t K_t^{\upsilon}, \tag{7.1.12}$$

where, $\upsilon := \frac{\sigma(\eta-1)}{(\eta-1)\sigma+1} < 1$ and,

$$z_t := Y_t A_t^{\frac{\eta-1}{(\eta-1)\sigma+1}} \left\{ \left[Y_t^{\frac{1-\sigma}{\eta\sigma+1-\sigma}} \left(\frac{\eta-1}{\eta}\frac{1-\sigma}{w_t}\right)^{\frac{\eta(1-\sigma)}{\eta\sigma+1-\sigma}} \right]^{\frac{\eta-1}{\eta}} \right.$$

$$\left. - w_t \left[Y_t^{\frac{1-\sigma}{\eta\sigma+1-\sigma}} \left(\frac{\eta-1}{\eta}\frac{1-\sigma}{w_t}\right)^{\frac{\eta(1-\sigma)}{\eta\sigma+1-\sigma}} \right]^{\frac{1}{1-\sigma}} \right\} \geq 0. \tag{7.1.13}$$

Since,

$$\left[Y_t^{\frac{1-\sigma}{\eta\sigma+1-\sigma}} \left(\frac{\eta-1}{\eta}\frac{1-\sigma}{w_t}\right)^{\frac{\eta(1-\sigma)}{\eta\sigma+1-\sigma}} \right]^{\frac{\eta-1}{\eta}} \geq w_t \left[Y_t^{\frac{1-\sigma}{\eta\sigma+1-\sigma}} \left(\frac{\eta-1}{\eta}\frac{1-\sigma}{w_t}\right)^{\frac{\eta(1-\sigma)}{\eta\sigma+1-\sigma}} \right]^{\frac{1}{1-\sigma}}, \tag{7.1.14}$$

$z_t \geq 0$ and it is always convenient for shareholders to operate at maximum capacity in each period. Besides, $\upsilon < 1$ implies that equilibrium revenues are strictly increasing but concave in K_t, which is a form of decreasing returns to scale (DRS).

To simplify the notation, we suppress the asterisks to denote optimal investment decisions. Thus, given the expression for z_t in Eq. (7.1.13), shareholders' problem can be formulated as,

$$\begin{cases} \hat{V}^E(K_t, S_t, U_t) = \max\left\{ \max_{U_{t+1}, S_{t+1}, K_{t+1}} \{D_t \right. \\ \qquad\qquad\qquad\qquad \left. +\mathbb{E}_t\left[\frac{M_{t+1}}{M_t}\hat{V}^E(K_{t+1}, S_{t+1}, U_{t+1})\right]\right\}, R_t^E \Big\} \\ s.t. \\ D_t = NI_t + p_t\Delta_{t+1}^U + \Delta_{t+1}^S - (1+\kappa)(K_{t+1} - K_t) - \xi U_t & \text{Dividends} \\ NI_t = \left[z_t K_t^\upsilon - c_t S_t - r_t U_t - (\kappa+\delta)K_t - \phi(K_t, K_{t+1})\right](1-\tau) & \text{Net Income} \\ S_{t+1} \leq \frac{(1-\alpha)(1-\delta)K_{t+1}}{1+c_{t+1}} & \text{CC} \\ R_{t_d}^E = \min\left\{K_{t+1}(1-\delta)(1-\alpha) - S_{t+1}(1+c_{t+1}) - U_{t_d}, 0\right\} & \text{Recovey Value.} \end{cases} \tag{7.1.15}$$

7.1.3 Optimal Investment and Financing Decisions

We assume that z_t follows a Markov process and $\frac{M_{t+1}}{M_t} = \frac{1}{1+r} f(z_{t+1}, \epsilon_{t+1})$, where $\{\epsilon_t\}_{t\geq 0}$ is a sequence of i.i.d. random variables and $f : \mathbb{R} \times \mathbb{R} \to \mathbb{R}^+$. Furthermore, we focus on the case in which $\tau r > \varphi > 0$, and it is then immediate to check that the CC is always binding, provided that the firm is solvent. Indeed, the marginal contribution to shareholders value of a unit of secured debt is equal to $\tau r - \varphi > 0$, and thus it is optimal for shareholders to issue as much as secured debt as possible (cf. Sects. 3.1.2 and 3.2.2). Consequently, $R^E = R^U = 0$, and Eq. (7.1.15) can be formulated as,

$$\hat{V}^E(K_t, U_t, z_t)$$
$$= \max\left\{ \max_{U_{t+1}, K_{t+1}} \left\{ D_t + \frac{1}{1+r}\mathbb{E}\left[f(z_{t+1}, \epsilon_{t+1})\hat{V}^E(K_{t+1}, U_{t+1}, z_{t+1})\,|z_t\right]\right\}, 0\right\} \tag{7.1.16}$$

where $D_t = NI_t + p_t\Delta_{t+1}^U + [\gamma - (1+\kappa)](K_{t+1} - K_t) - \xi U_t$, $\gamma : \frac{(1-\alpha)(1-\delta)}{1+c}$, $c := r + \varphi$, $p_t = p(K_{t+1}, U_{t+1}, z_t)$ and,

$$NI_t = \left[z_t K_t^\upsilon - rU_t - (\kappa + \delta + c\gamma)K_t - \phi(K_t, K_{t+1})\right](1-\tau). \tag{7.1.17}$$

Let $W_t := D_t + \frac{1}{1+r}\mathbb{E}_t\left[f(z_{t+1}, \epsilon_{t+1})\hat{V}^E(K_{t+1}, U_{t+1}, z_{t+1})\,|z_t\right]$. As is evident, W_t is a function of K_{t+1}, U_{t+1}, that is, $W : \mathbb{R}^+ \times \mathbb{R}^+ \to \mathbb{R}$. Let W_t^* be the maximum value that W_t can take over the positive orthant $\mathbb{R}^+ \times \mathbb{R}^+$, which is the domain set for the choice of K_{t+1} and U_{t+1}. If $W_t^* \leq 0$, then it is convenient for shareholders to exercise their option to default. Thus, we can introduce the dummy variable ψ_t

characterizing shareholders willingness to keep the firm solvent at a generic date t,

$$\psi_t := \begin{cases} 1 & W_t^* > 0 \\ 0 & W_t^* \leq 0. \end{cases} \tag{7.1.18}$$

Notice that, when $\psi_t = 1$, we have $\hat{V}^E(K_t, U_t, z_t) = W_t^*$. Hence, by assuming the equity value as a differentiable function, we can characterize the firm's equilibrium investment policy and capital structure in the continuation region.

Starting from the optimal capital stock process, we have the following first order condition,

$$\begin{aligned}(1+\kappa) + \theta(I_t)\left(\frac{I_t}{K_t}\right)(1-\tau) - \gamma - p_K(K_{t+1}, U_{t+1}, z_t)\,\Delta U_{t+1} \\ = \frac{1}{1+r}\mathbb{E}_t\left[f(z_{t+1}, \epsilon_{t+1})\,\hat{V}_K^E(K_{t+1}, U_{t+1}, z_{t+1})\right],\end{aligned} \tag{7.1.19}$$

which is again representative of the positive NPV rule in capital budgeting. The term $(1+\kappa) + \theta(I_t)\left(\frac{I_t}{K_t}\right) - \gamma - p_K(K_{t+1}, U_{t+1}, z_t)\,\Delta U_{t+1}$ is the marginal cost for shareholders of an additional unit of capital stock, while $\frac{1}{1+r}\mathbb{E}\left[f(z_{t+1}, \epsilon_{t+1})\,\hat{V}_K^E(K_{t+1}, U_{t+1}, z_{t+1})\,|z\right]$ is the associated marginal benefit. The latter can be obtained from the envelope condition for K_t,

$$\begin{aligned}&\hat{V}_K^E(K_t, U_t, z_t) \\ &= \left\{\left[\upsilon z_t K_t^{\upsilon-1} + \theta_t\frac{I_t}{K_t}(1-\delta) + \frac{\theta_t}{2}\left(\frac{I_t}{K_t}\right)^2 - c\gamma\right](1-\tau) + \tau(k+\delta) + 1 - \delta - \gamma\right\}\psi_t.\end{aligned} \tag{7.1.20}$$

Putting together, Eq. (7.1.19–7.1.20) lead to the following investment Euler equation,

$$\begin{aligned}&(1+\kappa) + \theta(I_t)\left(\frac{I_t}{K_t}\right)(1-\tau) \\ &\quad = \gamma + p_K(K_{t+1}, U_{t+1}, z_t)\,\Delta U_{t+1} + \frac{1}{1+r}\mathbb{E}_t \\ &\quad \times\left\{f(z_{t+1}, \epsilon_{t+1})\left[\left(\upsilon z_{t+1}K_{t+1}^{\upsilon-1} + \theta_{t+1}\frac{I_{t+1}}{K_{t+1}}(1-\delta) + \frac{\theta_{t+1}}{2}\left(\frac{I_{t+1}}{K_{t+1}}\right)^2 - c\gamma\right)\right.\right. \\ &\quad\quad \left.\left.(1-\tau) + \tau(k+\delta) + 1 - \delta - \gamma\right]\psi_{t+1}\right\},\end{aligned} \tag{7.1.21}$$

which combines all results obtained and discussed in the previous chapters. Here, we focus on the effect of debt on the investment decisions, while in Sect. 7.2 we discuss in more depth the joint effect of DRS and investment adjustment costs. On one hand, the presence of secured debt motivates shareholders to invest more compared to the unlevered case in which $\{S_t = 0, U_t = 0\}_{t\geq 0}$. However, the marginal benefit of investment is lost in case the firm will be insolvent at a later point in time. Hence, compared with the case in which there is no unsecured debt, we observe a debt overhang effect which reduces shareholders propensity to invest. In fact, without unsecured bonds ($U_t = 0$), shareholders would never default, as we showed in Sect. 3.1.2 (cf. Proposition 3.2). To know which effect will dominate, the model must be solved numerically. However, we can expect that, as the firm gets closer to its default threshold $z^b = z^b(K_t, U_t) : W_t^* = 0$, the debt overhang effect will dominate. Likewise, for values of z far from z_b it is reasonable to expect that the overinvestment effect prompted by the funding cost advantage of secured debt will dominate. Nevertheless, investment will be always lower compared to case in which $U_t = 0$.

The optimality conditions for U_{t+1} are equivalent to those obtained in Sect. 4.2,

$$\begin{cases} p_t + p_U(K_{t+1}, U_{t+1}, z_t)\,\Delta U_{t+1} \\ \quad + \frac{1}{1+r}\mathbb{E}\left[f(z_{t+1}, \epsilon_{t+1})\,\hat{V}_U^E(K_{t+1}, U_{t+1}, z_{t+1})\,|z_t \right] = 0 \quad \text{First Order Condition} \\ \hat{V}_U^E(K_t, U_t, z_t) = [-c - \xi - p_t(1-\xi) + \tau c]\,\psi_t. \end{cases} \tag{7.1.22}$$

In equilibrium, the price per dollar of unsecured debt is given by,

$$p_t = \frac{1}{1+r}\mathbb{E}\{f(z_{t+1}, \epsilon_{t+1})\,[c + \xi + p_{t+1}(1-\xi)]\,\psi_{t+1}|z_t\}, \tag{7.1.23}$$

and, given the conjecture $p_U < 0$, shareholders find optimal to issue additional unsecured debt in each period,

$$U_{t+1} - U_t(1-\xi) = \Delta_{t+1}^U = -\frac{\frac{1}{1+r}[1 - \vartheta(z_t, K_{t+1}, U_{t+1})]}{p_U(K_{t+1}, U_{t+1}, z_t)}\tau c, \tag{7.1.24}$$

where,

$$\begin{aligned} &\vartheta(z_t, K_{t+1}, U_{t+1}) := \mathbb{E}\{f(z_{t+1}, \epsilon_{t+1})\,\psi_{t+1}|z_t\} = \\ &\mathbb{E}^{\mathbb{Q}}\left\{ f(z_{t+1}, \epsilon_{t+1})\,\mathbb{I}\left(z_{t+1} > z^b(K_{t+1}, U_{t+1}) \right)|z_t \right\} = \\ &\overset{\mathbb{Q}}{\Pr}\left\{ z_{t+1} > z^b(K_{t+1}, U_{t+1})\,|z_t \right\}, \end{aligned} \tag{7.1.25}$$

is the risk-neutral probability of default for the next period. Provided that p is decreasing in the amount of unsecure debt outstanding, i.e. $p_U < 0$, we then have the following result for the firm's equilibrium capital structure. In any MPE, the firm always issues the maximum amount of secured debt as possible, while unsecured debt is issued gradually over time as long as shareholders do not find more convenient to exercise their option to default, as in DeMarzo (2019). In other words, the leverage ratchet effect continues to operates, but it is limited to the unsecured part of the firm's capital structure. As said, the effect of debt financing on investment is uncertain. On one hand, the tax benefits of debt lowers the marginal cost of investment. On the other, the possibility of default acts in the opposite direction. This result combines the entire dynamic capital structure theory developed up to know, and can be extended to more generic conditions.

7.2 Borrowing Constraints

We consider a specific case of the model presented in the previous section, in which the firm is not allowed to issue unsecured debt (cf. Sect. 7.2.1). In this perspective, the meaning we attribute to borrowing constraints is that the firm's capital structure is constrained by $\{U_t = 0\}_{t\geq 0}$ and Eq. (7.1.4). The discussion of this specific case is preliminary to numerical solution and structural econometrics methods, we discuss in Sect. 7.3. In this regard, although we could easily allow for a time-varying risk-free rate and cost of debt, the state space would increase in its dimension and the collateral constraint $S_{t+1} \leq \gamma_{t+1} K_{t+1}$ could be occasionally binding, and therefore numerical solution methods could be harder to implement. The latter are essential in presence of investment adjustment costs, as the model does not admit a (fully) closed form solution despite the firm is always solvent.

In Sect. 7.2.2 we show that the model has substantial implications for the cross-section of stock returns that are very close to those of Sect. 4.3.1. Namely, expected stock returns are function of market multiples and expected fundamentals. One interesting consequence is that, as long as we are just interested in the relation between stock returns and firm's characteristics, there is no need to solve the model numerically. Nevertheless, we might be interested to estimate the "impact" of investment adjustment costs. On this point, Sect. 7.3.3 deals with structural econometric methods, in which we discuss the Generalized Methods of Moments (GMM).

7.2.1 The Model

In the general model of Sect. 7.1, the subprogram for optimal pricing and production decisions is not depending on unsecured debt. By imposing the additional borrowing constraint $\{U_t = 0\}_{t\geq 0}$, which prevents the firm to unsecured debt financing, and recalling that $z_t K_t^{\nu} \geq 0$, we can use Proposition 3.2 to rule out the case of default.

Therefore, shareholders' problem becomes,

$$\hat{V}^E(K_t, z_t) = \max_{U_{t+1}, K_{t+1}} \left\{ D_t + \frac{1}{1+r} \mathbb{E} \left[f(z_{t+1}, \epsilon_{t+1}) \hat{V}^E(K_{t+1}, z_{t+1}) | z_t \right] \right\}, \tag{7.2.1}$$

where,

$$\begin{cases} D_t = NI_t + [\gamma - (1+\kappa)](K_{t+1} - K_t) \\ NI_t = \left[z_t K_t^{\upsilon} - (\kappa + \delta + c\gamma) K_t - \phi(K_t, K_{t+1}) \right] (1-\tau), \end{cases} \tag{7.2.2}$$

and it is immediate to show that the Euler equation characterizing the optimal investment becomes,

$$(1+\kappa) + \theta(I_t) \left(\frac{I_t}{K_t} \right) (1-\tau) = \frac{1}{1+r} \mathbb{E}_t \{ f(z_{t+1}, \epsilon_{t+1})$$

$$\left[\left(\upsilon z_{t+1} K_{t+1}^{\upsilon-1} + \theta_{t+1} \frac{I_{t+1}}{K_{t+1}} (1-\delta) + \frac{\theta_{t+1}}{2} \left(\frac{I_{t+1}}{K_{t+1}} \right)^2 \right) \right. \tag{7.2.3}$$

$$\left. \left. (1-\tau) + \tau(k+\delta) + 1 - \delta + \gamma(\tau c - \varphi) \right] \right\}.$$

Define operating profits as revenues minus production and depreciations expenses (EbIT). Absent investment adjustment costs, by the envelope theorem the firm sets K_{t+1} to the level maximizing the expected discounted value of the next period's operating profits, net of the opportunity cost of invested capital $(1+\kappa)(1+r)$. Investment adjustment costs can be seen as a friction which limits shareholders flexibility to adjust the future capital stock to its first-best level in terms of operating cash flows. For this reason, we should expect that the firm's monopolistic power will be partly dissipated by second-best capital adjustments, that is, the firm will respond less aggressively to fluctuations in aggregate demand (Y_t), productivity (A_t) and factors' prices (w_t), the three stochastic components of z_t the firm takes as given. To understand the underlying economic reasoning, consider the following example. Imagine that Y_{t+1} to be unusually high only for date $t+1$ with probability close to one, and then will certainly revert to much lower values. Absent investment adjustment costs, the firm will benefit from a one-off increase in its output capacity and then from a subsequent reduction. With investment adjustment costs, any change in output capacity is a net cost for the firm. For very large values of (θ^+, θ^-), shareholders will probably find more convenient to keep the capital stock as constant and to do not respond to fluctuations in aggregate demand.

The previous considerations suggest that the value of the firm include elements from both the results in Sects. 3.2.2 and 4.3.1. From Sect. 3.2.1 we recall that,

$$\left[\theta_{t+1}\frac{I_{t+1}}{K_{t+1}}(1-\delta)+\frac{\theta_{t+1}}{2}\left(\frac{I_{t+1}}{K_{t+1}}\right)^2\right]K_{t+1}=$$

$$\theta_{t+1}I_{t+1}\left[1-\delta+\frac{I_{t+1}}{K_{t+1}}\right]-\frac{\theta_{t+1}}{2}\left(\frac{I_{t+1}}{K_{t+1}}\right)^2K_{t+1}=\theta_{t+1}\left(\frac{I_{t+1}}{K_{t+1}}\right)K_{t+2}. \tag{7.2.4}$$

We can then multiply both sides of Eq. (7.2.3) by K_{t+1}, thereby obtaining,

$$\mathbb{E}_t\left\{\frac{M_{t+1}}{M_t}y_{t+1}\right\}=\left[(1+\kappa)+\theta(I_t)\left(\frac{I_t}{K_t}\right)(1-\tau)\right]K_{t+1}-$$

$$\mathbb{E}_t\left\{\frac{M_{t+1}}{M_t}\left[(1+\kappa)+\theta(I_{t+1})\left(\frac{I_{t+1}}{K_{t+1}}\right)\right]K_{t+2}\right\}+(1-\upsilon)(1-\tau)\mathbb{E}_t\left\{\frac{M_{t+1}}{M_t}z_{t+1}K_{t+1}^{\upsilon}\right\} \tag{7.2.5}$$

where y_t denotes the free cash flows to the firm, that is,

$$y_t=\underbrace{\left[z_tK_t^{\upsilon}-\frac{\theta_t}{2}\left(\frac{I_t}{K_t}\right)^2K_t\right](1-\tau)-(1+\kappa)(K_{t+1}-K_t)+\tau(\delta+\kappa)K_t}_{x_t\text{: unlevered free cash flows}}+\gamma(\tau c-\varphi). \tag{7.2.6}$$

As an application of the general result from Sect. 2.4, the equilibrium value of the firm (V_t) must be equal to,

$$V_t=V_t^E+F_{t+1}=\sum_{j=1}^{\infty}\frac{M_{t+j}}{M_t}\left[x_{t+j}+(\gamma\tau c-\varphi)K_{t+j}\right]=\sum_{j=1}^{\infty}\frac{M_{t+j}}{M_t}y_{t+j}, \tag{7.2.7}$$

that is,

$$V_t=\left[(1+\kappa)+\theta(I_t)\left(\frac{I_t}{K_t}\right)(1-\tau)\right]K_{t+1}+(1-\upsilon)(1-\tau)\mathbb{E}_t\sum_{j=1}^{\infty}\frac{M_{t+j}}{M_t}z_{t+j}K_{t+j}^{\upsilon}. \tag{7.2.8}$$

The term $\left[(1+\kappa)+\theta(I_t)\left(\frac{I_t}{K_t}\right)(1-\tau)\right]K_{t+1}$ is the NPV of free cash flows to the firm if there was perfect competition in the firm's product market, and, consequently, the term $(1-\upsilon)(1-\tau)\sum_{j=1}^{\infty}\frac{M_{t+j}}{M_t}z_{t+j}K_{t+j}^{\upsilon}$ is instead the NPV of the additional cash earnings coming from the firm's market power. The lower η, the higher the firm's market power and the NPV of monopoly rents (NPVMR), $\Theta_t := (1-\upsilon)(1-\tau)\mathbb{E}_t\sum_{j=1}^{\infty}\frac{M_{t+j}}{M_t}z_{t+j}K_{t+j}^{\upsilon}$ (cf. Sect. 4.3.1). Notice that for

$\theta(I_t) = 0$, we are going back to the model presented in Sect. 4.2, while for $\eta \to \infty$ the DRS coefficient υ converges to one and we obtain the model presented in Sect. 3.2.

Contrary to the case without adjustment costs (cf. Chap. 4), shareholders' problem is no longer static. As it clear from Eq. (7.2.3), today's investment decisions (I_t) are function of tomorrow's investment decisions (I_{t+1}). By induction, investments at each date t (I_t) are function of the distribution of all future shocks $\{z_s\}_{s>t}$. For this reason, the model must be solved through numerical methods. This is another difference with the case without adjustment costs, in which the use of numerical methods could be avoided as long as $\mathbb{E}_t\left[f\left(z_{t+1}, \epsilon_{t+1}\right) z_{t+1}\right]$ admits a closed-form expression.

It is important to observe that, holding everything else constant, the value of the firm is strictly decreasing in the investment adjustment costs. In other words, we should not be fooled by the structure of Eq. (7.2.8), in which the term $\left[(1+\kappa)+\theta\left(I_t\right)\left(\frac{I_t}{K_t}\right)(1-\tau)\right] K_{t+1}$ adds on top of NPVMR. The latter will be indeed lower compared to the frictionless cases, based on what already observed before for what concerns optimal investment decisions. The larger the investment adjustment costs are, the less the firm will exploit its ability to adjust the capital stock in response to the conditional distribution of all future shocks $\{z_s\}_{s>t}$. Another way to see this is to observe that investment adjustment costs can be seen as an additional constraint to investment decisions. Indeed, holding z_t constant, shareholders can obtain dividends as in absence of investment adjustment costs if and only if $K_{t+1} = (1-\delta) K_t$. Since investment adjustments reduce the total free cash flows to the firm, shareholders value and the value of the firm will be necessary lower compared to the case in which investment adjustment costs are absent.

7.2.2 The Cross-Section of Stock Returns

We re-examine the relationship between stock returns and firm's characteristics, such as expected profitability indicators and valuation multiples, basically adjusting the routine developed in Sect. 4.3.1 to the more general case in which investment adjustment costs are present. Let $r_{t+1}^E = \frac{D_{t+1}+V_{t+1}^E}{V_t^E}$ be the stock return; then, by combining the firm's budget constraint with Eq. (7.2.8), we obtain the following equation,

$$\begin{aligned} & \frac{V_t^E}{V_t}\left(1+r_{t+1}^E\right)+S_{t+1}[1+c(1-\tau)] \\ & =\frac{\left[z_{t+1} K_{t+1}^{\upsilon}-\frac{\theta_{t+1}}{2}\left(\frac{I_{t+1}}{K_{t+1}}\right)^2 K_{t+1}-(\kappa+\delta) K_{t+1}\right](1-\tau)+\Lambda_{t+1}}{V_t}, \end{aligned} \tag{7.2.9}$$

where Λ_t is the NPV of the total extra-profits compared with the case of perfect product market competition *and* no-adjustment costs, that is,

$$\Lambda_t := \theta_t \left(\frac{I_t}{K_t} \right) (1 - \tau) K_{t+1} + \Theta_t. \tag{7.2.10}$$

Notice that in Sect. 4.3.2 there was no need to stress the absence of investment adjustment costs, for the simple reason that they were absent regardless η was finite or diverging.

If we let $\varrho_{t+1} := \frac{\Lambda_{t+1}}{\Lambda_t} - 1$, and take conditional expectations of both sides of Eq. (7.2.9), we find that, in general, expected stock returns are related to *value*, *quality* and *growth* factors according to,

$$\mathbb{E}_t \left(r^E_{t+1} \right) = BP_{t+1} \cdot \mathbb{E}_t \left(RoE_{t+1} \right) + (1 - BP_{t+1}) \cdot \mathbb{E}_t \left(\varrho_{t+1} \right), \tag{7.2.11}$$

where $RoE_{t+1} := \frac{NI_{t+1}}{V_t - S_{t+1}}$ and $BP_{t+1} = \frac{(1+\kappa)K_{t+1} - S_{t+1}}{V^E_{t+1}}$ are the return on equity (RoE) and the book-to-price-ratio (BP), respectively. As in Sect. 4.3.1–4.3.2, expected stock returns are a weighted average of the firm's expected RoE and growth in extra-profits. Firms with high expected RoE are considered *quality* stocks, while firms with high book-to-price ratio are typically intended as *value* stocks. Firms with high expected sales or earnings growth rates, which are both proxies of ϱ_{t+1}, are instead considered as value *growth* stocks. Holding the cost of equity constant, growth stocks have lower book-to-price ratio and the other way around, consistent with the classic interpretation of high and low book-to-price stocks (Fama and French 1993). Nevertheless, the same holds for high quality stocks, so we should avoid to link the returns of low book-to-price stocks to growth. Put differently, we should expect growth (ϱ_{t+1}), quality (RoE_{t+1}) and value (BP_{t+1}) factors to have separate explicative power in the cross-section of stock returns. See Sect. 4.3.1 for references on several empirical studies confirming the model prediction.

Finally, in presence of unsecured debt and leverage ratios that implies small default probabilities, it is possible to show that Eq. (7.2.11) is a good approximation of the actual relationship that arises in the general model. In short, anomalies such as quality, growth and value can be perfectly consistent with the efficient market hypothesis.

7.3 An Introduction to Numerical Solution Methods and Structural Econometrics

7.3.1 Discrete Dynamic Programming

The models studied in the previous two sections need both to be solved numerically. In this and the following sections we show a general procedure that can be implemented through any standard coding language, starting here from the case in which borrowing constraints are present (cf. Sect. 7.2). The extension on unsecured and defaultable debt is not so straightforward, and we will only layout some general consideration.

Numerical methods require intermediated computer programming skills at least in one fast and flexible language (e.g. C++, Python). Interpreted languages (e.g. Python) tend to be a bit slower compared to compiled languages (e.g. C++). However, the former are usually easier to implement and platform-independent. For computational intensive applications, especially those in which the same model must be solved plenty of times for different configuration of its free parameters (e.g. Simulated Methods of Moments), compiled languages should be preferred. Otherwise, interpreted languages could be considered as a more hands-on alternative. Sometimes, a good compromise is the choice of an interpreted language that can be also executed as a compiled program. *Python* is one possibility, and an example is provided in Appendix at the end of this chapter.

There are different ways to solve numerically stochastic dynamic programming (SDP) problems. Here, we consider the method of value function iteration (VFI), which is very common in the literature. The VFI is the easiest solution method, but it is also quite slow in general. Nevertheless, its speed can be improved with refined algorithms such as the *policy iteration*, multi-grid VFI or approximate dynamic programming (e.g. projection methods).

Consider again the model in Sect. 7.2. Let assume also that $\{z_t\}_{t\geq 0}$ follows a finite Markov chain of size M, that is, $z_t \in \left\{z_j\right\}_{j=1}^M$ for each date $t \in \mathbb{N}$. In this way, the *state space* of the model is restricted to two dimensions, i.e. (K_t, z_t), one of which can take only a set of countable values (z). On this point, several continuous Markov processes can be approximated as finite Markov chain. For instance, a stationary first-order autoregressive process (AR1), such as,

$$z_t = \rho z_{t-1} + \epsilon_t, \ |\rho| < 1, \tag{7.3.1}$$

where $\epsilon_t \sim_{i.i.d.} \mathcal{N}\left(0, \sigma^2\right)$, can be discretized using Tauchen (1986) or Tauchen and Hussey (1991) method. We denote by $\mathrm{P} = \left[\mathrm{p}_{i,j}\right]$ the transition matrix of z_t,

$$\mathrm{p}_{i,j} = \Pr\left\{z_{t+1} = z_j | z_t = z_i\right\}. \tag{7.3.2}$$

which we restrict to be *irreducible* and *aperiodic*. *Irreducible* means that $\forall (i, j)$, $\exists n \in \mathbb{N}$ such that $\Pr\left\{z_{t+n} = z_j | z_t = z_i\right\} > 0$, that is, each state has a positive probability to occur in the future given the current state. *Aperiodic* means that in each period every state $z_i \in \left\{z_j\right\}_{j=1}^M$ can materialize. A Markov chain that is irreducible and aperiodic converges to a long-run distribution. The long-run probability of each state $z_i \in \left\{z_j\right\}_{j=1}^M$ converge to the related unconditional probabilities, we can obtain from the normalized eigenvector associated to the unit eigenvalue of $P^{\intercal}$. In this way, we can define a deterministic version of the model in which z_t is always equal to its expected value, and compute the related steady-state.

It turns out that *discretizing* the original dynamic programming problem is very useful, then,

$$\hat{V}^E(K, z_i) = \max_{K' \geq 0} \Bigg\{ \left[zK^{\upsilon} - (\kappa + \delta + c\gamma) K - \phi(K, K')\right]$$

$$(1-\tau) + [\gamma - (1+\kappa)] (K' - K) + \sum_{j=1}^{M} \frac{\pi_{i,j}}{1+r} \hat{V}^E(K', z_j) \Bigg\} \tag{7.3.3}$$

where $\pi_{i,j} := f(z_i) \, \mathrm{p}_{i,j}$ is the risk-neutral probability to observe $z_{t+1} = z_j$ conditional upon $z_t = z_i$.

The first step to obtain a discrete approximation of the problem in Eq. (7.3.3) is to introduce a grid $\mathcal{K} = \{K_1, K_2, ..., K_{G_K}\}$ of $G_K \in \mathbb{N}$ admissible values for K. The grid should be large enough to include the *deterministic steady-state* of the model. The latter is defined as the steady-state of the solution for the deterministic version of the problem in Eq. (7.3.3), in which z_t is always equal to its unconditional expected value $\bar{z}$. Adapting the investment Euler equation (cf. Eq. 7.2.3) to the deterministic case,

$$(1+\kappa) + \theta(I_t)\left(\frac{I_t}{K_t}\right)(1-\tau) = \frac{1}{1+r} \Bigg\{ \tau(k+\delta) + 1 - \delta + \gamma(\tau c - \varphi)$$

$$\left[\upsilon z_{t+1} K_{t+1}^{\upsilon-1} + \theta_{t+1} \frac{I_{t+1}}{K_{t+1}} (1-\delta) + \frac{\theta_{t+1}}{2} \left(\frac{I_{t+1}}{K_{t+1}}\right)^2\right] (1-\tau) \Bigg\}, \tag{7.3.4}$$

we can obtain the deterministic steady-state value $(\bar{K})$ for K_t as,

$$\bar{K} = \left\{ \frac{\begin{array}{c}(1+r)\left[(1+\kappa) + \theta\delta(1-\tau)\right] \\ -\left[\left(\theta\delta + \frac{\theta}{2}\delta^2\right)(1-\tau) + \tau(k+\delta+\gamma c) + 1 - \delta - \gamma\varphi\right]\end{array}}{\upsilon \bar{z}(1-\tau)} \right\}^{\frac{1}{\upsilon-1}}. \tag{7.3.5}$$

We then obtain K_{G_K} as a sufficiently large multiple of $\bar{K}$, while K_1 is set close to zero. Let $\mathcal{G} = \mathcal{K} \times \mathcal{Z}$ be the *grid* of the problem, where $\mathcal{Z} := \{z_j\}_{j=1}^{M}$ is the support of z_t, and focus on the solution of the discrete approximation of Eq. (7.3.3),

$$\hat{V}^E(K, z_i) = \max_{K' \in \mathcal{K}} \left\{ \left[zK^\upsilon - (\kappa + \delta + c\gamma)K - \phi(K, K')\right](1-\tau) + [\gamma - (1+\kappa)] \right.$$
$$\left. (K' - K) + \sum_{j=1}^{M} \frac{\pi_{i,j}}{1+r} \hat{V}^E(K', z_j) \right\}, \tag{7.3.6}$$

following Algorithm 1.

Algorithm 1 Value function iteration

(1) Set equal to $n \in \mathbb{N}$ the maximum number of iterations. Denote each iteration by s.
(2) Choose a guess $H^{(0)}$ for $\hat{V}^E$ and set $s = 0$.
(3) For each $\mathbf{g} = (K_{g_1}, z_{g_2}) \in \mathcal{G}$ obtain,

$$H^{(s+1)}(K_{g_1}, z_{g_2}) = \max_{K' \in \mathcal{K}} \left\{ \left[zK^\upsilon - (\kappa + \delta + c\gamma)K - \phi(K, K')\right](1-\tau) + \right.$$
$$\left. [\gamma - (1+\kappa)](K' - K) + \sum_{j=1}^{M} \frac{\pi_{i=g_2,j}}{1+r} H^{(s)}(K', z_j) \right\}.$$

(4) Interpolate the values $\{H^{(s+1)}(K, z)\}_{(K,z) \in \mathcal{G}}$ obtained before to get a new guess $H^{(j+1)}$ for $\hat{V}^E$.
(5) Evaluate the "distance" between $H^{(j+1)}$ and $H^{(j)}$ as $||H^{(j+1)} - H^{(j)}||$.
(6) If $||H^{(j+1)} - H^{(j)}|| < vtol$, where $vtol > 0$ is a tolerance parameter stop. Else, if $j \leq n - 1$ set $j \leftarrow j + 1$ and repeat steps 3-to-5.

If $||H^{(j+1)} - H^{(j)}|| < vtol$ after $s \leq n$ iterations the algorithm has (numerically) converged to a discrete approximation of the cum-dividend equity value function of the original optimization problem. Sometimes, it is convenient to start with a coarse grid $\mathcal{K}$ and the repeat Algorithm 1 for a finer grid, using as initial guess for $\hat{V}^E$ the results obtained with the coarse grid. This is the multi-grid algorithms case. Chow and Tsitsiklis (1991) shows that a similar approach could be faster in several circumstances. Appendix at the end of the chapter provides an example on how to implement Algorithm 1 using Python, which can be adapted to the multi-grid case by considering multiple calls of the function solve_model(Gk,n,Ve0) for increasingly larger values Gk for G_k.

7.3.2 The case of Defaultable Debt

This section introduces an algorithm to solve the general version of the model in which the firm is allowed to issue unsecured debt. Compared to more standard SDP problems, here we have the additional complication that the price of unsecured debt is endogenous to shareholders' decisions. Heuristically, we can imagine a two-steps procedure in which we make a first guess for the price of unsecured debt and we apply the VFI algorithm to obtain a candidate solution for the equity value function. Then, based on the latter, we obtain the optimal default threshold and compute the resulting price of debt from Eq. (7.1.23). If the latter results sufficiently close to the original guess, then we have a good numerical solution, otherwise we repeat the procedure until the price of debt converges.

More specifically, we let $i = 1, 2, ..., N$ the index identifying algorithm iterations, each one consisting in several "instructions", we define as sub-program. We choose an appropriate discretization $\mathcal{G} = \left\{ \{K_{g_1}\}_{g_1=1}^{G_1}, \{U_{g_2}\}_{g_2=1}^{G_2}, \{z_{g_3}\}_{g_3=1}^{G_3} \right\}$ of the state-space for (K_t, U_t, z_t), where $G_1 \cdot G_2 \cdot G_3$ provides the number of gridpoints $\mathbf{g} = (g_1, g_2, g_3) \in \mathcal{G}$ involved in the numerical solution process. Then, we guess a candidate function $p^{(0)}$ for the price of debt, and then repeat Algorithm 2 until $||p^{(i)} - p^{(i-1)}|| < ptol$, where $ptol > 0$ is a tolerance parameter, or the maximum number of iterations $(i = N)$ is reached. In this way, we obtain a numerical approximation of $\hat{V}^E$, p and the firm's equilibrium policies which is valid for the subspace bounded by the extreme points of the grid $\mathcal{G}$.

Algorithm 2 Subprogram for the i-th iteration $(i \leq N)$

Step 1:	set equal to $n \in \mathbb{N}$ the maximum number of iterations for the subprogram.
Step 2:	choose a guess $H^{(j)}$ for $\hat{V}^E$ and set $j = 0$.
Step 3:	for each $\mathbf{g} \in \mathcal{G}$ solve for (U_{t+1}, K_{t+1}) using Eq. (7.1.21), Eq. (7.1.24), the guess $H^{(j)}$ for $\hat{V}^E$ and $p^{(i-1)}$.
Step 4:	use the values obtained before for U, K at each $\mathbf{g} \in \mathcal{G}$ to obtain $H^{(j+1)}$ from Eq. (7.1.16) and a suitable interpolation algorithm.
Step 5:	obtain $||H^{(j+1)} - H^{(j)}||$.
Step 6:	if $||H^{(j+1)} - H^{(j)}|| < vtol$, where $vtol > 0$ is a tolerance parameter, let's stop. Otherwise, if $j \leq n - 1$ set $j \leftarrow j + 1$ and repeat steps 3-to-5.
Step 7:	if the algorithm converged, use U, K, $H^{(j)}$ and Eq. (7.1.23) to obtain the price of debt at each grid point. Then, interpolate the results to obtain the function $p^{(i)}$.

Since in general it is hard to obtain precise theoretical results, here we limit our discussion on the way to follow to setting up the solution algorithm. The reader may refer also to Gamba and Mao (2020), Gomes and Schmid (2010, 2021), Gamba and Saretto (2020) or Xiang (2019), which provide examples of this solution methodology.

7.3.3 The Generalized Method of Moments

In this section we provide a brief overview of structural estimation methods, by considering the case in which the firm cannot issue unsecured debt (cf. Sect. 7.2). In Sect. 4.3.2 we showed a direct way to test the validity of,

$$\mathbb{E}_t\left(r_{t+1}^E\right) = BP_{t+1} \cdot \mathbb{E}_t\left(RoE_{t+1}\right) + \left(1 - BP_{t+1}\right) \cdot \mathbb{E}_t\left(\rho_{t+1}\right), \tag{7.3.7}$$

which required however to impose the additional assumption,

$$\mathbb{E}_t\left(\rho_{t+1}\right) \approx g_t^{STM} + \varepsilon_t \tag{7.3.8}$$

in order to proxy the expected value for $\rho_{t+1} = \frac{\Theta_{t+1}}{\Theta_t} - 1$. Here, we could follow the same approach for Eq. (7.2.11) and the expected growth in Λ_t, and test again for the joint validity of,

$$\begin{cases} \mathbb{E}_t\left(r_{i,t+1}^E\right) = EY_{i,t}^{NTM} + \left(1 - BP_{i,t}^{NTM}\right) g_{i,t}^{STM} + \varepsilon_{i,t} \\ \mathbb{E}_t\left(\varepsilon_{i,t}\right) = 0 \end{cases}, \tag{7.3.9}$$

where $EY_{t,t}^{NTM}$ and g_t^{STM} are the earnings yield of the stock, respectively, both computed by considering the consensus estimates for NTM earnings, and the consensus estimate for STM industry sales growth (cf. Sect. 4.3.2). If the Wald test for,

$$\begin{cases} H_0 : \mathbb{E}\left\{r_{i,t+1}^E - \left[EY_{i,t}^{NTM} + \left(1 - BP_{i,t}^{NTM}\right) g_{i,t}^{STM}\right]\right\} = 0 \\ H_1 : \mathbb{E}\left\{r_{i,t+1}^E - \left[EY_{i,t}^{NTM} + \left(1 - BP_{i,t}^{NTM}\right) g_{i,t}^{STM}\right]\right\} \neq 0, \end{cases} \tag{7.3.10}$$

does not provide sufficient evidence to reject H_0 in favor of H_1, we could not conclude whether Eq. (7.2.9) is more "realistic" than Eq. (7.2.10). The only thing we could say is that few characteristics are sufficient to explain expected stock returns, consistent with a certain class of equilibrium models. In other words, the econometric model in Eq. (7.3.9) is valid if investment adjustment costs are present or not. While for estimating conditional expected stock returns Eq. (7.3.9) i is enough, we may wonder whether investment adjustment costs are relevant or not. Structural estimation allows us to address this question.

Since we do not need to solve the model numerically, we allow for time-varying cost of debt ($c \to c_{t+1}$) and tax rate ($\tau \to \tau_t$), and we let $\lambda_{t+1} = \frac{(1-\alpha)(1-\delta)}{1+c_{t+1}} \mathbb{I}\left(\tau c_{t+1} \geq \varphi_{t+1}\right)$ as in Chap. 4. It is then immediate to show that the following investment Euler equation must be verified in equilibrium (cf. Sects. 3.2, 4.2, and 7.1),

$$
\begin{aligned}
&(1+\kappa)+\theta\left(I_t\right)\left(\frac{I_t}{K_t}\right)(1-\tau) \\
&=\frac{1}{1+r_{t+1}}\mathbb{E}_t\left\{f\left(z_{t+1},\epsilon_{t+1}\right)\left[\left(\upsilon z_{t+1}K_{t+1}^{\upsilon-1}+\theta_{t+1}\frac{I_{t+1}}{K_{t+1}}(1-\delta)+\frac{\theta_{t+1}}{2}\left(\frac{I_{t+1}}{K_{t+1}}\right)^2\right)\right.\right. \\
&\qquad\left.\left.\times\ (1-\tau)+\tau\left(k+\delta\right)+1-\delta+\lambda_{t+1}\left(\tau c_{t+1}-\varphi_{t+1}\right)\right]\right\}.
\end{aligned}
\tag{7.3.11}
$$

Now, the goal is to use the Generalized Methods of Moments (GMM) to estimate the vector of parameters $\boldsymbol{\omega}=\left(\alpha,\nu,\theta^-,\theta^+,\kappa,\delta\right)$, or a subset (e.g. κ is known), and test whether Eq. (7.3.11) is consistent with observed data. To do this, we have to specify $f\left(z_{t+1},\epsilon_{t+1}\right)$, as the risk-free interest rate r_{t+1} can be proxied by considering interbank rates or Treasury rates. Suppose we have a dataset $X=\left[\left(\left(f_{i,t},K_{i,t},I_{i,t},\tau_{i,t},c_{i,t+1}\right),\mathbf{h}_{i,t}\right)_{i=1}^N\right]_{t=1}^T$ of T observations for N different stock or portfolios of stocks indexed by $i=1,2,..,N$. Then, following the same approach as in Sect. 4.3.2, we have the following system of hypothesis to test,

$$
\begin{cases}
H_0:\mathbb{E}\left[\epsilon\left(\boldsymbol{\omega},f,K_t,I_t,\tau_t,c_{t+1}\right)\mathbf{h}_t\right]=\mathbf{0} & \text{Eq. (7.3.11) is valid}\\
H_0:\mathbb{E}\left[\epsilon\left(\boldsymbol{\omega},f,K_t,I_t,\tau_t,c_{t+1}\right)\mathbf{h}_t\right]\neq\mathbf{0} & \text{Eq. (7.3.11) is rejected,}
\end{cases}
\tag{7.3.12}
$$

where $\mathbf{h}_t\in\mathbb{R}^{n+1}$ is a vector of $n+1>dim\left(\boldsymbol{\omega}\right)$ distinct instrument variables, which includes a constant $\left(h_t^{(1)}=1\right)$, and,

$$
\begin{aligned}
&\epsilon\left(\boldsymbol{\omega},f,K_t,I_t,\tau_t,c_{t+1}\right) \\
&\quad:=(1+\kappa)+\theta\left(I_t\right)\left(\frac{I_t}{K_t}\right)(1-\tau_t) \\
&\qquad-\left\{\frac{1}{1+r_{t+1}}f\left(z_{t+1},\epsilon_{t+1}\right)\left[\left(\upsilon z_{t+1}K_{t+1}^{\upsilon-1}+\theta_{t+1}\frac{I_{t+1}}{K_{t+1}}(1-\delta)+\frac{\theta_{t+1}}{2}\left(\frac{I_{t+1}}{K_{t+1}}\right)^2\right)\right.\right. \\
&\qquad\qquad\left.\left.(1-\tau_t)+\tau\left(k+\delta\right)+1-\delta+\lambda_{t+1}\left(\tau_t c_{t+1}-\varphi_{t+1}\right)\right]\right\},
\end{aligned}
\tag{7.3.13}
$$

is equivalent to the pricing error in Sect. 4.3.2. Under some regularity conditions for the data generating process underlying X (cf. Chapter 13 in Miao 2020), the GMM estimator $\hat{\boldsymbol{\omega}}_{GMM}$ for the vector of parameters $\boldsymbol{\omega}$ is obtained according to the following Algorithm 2, which also describes how to test for the validity of the model and for the parameters' significance. In short, the GMM works as follows. We obtain a first estimate of the model parameters by minimizing the sum of squared pricing errors. Then, we obtain a consistent estimate of the variance-covariance matrix of pricing errors and improve our initial estimate for $\boldsymbol{\omega}$. Under appropriate regularity conditions, we have asymptotic results which allows us to perform hypothesis testing by using standard distributions.

Algorithm 3 The generalized method of moments

(1) For each moment condition $\mathbb{E}\left[\epsilon\left(\boldsymbol{\omega}, f, K_{i,t}, I_{i,t}, \tau_{i,t}, c_{i,t+1}\right) h_{i,t}^{(s)}\right] = \mathbf{0},\ i = 1, 2, .., N,\ s = 1, 2, .., n+1$, define $\Psi_{i,s}(\mathbf{w}) := \sum_{t=1}^{T} \epsilon\left(\mathbf{w}, f, K_{i,t}, I_{i,t}, \tau_{i,t}, c_{i,t+1}\right) h_{i,t}^{(s)}$.
(2) Define $\boldsymbol{\psi}(\mathbf{w}) := \left(\Psi_{i,s}(\mathbf{w})\right)_{(i,s)\in\{1,2,...,N\}\times\{1,2,...,n+1\}}$ as the vector collecting all the $N\times(n+1)$ moment conditions (we have N stocks and $n+1$ distinct moment conditions).
(3) Obtain the estimator $\mathbf{w_0}$ as $\mathbf{w}_0 = \operatorname{argmin}_{\mathbf{w}} \boldsymbol{\psi}(\mathbf{w})^{\mathsf{T}} \cdot \boldsymbol{\psi}(\mathbf{w})$, and a consistent estimator $\hat{S}\left(\hat{\mathbf{w}}_0\right)$ for the variance-covaraince matrix of $\boldsymbol{\psi}(\mathbf{w}_0)$.
(4) The GMM estimator for $\boldsymbol{\omega}$ is obtained as $\hat{\boldsymbol{\omega}}_{GMM} = \operatorname{argmin}_{\mathbf{w}} \boldsymbol{\psi}(\mathbf{w})^{\mathsf{T}}\, \hat{S}^{-1} \cdot \boldsymbol{\psi}(\mathbf{w})$, where $\hat{S}^{-1}$ is the inverse matrix of $\hat{S}\left(\hat{\mathbf{w}}_0\right)$.
(5) Estimate the statistic $J = T \cdot \left(\boldsymbol{\Psi}_{GMM}^{\mathsf{T}} \hat{S}^{-1} \boldsymbol{\Psi}_{GMM}\right)$, where $\boldsymbol{\Psi}_{GMM} = \boldsymbol{\psi}\left(\hat{\boldsymbol{\omega}}_{GMM}\right)$, which is asymptotically distributed as a χ^2 with $N \times (n+1) - dim(\boldsymbol{\omega})$ degree of freedoms.
(6) Let $\nabla\boldsymbol{\psi}$ be the gradient of $\boldsymbol{\psi}(\mathbf{w})$ evaluated at $\mathbf{w} = \hat{\boldsymbol{\omega}}_{GMM}$. A consistent estimator for the variance-covariance matrix of $\hat{\boldsymbol{\omega}}_{GMM}$ is $\Sigma_{GMM} = \frac{1}{T}\left(\nabla\boldsymbol{\psi} \cdot \hat{S}^{-1} \cdot \nabla\boldsymbol{\psi}^{\mathsf{T}}\right)^{-1}$.
(7) Under the null hypothesis that $\omega^{(l)} = 0,\ \omega^{(l)} \in \boldsymbol{\omega}$, $\omega^{(l)}$ is asymptotically normally distributed with expected value equal to zero and variance equal to the $l-th$ element of the main diagonal of Σ_{GMM}.

Whited (1998) shows that Investment Euler equations are very often rejected by real data, although the relationship between investment and stock returns is well known. To explain this we should keep in mind that testing Eq. (7.3.11) requires to impose specific assumptions relative to the structure of investment adjustment costs, the SDF and the production technology of the firm. Instead, the relationship between stock and investment returns as in Eq. (7.3.10) is independent from the SDF, and then its validity holds for more general technology and adjustment costs specifications. For this reason investment Euler equation typically fails to be consistent with empirical observations, while their implications for the cross section of stocks returns remain valid, being only partially affected by the specific hypothesis on the firm's technology and the SDF of the economy.

7.4 Non-Markov Perfect Equilibria

In this section, we provide a concise overview of non-Markov perfect equilibria. The model we present is a simplified version of Malenko and Tsoy (2020), which in turns relates to Tserlukevich (2008) as well as DH (DeMarzo & He 2016). The basic idea is the following. Consider the CT setting described in Sect. 6.3, and assume $\theta = 1$

for simplicity (i.e. zero recovery value). The MPE in DH yields the lowest possible payoff for shareholders. Indeed, as shareholders have the option to issue additional debt in the future, in the unique MPE of the model the value of this option is fully dissipated. Consequently, we may consider *grim trigger strategies* those strategies that *off the equilibrium path* are resulting in the unique MPE of the game.

Consider a dynamic game between two players, say Alice (A) and Bob (B). In a nutshell, a grim trigger for Alice has the property that, if Bob deviates from his commitment, then Alice will punish him forever. Of course, Alice's punishment strategy is credible if and only if it will be optimal for her given Bob's optimal response. In other words, a grim trigger strategy is credible if and only if its punishment component is part of a dynamic equilibrium. In our context, players are not Alice and Bob, as in the windsurfing example of Chap. 6, but bond holders and shareholders, respectively. The latter announces they will follow a certain policy, and the former, in case the latter will violate their commitment, will play as in the DH's MPE forever.

The difference with Markov perfect equilibria is clear. With grim trigger strategies, shareholders and debt holders behavior no longer depend exclusively on the *payoff-relevant* variables, but also on outcomes that will be never observed in equilibrium. Recalling the windsurfing example in Chap. 6, non-Markov perfect equilibria should be considered when agents can establish long-run relationships. From a game theoretic perspective, we are going to make use implicitly of a Folk theorem. Folk theorems is a common name in dynamic games for "anything goes" results. Namely, in several situations, almost all efficient outcomes of a game can be supported by appropriate grim trigger strategies. An example is tacit collusions in dynamic oligopolies; see Fudenberg and Tirole (1991), Osborne and Rubinstein (1994), for a detailed exposition of the Folk theorem and Tirole (1988) for its applications in industrial organization.

7.4.1 The Setting

The basic setting of the model is the same as in Sect. 6.3.4, excluding the tax deductibility of interests expenses when $cF(t) > Y(t)$. For reasons that will be clear later, we set $c = r$ without loss of generality. Furthermore, we restrict the analysis to the case in which the risk-neutral drift of operating earnings (EbIT) is positive, $0 < \mu < r$, and $\xi = 0$. Suppose that shareholders commit to a leverage policy that consists in holding constant the Debt-to-EbIT ratio, or leverage, $l(t) := \frac{F(t)}{Y(t)} = l_0$. If such a policy was credible, the price of debt will be equal to one as we would never observe an event of default. To simplify the discussion, we will refer to $t = 0$ as the *inception date*, while to l_0 as target leverage ratio.

With Markov perfect strategies, we showed that commitment to $l(t) = l_0$ is time-inconsistent. Indeed, in the only MPE of the game, $l(t)$ is a function of past earnings (cf. Sect. 6.3.4). However, once we allow shareholders and bond holders to take into account off-equilibrium paths, shareholders' commitment to $l(t) = l_0$ has a chance to become dynamically consistent. The idea is the following. Suppose that committing to $l(t) = l_0$ yields always an higher equity market value, compared to the case of the unique MPE of the game. With Markov perfect strategies, shareholders would have the incentive to deviate from their commitment in order to profit from the capital loss inflicted to bond holders. However, if the latter "punished" shareholders "behaving[1]" as in the unique MPE of the game, shareholders may refrain to deviate from their commitment.

Let $V^E(t|l(t) = l_0)$ be the value of the equity given shareholders commitment to $l(t) = l_0$, while $V^E(t|MPE)$ that in case of a MPE; as long as the proceeds from issuing an amount $\Delta > 0$ in excess of the adjustment to keep $l(t) = l_0$ are less than $V^E(t|MPE) - V^E(t|l(t) = l_0)$, the grim trigger strategy described before ensures that $l(t) = l_0$ is time-consistent for shareholders. In the next section we show that the set of time-consistent constant leverage policies is characterized by $l_0 \leq r^{-1}$. Therefore, any time-consistent constant leverage policy translate into default-free unsecured debt, with price being always equal to one.

Furthermore, absent other restrictions on the tax deductibility of interest payments, we are going to show that $l_0 = 1$ is the optimal time consistent leverage policy, in the sense that shareholders prefer to commit to $l(t) = r^{-1}$ compared to any other level $l_0 < 1$. As a result, for each $t > 0$, that is, after an initial discrete amount of debt is issued to set $l(0) = l_0$, the equity market value is equal to the NPV of the tax shield on coupon payments. In other words, operating earnings are entirely pledged to obtain unsecured debt financing, and shareholders retain the corresponding tax benefits.

7.4.2 Constant Leverage Policies

A usual, a policy is a (possibly) state-contingent rule of behavior. A leverage policy is an $\mathcal{F}_t$−adapted stochastic process $l(t) = \frac{F(t)}{Y(t)}$, where $\mathcal{F}_t$ is the natural filtration of the EbIT process $Y(t)$. A constant leverage policy is such that $l(t) = l_0$, where $l_0 \geq 0$ is set at inception. Unlevered free cash flows are equal to $Y(t)(1 - \tau)$, as the firm's invested capital is assumed to be constant over time. Equivalently, the dynamics of $Y(t)$,

$$dY(t) = \mu Y(t)\,dt + \sigma Y(t)\,dW_t^{\mathbb{Q}}, \tag{7.4.1}$$

[1]Conditional upon shareholders deviating from their commitment, debt investors will conjecture that the firm will issue debt as in the only MPE of the game. As a result, shareholders will confirm this conjecture, eventually dissipating the value of the option to adjust the debt in the future.

is supported by an exogenous GBM process for the before-tax RoIC. A constant leverage policy implies the following debt dynamics,

$$dF(t) = \underbrace{\mu l_0 Y(t)\, dt}_{\text{Smooth Debt Adjustment}} + \underbrace{\sigma l_0 Y(t)\, dW_t^{\mathbb{Q}}}_{\text{Lump-sum adjustment at } t+dt} . \tag{7.4.2}$$

As long as the price of debt is equal to one, the term $\sigma \frac{l_0}{r} Y(t)\, dW_t^{\mathbb{Q}}$ is an *infinitesimal* lump-sum cash inflow (outlay, if negative) that the firm obtains (pays, if negative) from the adjustment of debt in response to the realization of the profitability shock dW_t. Notably, this sum is paid or earned by shareholders as an extraordinary dividend right before the new free cash flow $Y(t)\, dt$ starts to accrue. The presence of this term reintroduce a difference between the cum-dividend and ex-dividend market value of equity. For $t \neq 0$, this difference is in fact infinitesimal and can be omitted. However, at $t = 0$, the firm issues a discrete amount of debt to obtain the target leverage ratio l_0 based on the value of operating earnings $Y(0) = Y_0$. Therefore, at inception we have a difference between shareholders value and ex-dividend equity market value. To simplify the notation, we use V^E to denote the market value of equity for every $t \neq 0$, for which we do not need to distinguish between cum and ex dividend value (cf. Sect. 5.1), except for the term $\sigma \frac{l_0}{r} Y(t)\, dW_t^{\mathbb{Q}}$ which can be ignored, being infinitesimal with probability one.

Recall that the expected value of $W(t+h) - W(t)$ is null for every $h > 0$. Le assume to observe the value of equity right after the same instant's lump-sum adjustment $\sigma l_0 Y(t-dt)\, dW_{t-dt}^{\mathbb{Q}}$ has occurred. Then, it is immediate to show that (cf. Sect. 5.2) the value of equity is equal to,

$$rV^E(Y|l = l_0) = Y(1 - rl_0)(1 - \tau) + \mu l_0 Y + \mu Y V_Y^E(Y|l = l_0) + \frac{1}{2}\sigma^2 Y^2 V_{YY}^E(Y|l = l_0), \tag{7.4.3}$$

where $r > \mu$ is the risk-free rate. Under commitment to $l(t) = l_0$, the equity value function depends from $Y(t)$ only, and,

$$V^E(Y|l = l_0) = \frac{Y(1 - rl_0)(1 - \tau) + \mu l_0 Y}{r - \mu}. \tag{7.4.4}$$

Commitment to $l(t) = l_0$ implicitly assumes that shareholders never default in the future. Thus, a necessary condition for $l(t) = l_0$ to be time-consistent is that default is never enticing for shareholders. Let assume that $l_0 \leq r^{-1}$. Then, commitment to never default in the future is credible, as for any default boundary $Y_b < \infty$ shareholders would loose their continuation value $\frac{Y_b(1-rl_0)(1-\tau)+\mu l_0 Y_b}{r-\mu}$, which is strictly positive. In this regard, notice that the cash flow $\sigma \frac{l_0}{r} Y(t)\, dW_t^{\mathbb{Q}}$ is infinitesimal, and therefore it does not alter the conclusion in terms of cum-dividend equity market value, which is the only relevant metric for shareholders. On the other hand, if $l_0 > r^{-1}$, it is never rational for shareholders to adopt a constant leverage policy, as $Y(1 - rl_0)(1 - \tau) + \mu l_0 = [Y + (\mu - r) l_0](1 - \tau) < Y(1 - \tau)$.

7.4.3 *Time-Consistent Constant Leverage Policies*

A constant leverage policy l_0, is time-consistent if and only if shareholders do not have the strict incentive to deviate from it. As we showed before, a necessary condition is that $l_0 \leq r^{-1}$. Subject to this condition, shareholders never default along the commitment path. Recall that, following any deviation to $l(t) > l_0$, debt holders punish shareholders forcing the outcome of the unique MPE of the game. First of all, notice that buying back debt is always neutral for shareholders, as the price of debt is equal to one. Therefore, we can assume without loss of generality that discrete buybacks never occur in equilibrium. Hence, we must determine under which conditions it is optimal for shareholders to refrain from increasing debt by an amount $\Delta > 0$ and deviate from the constant leverage policy $l(t) = l_0$. To this end, let $p(Y, F + \Delta)$ be the price of debt in the only MPE of the game, that is,

$$p(Y, F + \Delta) = \left[1 - \left(\frac{y}{y_b}\right)^{-\gamma}\right] - \frac{\tau r}{r + \xi}\left[1 - \left(\frac{y}{y_b}\right)^{-\gamma}\right] < 1, \tag{7.4.5}$$

where, $y := \frac{Y}{F+\Delta}$, $\gamma = \frac{\left(\mu - \frac{1}{2}\sigma^2\right) + \sqrt{\left(\mu - \frac{1}{2}\sigma^2\right)^2 + 2r\sigma^2}}{\sigma^2}$ and $y_b = \frac{\gamma}{1+\gamma}\frac{c(1-\tau)+\xi}{r+\xi}(r - \mu)$ (cf. Sect. 6.3.4). Since in the case of commitment $\sigma l_0 Y(t - dt)\, dW^{\mathbb{Q}}_{t-dt}$ is infinitesimal, we can formulate the time-consistency requirement as,

$$\underbrace{\frac{Y(1 - l_0)(1 - \tau) + \mu \frac{l_0}{r} Y}{r - \mu}}_{\text{Shareholders Value | Commitment to } l_0} \geq \underbrace{V^{E,MPE}(Y, F + \Delta) + p(Y, F + \Delta)\Delta}_{\text{Shareholders Value | Deviation } \Delta > 0}, \tag{7.4.6}$$

The RHS of this inequality is equal to the value of the firm in the unique MPE of the game minus $p(Y, F + \Delta) F$. Hence, from Eq. (6.3.23), we can formulate Eq. (7.4.6) as,

$$[1 - p(Y, F + \Delta)] F \geq -\frac{1 - \tau}{r - \mu} Y \left(\frac{y}{y_b}\right)^{-\gamma}, \tag{7.4.7}$$

which is always true as $p(Y, F + \Delta) < 1$. Therefore, every constant leverage policy such that $l(t) = l_0 \leq r^{-1}$ is time consistent.

In other words, when the unique MPE of the game is used to punish shareholders' defection, the commitment to any policy $l(t) = l_0 \in [0, r^{-1}]$ is time-consistent. Therefore, the optimal time-consistent constant leverage policy is the one that maximizes shareholders value at $t = 0$ subject to the incentive compatibility constraint $l_0 \in [0, r^{-1}]$,

$$\max_{l_0 \in [0, r^{-1}]} \left\{ \underbrace{V^E(Y_0, l_0)}_{\text{Ex-dividend equity value}} + \underbrace{l_0 \frac{Y_0}{r}}_{\text{Proceeds from initial debt's issuance}} \right\}, \tag{7.4.8}$$

that is,

$$\max_{l_0 \in [0, r^{-1}]} \left\{ \frac{Y_0(1-\tau) + \tau l_0 Y_0}{r - \mu} \right\}. \tag{7.4.9}$$

Since the objective function is linear and increasing in l_0, the optimal constant leverage policy is $l_0 = r^{-1}$. Such a policy maximizes the NPV of debt tax shield, in that the firm never pays taxes. Indeed, shareholders value is $\frac{Y_0}{r-\mu}$ at inception. As a matter of fact, for every date $t > 0$ the free cash flows to the firm are equal to its operating earnings. Consequently, the value of the firm is equal to $V(t) = \frac{Y(t)}{r-\mu}$, and the market-leverage ratio $\frac{F(t)}{V(t)}$ is constant and equal to $(r - \mu) l_0$.

7.4.4 Limits to Tax-Deductibility of Interest Expenses

The model presented is extreme in many respects. First, despite debt is unsecured, there is no default risk due to the possibility of continuously adjust leverage in response to infinitesimal shocks. Second, the interest coverage ratio $\frac{rF}{Y}$ is always equal to one. Companies with an interest coverage close to one are generally rated as junk or close to, with high credit spreads that must compensate bond holder for the risk of incurring a certain loss in case the firm defaults. Third, taxation becomes irrelevant to the value of the firm and its securities, and government obtains zero corporate tax revenues.

In several jurisdictions, the tax deductibility of interest expenses is limited up to a certain fraction of operating earnings. For instance, companies that are headquartered in Italy for tax purposes faces a 30% limit. Recently, the same limit has been introduced also for US tax resident firms, although with a slight difference in terms of the relevant definition of operating earnings, which can be ignored at this level of analysis. Let $r\bar{l} < 1$ be the maximum interest expenses that can be deducted from corporate taxes as a fraction of the same period's operating earnings. Then, every $l_0 \in [\bar{l}, r^{-1}]$ is equivalent to $\bar{l}$, since it does not generates any additional free cash flow to the firm. Therefore, without loss of generality, we can limit the search of the optimal time-consistent constant leverage policy to the domain $\left[0, \bar{l}\right]$,

$$\max_{l_0 \in \left[0, \bar{l}\right]} \left\{ \frac{Y_0 \left(1 - \tau\right) + \tau l_0 Y_0}{r - \mu} \right\}. \tag{7.4.10}$$

Again, the objective is linear and increasing in l_0. Thus, the optimal time-consistent constant leverage policy is $\bar{l}$, as it is the one minimizing the future tax burden. The value of the firm is equal to,

$$V\left(t\right) = \frac{Y\left(t\right)\left(1 - \tau\right) + \tau \bar{l} Y\left(t\right)}{r - \mu} \tag{7.4.11}$$

and the market-leverage ratio is constant and equal to $\frac{F(t)}{V(t)} = \frac{\bar{l}(r-\mu)}{1+(\bar{l}-1)\tau}$. The trade-off theory is back, although a constant leverage ratio is no longer the consequence of an explicit trade-off between the tax benefits of debt and bankruptcy, agency or transaction costs. Instead, the trade-off arises between the alternatives of reducing debt in response to a negative shock, and defecting and being punished with the occurrence of most hurting equilibrium of the game.

As in the discrete time case (cf. Sect. 3.1.3), the weighted average cost of capital (WACC) is equal to,

$$wacc\left(t\right) = \frac{V^E\left(t\right)}{V\left(t\right)} \mathbb{E}_t\left[r^E\left(t\right)\right] + \frac{F\left(t\right)}{V\left(t\right)} r\left(1 - \tau\right), \tag{7.4.12}$$

as debt is risk-free and trades at par value. The proof is straightforward and the reader may refer to DeMarzo (2005) for more technical details. In this specific case, we obtain,

$$wacc\left(t\right) = \left(1 - \lambda\right) \mathbb{E}_t\left[r^E\left(t\right)\right] + \lambda r\left(1 - \tau\right), \tag{7.4.13}$$

which is the standard practitioners formula except that the cost of debt is equal to the risk-free rate, as there are no transaction costs.

7.4.5 Final Considerations

Malenko and Tsoy (2020) introduces jumps in the unlevered free cash flows process (cf. Eq. 7.4.1), and consider the class of $s - S$ restructuring policies. An $s - S$ policy in their paper consists in maintaining the interest coverage ratio $\left(\frac{rF}{Y}\right)$ between a lower (s) and an upper (S) threshold. Provided that jumps are not so extreme to lead shareholders to prefer default, the DH equilibrium could be used as a punishment device to support an equilibrium of this type. Hence, once we depart from Markov

Perfect strategies, we can use the DH equilibrium to support a vast array of subgame perfect equilibria, in which the firm may adjust its leverage according to very different rules. Despite this construction may be used to rationalize several observed patterns, its flexibility could be detrimental to stable predictions. After all, if we can rationalize several different leverage patterns, we can no longer predict which one will occur in a specific situation.

Appendix

In this appendix we provide a Python code to implement Algorithm 1 in Sect. 7.3.1. For simplicity, we considered he case in which investment adjustment costs are symmetric, that is, $\theta^+ = \theta^- = \theta$. To run the program is sufficient to:

(1) copy-paste the code below within a text file, and save it with the *.py* extension (e.g. *algo1.py*);
(2) open a Python console (e.g. *ipython*) and import the module created before (e.g. *import sys; sys.path.append("//Users//myname//Documents//"); import algo1* if algo.py is saved in the folder */Users/myname/Documents/*)
(3) the user should run the function solve_model(Gk,n,Ve0) (e.g. *out=algo1.solve_model(50,100,None)*) to obtain the numerical solution of the model.

See the documentation of the function solve_model for the usage of its arguments and the values returned from its call.

```
#!/usr/bin/env python
# -*- coding: UTF-8 -*-
# coding: utf-8
# author(s): @umberto.sagliaschi , @roberto.savona

import numpy as np, pandas as pd, scipy as sci
from scipy.interpolate import interp2d
from scipy import optimize
from numpy import linalg


# Parameters
r = 0.02 # Real risk-free rate
delta = 0.20 # Depreciation rate
alpha = 0.3 # Liquidation costs, as a fraction of K\cdot(1-\delta)
tau = 0.25 # Tax rate
theta = 0.05 # adjustment cost parameter
upsilon = 0.5 # DRS coeffieicent
kappa = 0.3 # Working capital to fixed assets ratio
n = 100 # Max inner loop iteration
ptol = 10e-5 #Tolerance: price per dollar of unsecured debt
vtol = 10e-5 #Tolerance: equity value unction given price of unsecured
    debt

# Composite parameters
varphi=0.005
c = r+varphi # \varphi=0
gamma = (1.-alpha)*(1.-delta)/(1+c) #Same of lambda since \varphi=0.
```

```python

# z_grid is the support of z. Tmat is a transition matrix for the shock under the risk-neutral probability measure.
z_grid = [0.5,1.,1.5]
Gz = len(z_grid)
TMAT = [[0.3,0.2,0.5],
        [0.4,0.2,0.4],
        [0.5,0.2,0.3]]
TMAT = np.array(TMAT)


def K_steady_state():
    '''
    Solve for the deterministic steady-state of the model
    '''
    #Get unconditional probabilities
    eigenval, eigenvecs = np.linalg.eig(TMAT.T)
    probs_unc = eigenvecs[(np.abs(eigenval - 1.)).argmin()]
    probs_unc = probs_unc/probs_unc.sum()

    #Compute the unconditional expected value of z
    z_bar = np.dot(probs_unc, z_grid)

    #Compute the deterministic steady state of the model
    A1=(1.+r)*((1+kappa)+theta*delta*(1-tau))
    A2 = (theta*delta+0.5*theta*(delta**2.))*(1.-tau)+tau*(kappa+delta+gamma*c)+1-delta-gamma*varphi
    K_hat = ((A1-A2)/(upsilon*z_bar*(1.-tau)))**(1./(upsilon-1))


    return K_hat

def solve_model(Gk=50,n=n,Ve0=None):
    '''
    Algorithm 1 is run by calling this function, which returns \hat{V}^{E} and the equilbrium policy K'=K'(K,z).
    Solve the model for a given size of the grid for the capital stock (Gk).
    The parameter n controls the maximum number of iterations. Ve0 is a guess for the value function.
    The algorithm can be iterated for finer grids (i.e. increasing values of Gk) takiing as given the equity value function obtained at the precedent step. In this way we can mimick the Chow and Tsitsiklis (1991) approach.
    '''
    assert(tau*c>=varphi)
    # Grid
    K_grid = np.linspace(0.01, K_steady_state() * 2 * max(z_grid) / min(z_grid), Gk)
    K_step = np.mean(np.diff(K_grid))

    #Guees
    if Ve0 is None: Ve0 = lambda K,z: D(K=K,K_end=0,z=z)
    Ve0 = np.vectorize(Ve0)(*np.meshgrid(K_grid,z_grid))
    Ve0 = interp2d(K_grid, z_grid, Ve0, bounds_error=True, fill_value=None)

    return VIT(K_grid,Ve_guess=Ve0,n=n,vtol=vtol),K_grid

def VIT(K_grid,Ve_guess=None,n=n,vtol=vtol):
    """
    Perform Steps 1 to 7.
    """
    j=1
    Ve=Ve_guess
    eps = np.inf
    while (eps > vtol) and (j<=n):
```

```
        print("%i␣iterations ,␣eps=%f" % (int(j), eps), end="\r")
        Ve_new = T(Ve=Ve, K_grid=K_grid) # Bellman operator
        NEW=Ve_new(K_grid, z_grid)
        OLD= Ve(K_grid, z_grid)
        diff_squared = list(map(lambda x: x ** 2., NEW-OLD))
        eps = np.sum(diff_squared)
        Ve = Ve_new
        j += 1 # update counter

    K_next = T(Ve, what='K', K_grid=K_grid)

    return Ve, K_next

def T(Ve, K_grid, what='Ve'):
    """
    Perform Step 3. for all gridpoints g\in\mathcal{G}
    """
    T_local = lambda K, z: solve_local(Ve=Ve, K=K, z=z, K_grid=K_grid, what=
        what)
    out_grid = np.vectorize(T_local)(*np.meshgrid(K_grid, z_grid)) #
        Evaluate v'=Tv over the grid
    # Interpolate v_g to obtain Ve_new
    out = interp2d(K_grid, z_grid, out_grid, bounds_error=True, fill_value
        =None)#RegularGridInterpolator(points=(K_grid, U_grid, z_grid),
        values=Ve_grid, bounds_error=False, fill_value=0)
    return out

def solve_local(Ve, K, z, K_grid, what='Ve'):
    """
    Perform the instructions at Step 3. for a given gridpoint g\in\mathcal
        {G}
    """
    # Conditional probabilities given current realization for z_{t}
    cond_probs = TMAT[z_grid.index(z)]

    def f(K_end):
        EXP = np.sum([Ve(K_end, z_grid[i])*cond_probs[i] for i in range(0,
            Gz, 1)])

        return -(D(K=K, K_end=K_end, z=z) + (1./(1.+r))*EXP)

    # Find optimal controls conditional upon the firm being solvent
    opt = optimize.fminbound(f, min(K_grid), max(K_grid))
    K_end = min(K_grid, key=lambda x: abs(x-opt))
    EXP = np.sum([Ve(K_end, z_grid[i])*cond_probs[i] for i in range(0, Gz,
        1)])

    # Obtain the cum-dividend equity value
    Ve = max(D(K=K, K_end=K_end, z=z) + (1./(1.+r))*EXP, 0.)

    if what=='Ve':
        return Ve
    else:
        return K_end

def D(K, K_end, z):
    """
    This function compute dividends a function of:
    - K, the capital stock at the beginning of the date considered;
    - K_end, the capital stock at the end of the date considered;
    - z, the current realization for z_{t};
    """
    I = K_end - (1.-delta)*K #Investments
    phi = 0.5*theta*(I**2.)/K #Investment adjustment costs
    NI = (z*(K**upsilon)-(kappa+delta+c*gamma)*K-phi)*(1.-tau) #Net Income
    Delta_IC = (1.+kappa)*(K_end-K) #Change in Invested Capital
```

```
    Delta_PFN = gamma*(K_end-K) #Proceeds from debt capital structure adjustments
    DIVIDENDS = NI + Delta_PFN - Delta_IC

    return DIVIDENDS
```

References

Chow, C.-S., & Tsitsiklis, J. N. (1991). An optimal one-way multigrid algorithm for discrete-time stochastic control. *IEEE Transactions on Automatic Control, 36*(8), 898–914.

DeMarzo, P. M. (2005). Discounting tax shields and the unlevered cost of capital. *SSRN Electronic Journal.*

DeMarzo, P. M. (2019). Presidential address: Collateral and commitment. *The Journal of Finance, 74*(4), 1587–1619.

DeMarzo, P. M., & He, Z. (2016). Leverage dynamics without commitment. *NBER Working Papers*, 22799.

Fama, E. F., & French, K. R. (1993). Common risk factors in the returns on stocks and bonds. *Journal of Financial Economics, 33*(1), 3–56.

Fudenberg, D., & Tirole, J. (1991). *Game theory*. MIT Press.

Gamba, A., & Mao, L. (2020). Debt covenants and the value of commitment. *SSRN Electronic Journal.*

Gamba, A., & Saretto, A. (2020). Growth options and credit risk. *Management Science, 66*(9), 4269–4291.

Gomes, J. F., & Schmid, L. (2010). Levered returns. *The Journal of Finance, 65*(2), 467–494.

Gomes, J. F., & Schmid, L. (2021). Equilibrium asset pricing with leverage and default. *The Journal of Finance, 76*(2), 977–1018.

Li, E. X. N., Livdan, D., & Zhang, L. (2009). Anomalies. *Review of Financial Studies, 22*(11), 4301–4334.

Li, S., Whited, T. M., & Wu, Y. (2016). Collateral, taxes, and leverage. *Review of Financial Studies, 29*(6), 1453–1500.

Livdan, D., Sapriza, H., & Zhang, L. (2009). Financially constrained stock returns. *The Journal of Finance, 64*(4), 1827–1862.

Malenko, A., & Tsoy, A. (2020). Optimal time-consistent debt policies. *SSRN Electronic Journal.*

Miao, J. (2020). *Economic dynamics in discrete time*. MIT Press.

Osborne, M. J., & Rubinstein, A. (1994). *A course in game theory*. MIT Press.

Tirole, J. (1988). *The theory of industrial organization*. MIT Press.

Tserlukevich, Y. (2008). Can real options explain financing behavior? *Journal of Financial Economics, 89*(2), 232–252.

Whited, T. M. (1998). Why do investment euler equations fail? *Journal of Business and Economic Statistics, 16*(4), 479.

Xiang, H. (2019). Time inconsistency and financial covenants. *SSRN Electronic Journal.*

Zhang, L. (2005). The value premium. *The Journal of Finance, 60*(1), 67–103.

The manufacturer's authorised representative in the EU is Springer
Nature Customer Service Centre GmbH, Europaplatz 3, 69115 Heidelberg,
Germany. If you have any concerns regarding our products, please
contact ProductSafety@springernature.com

Printed and bound by CPI Group (UK) Ltd, Croydon, CR0 4YY
30/09/2026
02225690-0002